W9-AFC-872

Notable Family Networks in Latin America

Notable Family Networks

IN

LATIN AMERICA

DIANA BALMORI

STUART F. VOSS

MILES WORTMAN

The University of Chicago Press

CHICAGO AND LONDON

DIANA BALMORI is visiting fellow in history and visiting lecturer in architecture at Yale University. STUART F. VOSS is professor of history at the State University of New York, Plattsburgh. MILES WORTMAN is visiting professor of Latin American history at Baruch College (City University of New York) and a political analyst with Multinational Strategies, Inc.

The University of Chicago Press, Chicago 60637
The University of Chicago Press, Ltd., London

Library of Congress Cataloging in Publication Data
Balmori, Diana.
  Notable family networks in Latin America.
  Bibliography: p.
  Includes index.
  1. Family—Latin America—History—Case studies.
2. Elite (Social sciences)—Latin America—History—
Case studies.   I. Voss, Stuart F.   II. Wortman, Miles L.,
1944–   . III. Title.
HQ560.5.A15   1984   306.8'5'098   84-2423
ISBN 0-226-03639-1 .

CONTENTS

ACKNOWLEDGMENTS

We are grateful to the New York State Latin Americanists (NYSLA), the regional association that provides the main forum for the state's Latin Americanists. Through NYSLA, we three authors met and were able to establish regular contacts, which were important in early stages of the project.

Thanks are also due to SUNY-Oswego president, Dr. Virginia Radley, dean of arts and sciences, Dr. Donald Mathieu, and history chairman, Paul Morman, for granting leaves of absence for writing and for over-all support of intellectual activities at a time when little other encouragement was present. In like manner, the administration of SUNY-Plattsburgh, through the granting of a sabbatic leave, clerical support, and travel funds, contributed much-needed assistance. The chair of the history department, Dr. Douglas Skopp, was most helpful in facilitating this support. We would also like to thank our cartographer Kathe Fairweather and our indexer Mary Lombardi. Finally, we would like to express our deep appreciation to the University of Chicago Press for their unstinting support on this very complex manuscript from its early stages.

We are listed alphabetically since this book is the product of our equal coauthorship.

INTRODUCTION

They are the *casta divina*: thirty families who dominated nineteenth-century henequén production, land marketing, and capital in Mérida.[1] They are the Grupo Monterrey, who controlled the regional economy of Monterrey during Porfirio Díaz's time. They are the Paraíba Oligarchy: thirty-six families of nineteenth-century Brazil who dominated cotton production and marketing; monopolized elective offices and appointive posts at all levels; appropriated all local tax revenues to themselves; conducted a *política de familia*, that ensured their control of municipal positions and of the positions of colonels, justices of the peace, and bosses at the local level in Paraíba; and forged an alliance (Rio, São Paulo, and Mínas) that controlled the presidential office from 1889 to 1930.[2] They are the Ochocientos, the Quinientos, or the Casa Otomana of nineteenth-century Chile, the clan of interrelated families dominated and led by the Larraín Salas, and the same cabal that, Mary Lowenthal Felstiner says, brought "kinship politics into the revolution of Independence and limited government to the elite."

All these groups of families formed societies organized by kinship alliances and filled political and social positions on the basis of kinship qualifications. Historians of nineteenth-century Argentina and Chile call them "family clusters," the interconnected families that rose to power and dominated both nations.[3] Examining these diverse family groups in isolation at different times and in different parts of Latin America, we conclude they are the basis of a particular socioeconomic structure, one that reached its maximum development in the nineteenth century. We call these groups "family networks." We also call this piece *Notable Family Networks* to show that we are not looking at all families or at all time periods of Latin American history.

1

Family networks were associations of families allied through business, marriage, spatial proximity, and later through memberships in organizations. They emerged at the end of the eighteenth century and then developed over three generations, dominating different regions in Latin America until the first decades of the twentieth century. These networks spawned groups that could become preeminent and gain control over towns or regions. Although not necessarily notable at the outset, the families used the process of family amalgamation to attain notability.

This study does not focus on isolated families, but on the interconnections between families and on the process through which they formed their networks. We have employed the concept "notability" because Hispanic society used it and gave it social value.[4] Other concepts also identify the members of these families: the *homens bono* or the *hombre acaudalado*.

To look at the families, we have adopted a generational structure that lets us observe them over time. This time span starts around 1750 and covers approximately three generations. The generations studied here are not historical generations, though they relate to a general timetable (1750–1880). They are direct, or genealogical, generations that cover the three-generation span as one unit of time. In that span, the group of families rose, peaked, and started to decline. The members of the first generation were usually new arrivals, mainly Spanish, but also some non-Hispanic immigrants. Also included were a few immigrants from other areas or regions of Latin America. The second-generation families were the families of sons of the first, and so on.

This work posits no generational theory, though the era, ending at the turn of the twentieth century, was rich in generational theories proposed by men like Auguste Comte, John Stuart Mill, Wilhelm Dilthey, Ortega y Gasset, and Julián Marías.[5] Perhaps something happened in the nineteenth century that fostered this view of a time. One could argue for an important, special cohort of individuals that marched in unison for a generation.[6] At any rate, we employ no theoretical construct of generations or of the length of generations. We deal only with direct descent.

The second generation built the network and consolidated the group by developing coherent patterns of marital alliances and occupational endeavors; these family members also created new ways to generate capital for the family enterprise. Here, the patterns operate most strongly (that is, a higher number of the members of the second generation did the same thing).

The third generation gathered the fruit of the second generation's efforts and reached the peak of power. Generational theory maintains that the third generation is *the* generation. (In the Argentine case in this study, the third generation is called *La generación del 80*.) Although this generation gained the highest level of control, it depended on the actions and changes of the second to do so.

The Family as the Basic Unit of Historical Analysis

Most historical scholarship on families appears in discussions of other topics: as part of the studies of great estates run by particular families over a period of generations, as part of research on mercantile enterprises that also happened to be family operations, or as part of studies of the elites that dominated a city, economy, or region. Here, we focus on the family as the basic enterprise and observe its activities in large estates, mercantile operations, political parties, cities, or regions.

Until quite recently, the family has not been considered a principal agent in Latin America's history and, thus, a basic unit to be analyzed. Instead, historians have viewed it as a private entity—shaped by historical forces, as are other societal institutions, but affecting history (or public activity) only indirectly through the individuals it nurtured.

Individuals, particularly great personages, have played a central role in Latin American historiography. Scholars initially used biographies or collections of episodic stories about individuals to understand public events. This approach lent itself to political and military history, which became the dominant topical genre. The historiographical climate reinforced this tendency. In a comparatively young field where many existing sources have not been examined and organized and are not easily defined and readily handled, the emphasis on the individual's role in shaping Latin American history has remained prevalent.

Through much of this century, the view of Latin American history has shifted its focus from the individual to collective action. In part, this move reflects a general shift in historiography from attention to the role of institutions, through which individuals acted and by which they were influenced, to the role of social groups, such as socioeconomic classes, social-cultural castes, and corporate entities. Consequently, studies of "elites" have become prominent. In using this mid-twentieth-century analytical tool on Latin America's past, historians have discovered families: prominent, important, "notable" families who assumed a role more extensive than that depicted in contemporary social science models for collective action.

Between the mid eighteenth and early twentieth centuries, these notable families played an important part in the history of Latin America.

They operated like their predecessors and for similar objectives. But because of the relative vacuum of sociopolitical structures in the nineteenth
century and through their own creative adaptions to it, they created a
network that functioned as a social organization in its own right. Because of their networks, these notable families may be the pivot around
which Latin American history moved from the late colonial period
through the early twentieth century.

This discovery, however, has created a problem: families do not function easily as basic units of historical analysis. They do not lend themselves to customary biographical study or to more recent structural or
group analysis. Their activities fall somewhere between individual and
collective action. How does one then fit these notable families into the
general schema and hypotheses upon which, until now, Latin American
history has been organized?

On one level, the family acts like a group and is a collective entity. As a
result, much of the current work on the Latin America family uses the
tools and models of social science research: marriage strategies, organizational modes, social relations, investment patterns, and political participation. The family is also a private entity. It is highly personal and, to
a certain extent, unique in its interests and concerns. At this level, its
public decisions contain a decidedly personal tone, and its contracts always involve more than business. A family's past is concrete and immediate; its future can be planned specifically, determined flexibly. Familial ideas and concerns are tinged with individual concerns.

The family, particularly the prominent family with greater resources
to influence the public realm, seems to occupy a separate category.
While it acts collectively, specific individuals do the acting; family members are not like the nameless and interchangeable members of a class or
group. Nevertheless, when the family is the central reference point for
individuals, their influence upon the public realm is seldom the result of
individuality; rather, it is a consequence of their participation in the
family. These individuals act in the public realm because they are private individuals related to one another. They act in concert as relatives,
not as members of a group or institution. The family not only nurtures
them privately to participate in the public realm, it provides a framework through which and for which family members function in the public realm.

Existing research and daily experience suggest that families are of central importance in understanding the history of Latin America. Analysis
of prominent families and the roles they played between the mid eighteenth and early twentieth centuries reveals explanations for several

problems that have arisen as historiography has turned to studies of collective action and of groups, structures, and movements. For example, researchers have described the nineteenth century as a period of ideological struggle between liberals and conservatives and between modernizers and traditionalists, or of class struggle among various socioeconomic groups or between those tempted into dependency and those upholding autonomy. But close examination shows no set of ideological or class lines, and where they nominally existed, groups and individuals continually moved back and forth across them. Notable families, however, provide a clue to understanding what actually occurred.

Numerous studies of elite families also have been undertaken in recent years. They examine both individual families and groups or clusters of families in a given locale or region. These studies examine the nature of familial modes of operation and, to a lesser extent, their impact on the rest of society. They reveal an essential continuity in Latin America's past and provide clues that help answer more complex, and customarily muddled, historical questions.

In this study, we define the family as a social unit based on blood and marriage. It extends vertically in time through blood ties (children and parents) and laterally through blood and marriage ties (spouse, brothers, sisters, cousins, brothers-in-law, and sisters-in-law). Extension by descent or marriage is not constant. Even a cursory look at a family over three or four generations reveals shifts in the importance of links in different generations: brother-in-law (lateral) connections are particularly important in sibling exchanges between two families; those between uncles and nieces make generational links more important and lead to the consolidation of two branches of the family fortune. A pattern may be a strategic response to testamentary or inheritance laws (as in the uncle-niece case) or a move to consolidate contiguous land holdings (as in the sibling exchange). The kinship patterns, however, are not so much the result of specific inheritance laws or land-ownership regulations as they are a result of the families' flexible organization and ability to adapt to changing rules. They responded to change through kinship associations, and kinship became a form of survival and success.

The connections created by marriages, children, and collateral kinships assured the existence of a support group during unstable times when institutions collapsed and re-formed into new structures. In different regions, groups of interconnected families rose to prominence in the late eighteenth century and formed powerful groups that, principally through the municipalities (*cabildos*), had to be heard or convinced or patronized by the royal government. When royal authority and its rep-

resentative institutions collapsed, kinship ties placed a group of interconnected families in a new situation. By the time the second generation
entered adulthood in the 1830s, the family network had become the ultimate arbiter. It gradually took over political, military, and legislative
functions; it created political parties and determined which alternatives
and oppositions within a small kin group would be played out. Always,
it assured that the outcome would remain in the hands of one or another
part of the family network.

Characteristics and Temporal Uniqueness of the Notable Families

Asserting that certain families—some dating back to the foundations
of colonial society—possessed notability, we need to describe what characteristics made a family notable and how these families differed from
others. The distinctions between the notable and the non-notable throughout the colonial and modern period were real. Moreover, by the nineteenth century, many notable families formed networks through which
they and their allies extended their power into government—of town,
city, region, or nation—and became the ultimate arbiters of its direction.[7]

The network also had a hierarchy of power within it. Some families
were more dominant than others; members of certain families emerged
as the top officers of the main institutions; other families disappeared
from sight by the fourth generation. Those families that succeeded did
more than just belong to the network. Their members held a significant
number of directorships and political posts and also held and owned
large amounts of land. The number and variety of marriages that took
place, particularly in the second generation, also indicated long-term
success and power.

Since the second generation usually contained the greatest number of
children, its families had the greatest opportunity to establish alliances.
The alliances were often complementary: those with mercantile holdings married those with land; those with land wed those with capital or
urban properties, a military command (which sometimes implied access
to new land opened up for settlement) or a political post. These combinations were crucial. Those who married within the same professional
group or, in the case of non-Hispanic immigrants, within the same group
of immigrants, were more marginal to the group as a whole and, consequently, less successful.[8]

Though the statement oversimplifies a complex situation with many
gradations, we could say that the difference between being notable and

being non-notable depended upon the family and the network. Individual notability was tied to wealth, achievement, or post, but it was also anchored most firmly and lastingly in a series of alliances. These alliances gave the individual the resources to overcome instability and reverses of fortune. Thus notability was ultimately tied to membership in the network. Individual and family success meant attaining such membership, primarily by marrying into a network family.

Both those within and those without the network acknowledged the peculiar set of characteristics that constituted notability. It had less to do with the families' prominence in local newspapers and in public displays on the plazas than with the way they adapted and combined strategies as an integrated whole. They created and coordinated a structured mode of operation.[9] This phenomenon is not peculiarly Hispanic. Noah Webster said that society in postindependence United States was made up of a "combination of families." Even the most superficial examination of colonial and early independence families, particularly in Boston, shows kinship strategies and alliances analogous to those in Latin America. Here also, an interconnected group emerged in positions of social and economic control.[10] A society of notable families and their particular social strategies for emergence and control as an integrated, interconnected group is not a theme foreign to English historians either.[11]

Nevertheless, these non-Iberic cases do not truly compare with the Latin American ones. The Ibero-American cases come later than those in the United States, for example; and in some Central American countries, the process has only just ended. Even if the family network were a multicultural phenomenon, it would have different consequences for Latin America late in the nineteenth century than for another society in which it had occurred earlier.

Such family cohesion was indeed unusual outside the networks. For non-notables, family simply was less important and less visible. Several historians have found that the extended family was not as common in past centuries as was once thought, except among the wealthy and powerful. The few existing Latin American studies that try to measure family structure demographically—principally those of Elizabeth Kuznesof and Donald Ramos—show that at the level below notability, family seems to have been less important, and "household" is a better term to define groups united under one roof. All studies point to the distinctiveness of the organizational structure of the notables' families.[12]

Very little information in our discussion is new to historians who have studied Latin American families in the colonial period or in the nineteenth century. The marriage strategies and the kinship associations in politics, commerce, and the professions will seem familiar to them. But in the nineteenth century, the same family strategies and combination of families made the network more cohesive and helped them control regional and national government. It was a difference of degree, not of substance or of operational mode, and the degree of cohesion allowed for concerted action at the highest level.

Since the postconquest period, the family has been an important organizational form in Hispanic-American society. It was the strongest organization in society when all other state structures were too distant (overseas in the peninsula) or too weak. Given these historical circumstances, the traditional Iberian family structure assumed a variety of forms. As the New World was settled, the family also developed systematic modes of operation. Although these were sometimes adapted to specific circumstances, they were variations within an already established repertory.

Individuals working in a loosely organized association had largely accomplished the conquest of Ibero-America, but families acquired the wealth and power and status that accrued from it. These families established their political and economic base in the new *municipios* that were created whenever a minimum number of Hispanic settlers warranted them. Well into the eighteenth century, they and those who joined or succeeded them sought nobility, the traditional peninsular status and title that conferred wealth, prestige, and power (often jurisdiction) over others. They claimed these rewards (as had their counterparts in the peninsular reconquest) for the services their family members performed for the crown: conquering, consolidating settlements, and exploiting new-found wealth. Though the families gained legal privileges granted and guaranteed by the crown, very few gained the prized "noble" status. The crown simply refused to repeat the mistake its predecessors had made in the peninsula. Thus most of the prominent families in the towns and cities of the New World became "notables," or the equivalent of the urban gentry of the peninsula.

These early "American" notables, however, did resist royal encroachment upon their prerogatives and did dominate their localities, largely by controlling the district office of *corregidor* (or *alcalde mayor*). A number of recent studies reveal that the power of prominent families grew steadily in their localities, reaching its zenith in the first half of the eighteenth century before the Bourbons undertook extensive reforms and imperial reorganization. Many of these same studies also show considerable turnover among the notable families: they maintained their prominent position for only two or three generations.[13]

The bureaucratic, economic, and intellectual revolutions promoted by the Bourbon dynasty in the late eighteenth century presented an arduous challenge to the established notable families. They had to deal with newcomers (a great many from the peninsula, particularly from its northern and eastern towns and cities), who seized upon the new circumstances created by the social upheaval. These newcomers formed families that attained preeminence in their localities. They also maintained a strong sense of the traditional Iberian urban patriciate. They measured themselves by the patriciate's criteria of wealth, public activity, and refinement. Some fit the model upon arrival. Others attained it in their lifetimes.

The repertory of family structures is not what separates these new notables from their predecessors. From the conquest to the mid eighteenth century, established families employed many of the same strategies used by our family networks. The numerous case studies cited in the bibliography reveal these patterns (chapter 5 treats several of these studies). By 1750, other important patterns were evident but not as widespread or as complex as they would become for the family networks. These include the use of diversification, complementarity, and the integration of domestic and foreign interests.

Moreover, in the colonial period, the groups of families that gained strength and came the closest to ruling were those in the poorest and most neglected areas, where the Iberian government structures were weaker. Areas such as Northwest Mexico, Northwest Argentina, and El Salvador all showed powerful family networks. New Mexico before Mexican independence in 1821 (and, of course, before acquisition by the United States) provides a perfect picture of family networks that evolved in such backwaters:

> These tiny settlements, focused around a square or plaza, were often dominated by a single large family clan whose members worked together to raise blue maize and chili peppers on small irrigated plots. Other members chose to ranch sheep on common lands fringing the town.
>
> Given such conditions, it was inevitable that a small ruling class comprised of some fifteen or twenty intermarried families would come to dominate New Mexico. By 1810 everyone knew that Peralta was a Chavez bailiwick: it was clear that the Martínez clan dominated some of the Río Arriba settlements. Similarly, the Archuletas, Pereas, Oteros, Duráns, Senas, Montoyas, Ortízes, and Cabeza de Bacas were known as the patrons of the country. And no family was a more distinguished representative of this fortunate group than the Pinos.[14]

In the nineteenth century, conditions changed. First, the notion of notability altered. The fundamental criteria for the Iberian urban patriciate remained, but the range and integration of the notables' economic
interests increased measurably. The greatest departure from the traditional model took place in the way the families extended their political
power and influence and in the way they perceived themselves. They not
only consolidated their authority over local society, they expanded it to
state, regional, and national levels as well. Moreover, they reached out
to the industrialized, modernized societies of the North Atlantic world.
The network helped the families successfully adapt to the changing circumstances of the nineteenth century. It enabled them to cumulatively
transmit and enhance their notability. The expansion of notability reached
its apogee in the late nineteenth century when the notable networks attained maximum political power and influence and social prestige.

What is distinctive after 1750 is not the continuity or discontinuity of
individual patterns or strategies but the growing interconnection of both
into a more intricate, comprehensive, viable vehicle of organization:
networks that functioned as social organizations in the public realm and
in their own right. This complexity, extension, and power sets these networks apart from earlier ones.

The family network appeared during the transition from the colonial
to the modern period for a number of reasons. Industrialization and the
emergence of northern Europe as a new force encouraged trading in
cash. (In the early nineteenth century, Britain was most influential in
this area.) As holds in ships became larger, the kinds of goods used for
long-distance trade also changed. Within colonial society itself, the
Church's role weakened and the military was transformed. When the
Church no longer operated as a source of credit, the family took its
place. In addition, the Bourbon's semiprofessional army became a local
one and shifted from an urban to a rural base. This rural base also became a new source for export products. Consequently, a military official
posted in the Indian frontier could defend his family lands, obtain new
lands from Indian territory, and, in times of need, press *hacienda* or *estancia* labor into military service.

In sum, a combination of the right timing, the right commodity, and a
predisposition for developing family strategies produced the powerful
family networks in nineteenth-century Latin America. The historical
context also contributed to their development. The collapse of restrain-
ing institutions allowed the family strategies to develop fully, so a family
network could establish great power in all spheres. In addition, the con-
junction of family strategies (developed during the colonial period and

later) and the formation of the nation-state transformed these groups into organizations for which power and control of a region (even a nation) would be a one-time event. It did not occur before, and it would not be repeated again.

For a decade, intensive work in family studies has been done. Now a pressing need exists for a larger framework in which to place and understand the detailed studies that have been completed. In undertaking such a task, we neither provide definitive answers nor anything approaching complete coverage. The basic problems, questions, and perspectives simply have not been formulated and argued long enough, and extensive and varied studies do not exist for most regions. Consequently, our generalizations are tentative, and our synthesis will be tested by other works as they appear.

The first chapter of this study outlines the formation of the family network and the historical context in which it took place. Case studies of three very different areas follow in subsequent chapters: the capital city of Guatemala and its hinterland, provincial Northwest Mexico, and the pampa region around Buenos Aires. The diversity of these areas makes the general network patterns more visible and brings out regional variations, which provides a stronger test for the thesis. Unfortunately, there are as yet no regional studies that cover this length of time or that integrate notable family structure into the larger historical setting.[15] In the concluding chapter, we analyze existing family studies, using them to illustrate the family network's operation in a variety of circumstances and with the variations in the general patterns.

While the three areas covered in the case studies do not represent the whole of Latin America, they do cover a wide range and test the limits of our thesis. Argentina and Northwest Mexico were typical of nineteenth-century development in Latin America, though in different degrees and possessing divergent colonial backgrounds. The Buenos Aires region, for example, was a backwater during the colonial period. Later, it dominated the hinterlands and controlled the surrounding territory that had been considered more developed during the colonial era (e.g., Córdoba, Salta, Tucumán). Northwest Mexico, also a backwater region that came to play a significant role in national politics in the early twentieth century, never could gain complete control of the old, developed area.

In reading our three principal case studies, readers must keep two fundamental perspectives in mind. First, the network model is based upon sets of strategies that are woven into an integrated whole and not upon the particular choices of outcomes. The continuity lies in the pattern of diversification, not in the exact mix of economic activities that make up the diversification strategy; in complementarity, not in the particular activities that are complementary. Second, geographic scale must be accounted for when comparing, for example, the regional societies of Central America that became nations and those of the La Plata (excepting Paraguay and Uruguay) that did not. Through the course of the nineteenth century, when most republican political institutions were very layered in nature, the notable networks expanded their interests outward from their localities. Though most networks remained local, some achieved state and even national scope.

1

The Family Network

A Three-Generation Process

The description that follows outlines a three-generation model of notable families in a network. It delineates the borders of the model like a Gaussian curve: the details are missing because the necessary research work is minimal for this time period and these geographic locations. Consequently, we see an overall pattern but few of the ramifications or the twists and turns of variations in circumstance. We attempt to fill in the border through our inclusion of case studies and in discussions of the divergent patterns found in different areas. The more points future research will enable us to fill in, the more precisely we will trace the pattern and flesh out the model.

We would like to reassert that regional variations do exist. They depend on how closely regional or local interests allied themselves with the prevailing forces in the mainstream. We cannot go any further; we depend on future work to add to or correct the variations.

Our theoretical framework follows. It is based on three different case studies (chapters 2–4) and other existing work (chapter 5).

In many areas of Latin America, certain families established themselves as ruling groups and left a permanent mark in their regions or countries. The process began in the mid eighteenth century when a group of predominantly *nouveaux arrivés* allied themselves and formed family clusters that, in the second generation, led the way to the formation of independent nations and societies. In some regions, particularly smaller colonial entities that became nation-states (that is, in Central

America, Ecuador, and Uruguay), second-generation members attained key positions at the national level. Elsewhere, it was in the third generation that networks secured control of their national societies.

The networking process began in the mid eighteenth century, expanded through the independence period, became visible by the mid nineteenth century, and peaked in the late nineteenth century. The power of the network often transcended the traditional epochs of Latin American history, such as the wars of independence and the conservative-liberal period. In some of the older, more sophisticated colonial regions, first-generation alliances (the marriage of newcomers into older notable families) were important. But generally, the networks evolved out of a series of internal alliances made during the second generation. In the third generation, these alliances were formalized through institutionalization. Throughout Latin America, the generational patterns repeat themselves. They are evident in occupation, marriage, number of children, landholding, place of residence, clubs, and political office.

The family network was born out of the new opportunities offered in the enlightened era of the late eighteenth century, when bureaucratic reform, economic revolution, and new ideas transformed America. Development occurred in the same way and nearly simultaneously throughout Latin America, though the specific products of the regions and the families' economic activities (cattle production, mining, commercial agriculture, or trade) differed. In most areas, family power remained local. Elsewhere, the family network, using a main city as its base, eventually attained control of entire states, regions, and even nations.

When notable families emerged at the pinnacle of power, they resembled an aristocracy. But these were not nobles by privilege. They were notables who earned their position through competition. Once in power, they did not function as individual families. Rather, they created a series of informal and formal institutions (political parties, clubs, banks, insurance companies, and residential clusters) through which they further established themselves in the nation's economic activities.

The power of the networks extended into the early twentieth century, though the family lost some political and economic authority and all power over the national economy. Throughout this century, the families have had access to political and economic power by virtue of their large fortunes, their landholdings, and their names. To this day, they promote particular family members into positions of power. While they no longer work as a united network, a significant number of them still possess some of the largest fortunes in their countries.

Although the networking sequence began in the mid eighteenth century and ended in the last decades of the nineteenth, some family founders arrived earlier or later. These individuals contributed variations in the pattern. Clearly, those who entered the sequence in the 1780s worked in the right time and with the right circumstances. In these families—the majority—the patterns are so marked that we call them the mainstream. Those late in the generational sequence sometimes fell out of the main group by the end of the third generation. Those early in the sequence had greater and more lasting power, and the prestige attached to their families lingered even when they lost all economic power.

The generational patterns, which the groups shared, show the areas and the manner in which the group coalesced and acted in unison.

Generational Patterns

Occupation

The occupational sequence was standard. The first generation began in one economic activity and then later diversified. Most commonly, these men were traders who, by the end of their lives, had started to buy land. In areas such as Northwest Mexico and Brazil, many were estate or mine owners who branched into commerce. The second generation diversified further and employed complementarity far more extensively to integrate and enlarge the family enterprise. Merchants transformed land holdings into haciendas, estancias, or mines. Then, they integrated them into a trade network and increased their already established commercial activities. In Argentina, for example, an estancia was added to a trading house in the city. In Chile, a trading house in Santiago was added to the mines in the north, or mines or land were added to a trading house in the capital. In Guatemala, mines and indigo fields, from which the first generation derived its trade, were purchased by the second. The number of professional careers also increased, principally in the fields of law, medicine, engineering, and education.

Professional careers were especially prevalent in the third generation, but this move to the professions was common to society as a whole and not peculiar to the families. More individuals of this generation also held political office at the state and national levels, and family members engaged in lifelong political careers. Both occupational areas greatly aided the process of diversification and complementarity, especially as families acquired shares in joint-stock companies and held directorships, particularly in banks and railroads. Managers and administrators often operated holdings while family members made company policy, engaged in their professions, or governed.

Officeholding

Though economic activities, especially trade, constituted the main occupation of first-generation males, many also held office in the local cabildos. In addition, many held posts in the colonial government or served as military officers in the royal army created by the Bourbons (and in Brazil, in the militia of the colony and, later, the empire). As a rule, members of this generation did not hold high office. When they held an official post, they did so as a secondary occupation.

In the second generation, the potential for officeholding was greater, given the republican political institutions, which were multilayered and held separate powers. Nevertheless, for most notables, officeholding remained secondary. The political posts they held complemented or supported their economic activities. Principally because of the size of the countries, members in the small nation-states (like those in Central America) achieved national office in the second generation. But in the larger nations, the political offices held by notables tended to be provincial or municipal (from governor to state legislator, provincial deputy, director of customs, or city mayor or councilman). These individuals derived most of their influence from their financial power, and they employed it to influence the bureaucracy. In Argentina, the officeholding pattern was more narrow: an individual held only one office, usually late in life.

By the third generation, officeholding had become prevalent, not only in the localities, but at the state and national levels as well. More important, family members developed political careers, holding bureaucratic posts as well as elected offices. This complemented the notable families' expanding range of economic activities, for which government played an ever-growing role as stimulus and support.

Marriage

Marriage was the primary mechanism by which families fused into a single group or network. Nineteenth-century political parties inspired weak and ephemeral allegiances compared to those created by marriage, and business associations were relatively short lived and tenuous. In fact, it is because these other forms were so weak that marriage strategy was essential to family success.

Today, marriage is regarded as part of the private realm of life. We cannot easily see it forging a powerful group or a quasi-public corporation. It was, however, a vehicle for the formation of something akin to (in its specificity, not in its operation) a modern corporation. It can, in fact, be considered a business organization in a society that lacked a mass market. Through marriage and the family, individuals achieved what the formal business organizations and political parties of the time could not: a long-lasting association of power and money. These families were the forerunners of the modern corporation in Latin America.

Marriage usually subsumed social, economic, and political alliances. Indeed, until the beginning of the twentieth century, political parties can best be understood in the context of kinship ties. A cursory glance at nineteenth-century political parties (or clubs, as they were called below the national level) reveals network family members in all of them and predominant in one or even several. Thus, no matter which party prevailed, the networks had influence and political clout. Consequently, family members could survive and recover from political adversity; the network often served as the basis for their overall political hegemony.

The male of the first generation generally married into a family with whom he traded or worked. When he was an immigrant from the peninsula (a sizeable group in most parts of Ibero-America during this time), he married into a local established creole family, if possible. If the immigrant were a trader or merchant, as many of the *peninsulares* of this first generation were, he usually sought marriage to the daughter of a mercantile family. However, he might also marry into a family engaged in the development of local products such as livestock, crops, and minerals. In areas less developed, where the consolidated social group did not exist or where society was weak, as in Northwest Mexico, newcomers often married one another.

In the second generation, families used marital alliances to create the core of the powerful social and economic networks in each country. This generation clearly illustrates how the fusion of the families took place. Often it began when two siblings of one family married two of another. If one spouse died, the survivor frequently married a brother or sister of the deceased. In the second generation, there were many multiple marriages between families. Marriages between two families in two consecutive generations (first and second or second and third) also took place.

One frequent result of second-generation marriages was a move to the state or national capital. The alliances thus became regional (combining localities) and interregional. In some cases, the marriage tied a region to the economic interests of the capital city or, more commonly, joined a locality with the interests of a state capital.

Second-generation marriages were also increasingly interoccupational. Traders married into mining and landowning families, and vice versa. This pattern clearly contrasts with that of the first generation, which tended to marry in its locality or region and into families with the same occupational background. The first-generation marriages seem to have been based on custom, tradition, and availability, though some peninsular immigrants were actively recruited for marriage and themselves regarded marriage as a means of occupational placement. In the second generation, some longer-range economic planning appears in marriage patterns. Families in Northwest Mexico, or families in São Paulo such as the Prados, are examples of this marriage strategy.[1]

In the third generation, many network families turned in upon themselves. Marriage occurred most commonly between cousins and with members of other network families. Sometimes, the marriage crossed generations, joining uncle and niece or aunt and nephew. Much depended upon local circumstance. Linda Lewin's study of Northeast Brazil, for example, shows notable families shifting from endogamy to exogamy in response to markedly changed conditions. In Latin America throughout the nineteenth century, marriage outside the networks occurred frequently with prominent North Atlantic immigrants. Thus, network families created bonds with their European economic partners. In Argentina, some members of the third generation even married into European nobility. Though marriages with prominent foreigners began in the second generation, the practice became more widespread in the late nineteenth century.[2]

Children

Network families also used their children to further the family enterprise. The seventy-three children fathered by the four second-generation Almada brothers in Northwest Mexico (thirty-five of them by José María alone) allowed the Almada family to assume a central role in the Álamos network. Luis Terrazas made sure that the marriages of his twelve children cemented the state network in Chihuahua around his family. With them, he built a virtual economic empire in that Mexican state during the late nineteenth and early twentieth centuries.[3]

Some studies show that in notable families the number of children seems to diminish from one generation to the next. For the few places that we have some data, the number of children was generally high in the first generation. The median varied between seven and eleven in most places. The number of children was halved in the second generation. It fell again in the third, when many couples remained childless.[4] We do not know whether these generational changes in birthrate followed, were more pronounced than, or differed altogether from the national trend. Any firm generalizations about children require overall statistics. For the moment, we can only identify what seems to be a trend and urge attention to and research in this area.

By the third generation, the number of children generally was not as important as it had been: the family itself as a mechanism of mobility was less significant. Once the network was formed, the group's power and control began to flow through other channels than those of the family. Institutions—new business organizations, clubs, and political parties—replaced the family as places to form alliances. Thereafter, alliances were made economically, politically, or professionally only by men and only in very specific branches of such endeavors. This pattern became common in areas, Buenos Aires, for example, where economic growth and modernization had advanced farthest. In other areas (such as Northwest Mexico and Northeast Brazil), marriage alliances remained critically important to the third generation's accumulation of power.

Property

From the first to the third generations, holdings expanded from medium-sized retail or wholesale stores (or, to a lesser extent, from landed estates or mines) to vast corporations with multiple investments. By the second generation, the trading house had become an elaborate enterprise comprising the import-export business and the hacienda or mine. Vast tracts of land were often added. The third generation branched into railroad and bank stocks, as well as enormous amounts of urban real estate. Moreover, by the third generation, the family functioned as a corporate unit in the buying and selling of its stock, property, and other holdings. (Stock listings of various companies in different countries show that the largest stockholders came from the same families and were usually allied through marriage, class, and residence.) The third generation's ownership of government bonds, banks, utilities, and transportation facilities increased the networks' power. Railroads that had been laid to serve their urban base and reduce competition later enabled them to control the rest of the country, region, or province. Controlling the capital or provincial city and the credit of its banks, the third generation controlled the future.

The acquisition of urban real estate dramatizes the connections between family and city. Some of the purchases made during the first generation had been expanded greatly in the latter life of the second. The generational sequence gave the families the time needed for the valorization of their investments. The third generation quite literally controlled the cities in which they resided because they had great quantities of choice real estate in their hands. Consequently, this generation had a direct economic interest in the cities and their growth.

In some areas, this property pattern was not nearly so pronounced. For example, in the northeast and in the interior of Brazil, where diversification grew out of rural landed estates, agricultural interests remained the fundamental base of the family enterprise, though now increasingly as a resource for export production.[5]

Residences

The third-generation families changed both their types of house and their neighborhoods within cities, although the process, in some cases, started toward the end of the second generation. As with their often contiguous lands in the countryside, their urban houses were all located in a small area. Thus they provided a concrete metaphor for the nucleus of power and privilege the families had formed. Once a great number of families settled in a small sector of the city and the network was visibly set apart from the rest of society, the residences no longer served as mere houses. They became social monuments, grandiose places that reflected the wealth and power of the group.

House styles changed completely in the third generation. Patio houses of long Ibero-American tradition were replaced by mansions in the nineteenth-century European (mainly French and English) style. The architectural "inwardness" of the inside patios with their enclosing walls was abandoned for three-story structures that emphasized the façade. Houses and grounds increased in size even though families were smaller.

Clubs

The creation of clubs is a phenomenon of the late second generation and especially of the third. Founded after the second generation's marriages had taken place, they helped institutionalize the alliances. In areas such as Buenos Aires and Santiago, where institutionalized forms of alliance were more fully developed, the clubs eventually supplanted family connections and effectively replaced family residences as centers of social life. But in many regions, like Northwest Mexico, where some clubs had emerged in the third generation, family residences still functioned as centers of network social life, and family connections remained the basis of network solidarity. This was especially true for notable networks that did not extend beyond the district *cabeceras* of their localities or those in the many provincial centers that possessed neither the state capital nor a booming economy.

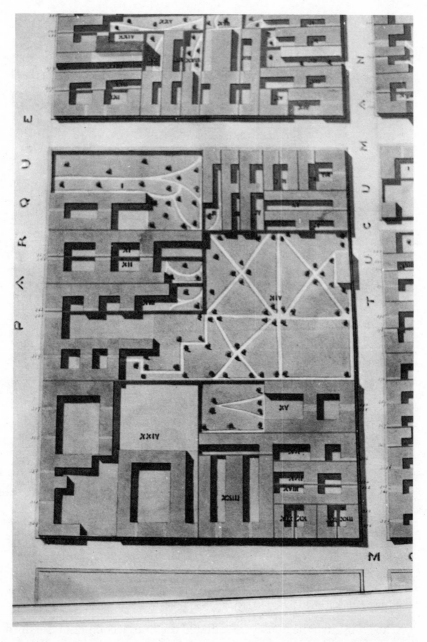

Cluster of Campos family houses, Buenos Aires, 1862. Houses I, XII, XIII, XIV, XV, XVI, six houses in one square block. Beare map 1860–70, Dirección de Arquitectura, Municipalidad de Buenos Aires, courtesy of Arq. José María Peña, director.

Late nineteenth-century Chihuahua City mansion in the new foreign styles adopted by third-generation members. Photograph courtesy of Edward Worthen.

The clubs, like the houses, manifested the faits accomplis of the third generation: alliances made by families in the network. Through marriage, wealth, schooling, and influence, the third-generation members achieved the social status that had been denied to the second generation and that they needed to form a club.

While the clubs institutionalized the family alliances, they also separated the group of families from the rest of society. As did the residential pattern of the second and third generations in the city, the club drew boundaries around the family network. This drawing of boundaries signified the completion of the process: growth was over, and the group would rule for another generation. Thereafter, individual families grew progressively weaker; however, their economic power continued to provide them with a platform by which they could reach important positions.

Family and State

Much can be written about the intricate relationship between the family networks and the state. Regarding the initial expansion of the notable family's power (most visible immediately after independence), all our data supports the view so well expressed by French historian André Bourgiére that the power of the family is inversely related to that of the state:

It is probably the single most important result of the recent preoccupation of historians with the problems of the family that the constant conflicts between the state and the family, the two competing institutions in the development of a society, have been brought to light. It appears that whenever the state no longer wields enough power to act and to protect its people, the family expands, assumes control of every aspect of the individual's life, and becomes a bastion. Whenever the state becomes stronger, the family shrinks, loosens the affective ties it had imposed on the individual, who then is more readily integrated into society as a whole.[6]

Studies of the Latin American family do not, as yet, allow for any such generalization, but Bourgiére's conclusions do find support in the family studies that span the independence period in Latin America. The relation of notable network families to political parties best illustrates the core of Bourgiére's hypothesis of the inverse relation between the family and the state. Family alliances took precedence over individual political leanings. Individual members, and even segments, of the family networks were especially visible when one or another party backed specific network interests. But these often momentary alliances with one or another party ultimately served the network as a whole rather than specific individuals or segments in it.

During the lifetimes of the notables of this study, the political life of their societies radically changed in structure, composition, and ideology. Consequently, the growing political presence of the families provided the principal continuity in the changing political reality of nineteenth-century Latin America. The first generation of the late colonial period primarily reacted to a state apparatus that was long established, although significantly altered under the Bourbons. After its demise in the struggle for independence, the founders of the families maneuvered— some more successfully than others—between a crumbling political regime and changed historical circumstances. Though they rarely introduced the new republican political system in the postindependence years, the second generation increasingly engaged in politics, adapting the emerging republican state to their families' interests. In the late nineteenth century, third generation members meshed the networks that linked their families together with the growing state bureaucracy, whose development they actively promoted. Consequently, the state apparatus became more private and the family networks assumed an increasingly corporate character.

In the colonial world, prominent families controlled a web of patronage at the municipal level.[7] Claims of clientage and kinship also frequently overlapped at the local level. Whenever possible, the families pursued linkage by promoting their interests to the royal officialdom. Corporate bodies figured significantly as vehicles through which notable families sought patronage, either directly from the institution itself or indirectly from the crown through these institutional bodies. A politics of petition ruled, and clientage gave them the most effective leverage for receiving requests. The new notables of the late colonial period were quite familiar with this political world, and they maneuvered in it with varying degrees of success.[8]

When the imperial political structure disintegrated throughout Latin America during the independence struggle (except in Brazil), the state apparatus rapidly changed, but the tactics and the spirit of clientage remained. In one sense, independence created a political vacuum. Some colonial institutions had been shattered, others shaken. Almost all groups found their customary modus vivendi with the state changed. Consequently, corporate institutions became far less effective for the political pursuit of family interest than they had been in the colonial period. In these circumstances, notable families seized the initiative to determine public affairs. The representative nature of the republican system and its separation of powers presented the notables with a wide range of offices at several levels of government. Through them, they could promote family interests.

The notables continued to rely on the customary practice of patronage. But they also began to employ their emerging family networks, usually in affiliation with political parties, as a comparatively efficient means for organizing political alliances and coalitions that furthered and protected their interests. Using existing clientele relations that linked them with large segments of the local population, notable families marshalled political support for electoral, demonstrative, and military purposes. Through their representatives and in accordance with their private interests, second-generation notable families influenced and, in some cases, determined the composition of the body politic, the particular political structures through which public affairs were conducted, and the values and goals of the system at all levels of government.

The increasing complexity and cohesion of the notable families enabled the third generation to attain even greater political influence and control over the state apparatus. The emergence of centralized state bureaucracies coincided with the network's growing political capability. Notable families identified the talents and abilities of their members and moved individuals into various facets of the family enterprise, including politics. The family network could then supply the professionally trained personnel that government needed. At the same time, patronage allowed the state bureaucracies to provide families with offices that required less expertise and could be filled by members of the ever-expanding networks. Nevertheless, the networks' level of cohesion and their increasingly corporate organization tempered the traditional patronage system by promoting and ensuring a measure of efficiency and merit.

By the early twentieth century, political structures were institutionalized in political parties, labor unions, business and professional associations, and the military. Accelerated economic growth in the late nineteenth century fostered the creation of these bodies and extended their influence to politics. Their underlying base was not, however, the corporate identities of the colonial world, but the grievances and needs of impersonal, socioeconomic interest groups. The notables' increasing neglect of client obligations, particularly to those below them, in favor of governmental mediation, further stimulated the new political reality. Consequently, fourth-generation notables found their grip on the political order slipping; interest groups challenged them from without and a steady evolution to a more modernized bureaucracy took place from within. After the third generation, notables found they could no longer maintain political hegemony. Yet they continued to employ family networks and client relations to retain influence in Latin American politics.

In large part, they did so through institutional structures, promoting their interest within the bodies and groups that played significant roles in the political life of their countries. Given this near total identification with government and the concentration of political and economic power, the family network's decline in power after the third generation demands explanation.

By the end of the third generation, the formalization of political structure led to the creation of organizations that opened the doors to other groups and interests and destroyed the cohesion previously obtained through the family alliances. Moreover, the third generation allied itself with the same old families, not with new ones (as had been the case of the second generation, which married into families unrelated by blood). Although their old connections were not lost and were transferred as a modus operandi to the organizations, their power was reflected only at the level of ownership and on boards of trustees of financial and cultural organizations. The growing importance of corporate management opened another avenue to a rising new group, allowing them to compete and gain control.

The generational structure of the family networks was most important for the joining of resources. Thus, the generational theories for explaining society that were so popular in the late nineteenth century (Ortega y Gasset's and Fichte's, for example) were not accidental. The family networks used old devices, developed partly in the context of familial relationships. By these means, clusters of families established themselves as the dominant power at local and regional levels and left an indelible mark on them. To this day, remnants of this power still propel individual members of the group into critical positions.

Adapting to Changing Circumstances

The development of the network was a function not only of the inner workings of the notable families but also of the changing pattern of larger historical circumstances. There was an interaction of general conditions and private familial circumstances. For their families to interconnect into networks that functioned with growing effect in the public realm, notables had to adapt creatively the individuality and peculiarities of their private world to the shifting circumstances of Latin American historical reality. The varying tempers and talents of individual family members, the sequence of life's common events (births, marriages, deaths), the unforeseen accidents (both windfalls and tragedies) were an abundant pool out of which a familial network could be created to turn events more and more to their advantage.

The initial period of adjustment for prominent families came with the conquest of the New World and its aftermath. They were confronted with a new environment—in all its physical, economic, and cultural dimensions. In the second half of the eighteenth century, the pace of change quickened as the Iberian crowns set out to redirect and reorganize colonial society and with the first significant penetration of the modernizing, industrializing currents emanating from the North Atlantic. With independence, the alterations and conflicts generated by royal reform continued, though no longer within an imperial context. External currents increasingly influenced the public realm of the new nation-states, to the point that by the late nineteenth century they had become momentous, if not preeminent. Through it all, the notable family networks not only survived, but prospered and came to predominate.

The Colonial Period

The pattern of family rule dates back to the earliest days of the colonies. An *hidalgo* mentality that sought privilege and the tribute of others as a reward for service greatly influenced both the conquistadores and the early colonists. Their ultimate goal was to become *grandees*, the upper nobility of the peninsula. These groups even used a vocabulary that defined the principal requisites: *limpieza de sangre*, "pure blood," the prime legal requirement for status, power, and office that was proven in countless notarized genealogies based upon baptismal records and, occasionally, creative imaginations; *hijos de los conquistadores*, "the descendants of the conquerors," whose right to favors was also based upon blood lines; and *vecinos*, the Iberian citizens of pure blood descended from the conquerors, distinguished from the mixed-blood castes, Indians, and blacks, who lacked the rights of citizenship.

Generalizing from the experiences of the Ibero-American settlements, we find that the conquerors laid out town plans that gave the best urban plots and rural land to the most powerful of their group; they founded municipal councils of cabildos, and while the offices were gained, theoretically, through election or purchase, they always fell to the most powerful; they established ecclesiastical cabildos to supervise the construction and maintenance of churches and cathedrals. Finally, they distributed the largest and best allotments of Indian labor to the most prominent conquistadores and their families; Indians in *encomiendas* worked for those vecinos licensed to pay tribute to the crown; Indians in slavery were owned outright by colonists; and, later on, government officials allotted Indians in *repartimiento* in a manner dictated more by custom than anything else.

Thus, in the earliest days, a few families secured wealth and power. Through the next two centuries, they passed to their descendants the townhouses, the lands, the labor, and the seats on the municipal and ecclesiastical councils. Tradition guarded their prerogatives. The Hapsburg monarchy respected this tradition, calling each colony a *reino*, "kingdom." It treated the leading families, the hijos de los conquistadores, like the nobles on the peninsula, though without conferring the privileges of peerage. Within each colony, traditional prerogatives, such as cabildo seats, were more important than wealth. For example, transient merchants could never secure their riches without marrying into the families that possessed such privileges. The crown's edicts even acknowledged the authority of traditions practiced "since time immemorial" as one component of imperial law. Colonists who violated written law could successfully defend the violation in court on the grounds of traditional behavior.

Prominent families used both positions on the Church boards and the help of their relatives in the ecclesiastical hierarchy to maintain their preeminence. Ecclesiastical tithes, donations, bequests, ritual fees, and sales of bulls yielded major sources of revenue, and these monies were reinvested in the colonial economy through loans and mortgages. Although owned by individual proprietors, most properties were at least partially mortgaged to the Church at five percent interest. For example, a farm or house, purchased for one thousand pesos with Church funds in 1570, paid an annual interest of fifty pesos two hundred years later, regardless of inflation. Their dominant positions within the Church gave leading families constant sources of capital and an influence in allocating Church resources. Similarly, wherever mortgaged property became vacant by default or death, these families decided who would take it. Thus they maintained their power over the economy.

This colonial hierarchy was fairly well defined within towns and cities. The most prestigious families were usually parishioners of the cathedral on the central plaza, while less important groups had churches in their respective neighborhoods. Within each parish, social strata were further defined by membership in *cofradías*, "sodalities" or "confraternities." These organizations were originally founded to fund the celebration of saints and to maintain chapels, masses, and feasts on saints' days, but they also financed their membership's baptisms, confirmations, marriages, interments, and memorials. As did the Church, the prestigious cofradía gathered large sums of money and invested it in members' enterprises. Only the most esteemed families belonged to the elite cofradías, and this pattern of limited membership was repeated in the groups of each parish, from the wealthiest creoles to the poorest mestizos. Stratification was thereby enforced.

In addition to contributing to the wealth and prestige of churches and cofradías, Christians were obligated to perform pious works, such as assisting the poor, infirm, or aged. But here again, the social structure affected charity; notable families donated money and their ecclesiastical sons and daughters to particular monasteries and their hospitals, while lesser families gave to other charities. Then as now, dances and fund-raising events run by society's grandes dames fulfilled a charitable function and excluded those less *grandes*.

Thus, through the aegis of the Church, ruling families maintained control of local economies, houses, land, and in some cases, mines. They also regulated social status in the churches and cofradías and dominated the secular bureaucracy of municipal government, the cabildos. There they licensed stores, taverns, slaughter houses, and meat providers; they set grain prices and gave out housing plots. In the largest cities, the cabildos administered Indian labor. The control of the urban markets, the best lands, and houses and labor provided the families with a foundation of power that passed from generation to generation.

In some areas, notably Mexico, peninsulares took over the failing farms or mines of the existing ruling families. In the second half of the eighteenth century, however, traditional society continued to dominate these new entrepreneurs. The newcomers could only gain the prereogatives of power through marriage; they could not change the social rules or break the stratification.

In the vast, besieged Hapsburg empire of the sixteenth and seventeenth centuries, the crown had to cement loyalty and did so by linking the fortunes of the local ruling families with its own. It further enhanced the power of these families by basing its authority on the nobility and notable families in traditional fashion, that is, by rewarding loyal families with additional privileges, such as titles, pensions, or tax farms. These favors were inheritable; some were renewed every two lives, guaranteeing loyalty. Many pensions lasted more than a century, and in many areas of Spanish America, notable families received more money from pensions than the crown did in taxes. In turn, the crown ensured that local ruling families recognized and defended royal authority.

These familial groups, however, were not socially stagnant. Traditional privileges served only as a foundation for their power. Severe economic losses over long periods of time led to the eventual decline of some notable families. Other lines ceased altogether, owing to disease or too zealous piety, which sent sons and daughters into the Church. To counteract adversity, some families merged their fortunes and drove out less vigorous ones. In various areas of America, they sought new blood to maintain or enhance family power. Spanish bureaucrats were particularly prized as additions to the family, since they carried with them additional influence in Spain, a new source of wealth, and perhaps most important, pure blood. Latent hostility between creoles and peninsulares did in general inhibit familial integration. Nevertheless, incorporation of newcomers, though limited in extent, provided the major source of change in the upper levels of the social structure in the first two hundred years of the Iberian empires in the New World.

Throughout Ibero-America, most of the notable families of the late sixteenth century continued to control the colonies through the early eighteenth. Kinship was the basis of organization in São Paulo, Chile, Caracas, and Mérida. Lima epitomized the continued rule of the early families in the eighteenth century. Three hundred notable houses reportedly existed in that city; the descendants of the conquerors ranked first among them, peninsulares second, and merchants third.

This social structure was not unusual. It derived from Spain, where familial power thrived in the royal court. The houses of Medina Celá and Osuna, for instance, greatly influenced the Council of the Indies and the Cabildo and Merchant Guild of Seville during these two hundred years. When Basque merchants settled throughout Spain and the New World, they used their family ties to link their prestige and authority at home with their commercial activities in the empire.

The social system of creole kinship, which was protected from competition and was inbred and fairly insular, clashed with the dynamism of the eighteenth-century bureaucratic, economic, and intellectual revolutions. The Bourbons, who gained the Spanish throne in 1700, brought the experience of Louis XIV and his bureaucrats to their struggle to curtail traditional rights and build state power. Throughout the early industrial revolution, the western European economy expanded. Its merchants came to Latin America armed with new capital and links to the metropolis. The merchants ideology of self-interested, laissez-faire trade (as described by Adam Smith) clashed with traditional prerogatives. At the same time, the enlightened view of natural rights beseiged the dominant counterreformation mentality of Ibero-America centered on traditional and divine rights.

The old families allowed merchants and bureaucrats into their midst. Either they accepted new beliefs and competed, or they lost power. Thus the revolution both conquered the old traditions and worked with them. Merchant immigrants entered established families, joining with the old to create a new power. Other newcomers fought against traditional authority to gain entrance to cabildos and had to wait a generation or two in order to marry into the upper echelon of society.

How, then, did the new process differ from the old? Previously, outsiders had come to America, they accepted and were then accepted and assimilated into traditional society. In the eighteenth century, new arrivals came, were accepted by traditional society, and transformed the system. They joined America with enlightened Europe. They brought in fresh monies from the dynamic capitalists in eighteenth-century Spain and fresh influence from the enlightened court.

They or their descendants formed new ruling groups. Some later led the creole fight in the 1812 Liberal Cortes. Others later led the independence movement. Merchants embracing the nineteenth-century free-trade ideology, these notable dynasties dominated political parties after independence. They introduced English merchants into the New World. Later still, they took part in industrialization. They—or at least some of them—still maintain power today. In sum, this change in strategies, so closely linked to the intellectual and economic changes of the period, was more important and longer lasting than the independence movement itself.

The revolution, for it was nothing less, was three pronged: bureaucratic, economic, and intellectual. The new Bourbon regime began the offensive in the early eighteenth century. It attacked Hapsburg institutions upon which the old ruling families' prerogatives rested. The Church provides the most obvious example. Throughout the century, the monarchy limited ecclesiastical prerogatives: first, by restricting membership in monasteries and, later, by controlling Church wealth. Some religious resources were taxed to help finance the growth in state power. Secular officials took over political positions that the Hapsburgs had left for the ecclesiastics. The Jesuits were expelled, the old families losing some of their children in the process. In Mexico and Central America, the state confiscated most Church and sodality funds, which consisted of outstanding debts, to fight the Napoleonic Wars. This *consolidación*, as it was called, along with the increased taxing of Church wealth, meant the loss of the old families' prime source of financial capital. They were ultimately compelled to look elsewhere, to the world market, for support.

Although the measures against the Church most obviously attacked traditional prerogatives, other actions took their toll as well. Most of the ancient pensions upon which notable families depended were stopped in 1720. The old families lost their right to the royal levies of tax farms and to Church tithes. The new Spanish bureaucrats gained control of all

these activities. The reform of the antiquated tax structure that depended almost exclusively upon mining and Indian tribute also affected the
families. The change extended taxes to society as a whole and to the
wealth of the creoles in particular. What had been a nominal tax on
trade that had resembled a tribute payment became a regular percentage tax on all colonial commerce. The families had to pay a levy on the
cattle, grains, cotton, wools, and other commodities they had controlled
since the conquest. The stagnant economy upon which traditional power had rested was thus compelled to compete or decline.

The old families resisted the higher levies and the expanding bureaucracy, particularly after mid century. Creoles revolted throughout the
Americas: in Peru, creoles inspired Tupac Amaru;[9] Caracas, Guatemala, and Mexico all endured spasms of rebellion. The revolts failed, for
the Bourbon monarchy that ruled absolutely and required obedience to
all its measures needed to finance increasingly numerous and prolonged
wars, regardless of traditional practices. Creoles might appeal these reforms and postpone them for a year or two, or until the decisive Intendancy Reforms of 1786, but they were eventually implemented.

The numbers and types of bureaucrats changed during this period.
David Brading estimates that the Bourbon reforms quadrupled the number of high-paying positions in Mexico. In the past, the Hapsburg monarchy had appointed Spanish officials trained in aristocratic Jesuit *cole-
gios* to expect the traditional prestige associated with bureaucratic work.
The new officials, from lower classes, from Salamanca, and from the
army, were trained in the discipline and ideals of an Enlightenment administration.

The nature of the economy changed as well. America's international
trade had been based on minerals; intercolonial commerce in wines,
grain, and cloth was not extensive. Under the Bourbons, the world economy expanded into Latin America, and attractive prices were offered
for other primary products. Cattle, which had propagated for two hundred years, roamed undisturbed on the Argentine pampa and were val-
ued highly, first for their hides and later for their meat. Cacao and indigo, farmed since the sixteenth century, suddenly rose in value, attracting
Spanish merchants to Caracas and Guatemala. The expanding European economy financed increased mineral exploitation, not only in Mexico
and Peru, but also in Honduras and New Granada. Cuba evolved from a
way station with two small cities to a major producer of tobacco and coffee. Soon after, it became the world's largest producer of sugar. The ac-
tivist Bourbon bureaucracy promoted the new trade. In the early years,

it licensed trade monopolies in the New World to peninsular interests and, later in the century, opened ports of the peninsula and the New World to colonial commerce, creating free trade within the empire.

New merchants came with peninsular capital and offered high prices for land and commodities. They financed old ruling families to expand production, paid high salaries to free laborers, and paid the laborers for basic commodities, whose price concomitantly rose. Although these credit arrangements had existed previously, the merchant-producer structure became paramount, replacing the Church-communal structure that had financed most enterprises.

The old Iberian creole society was not prepared to deal with such transformations in economic structure and conditions. Unaccustomed to change, it did not initially perceive their threatening nature. Increased prices for salaries and exportable commodities led to inflation, and inflation to an increased dependence upon the new market. Higher taxes added to the pressure upon the old families, who could once turn to the Church for funds. Now, however, the Church itself was in need, its resources eroded by inflation and government intervention.

For those with capital, the needs of an expanding state bureacracy and the expenses of intermittent eighteenth-century warfare created new opportunities. Positions in the chief colonial judicial body, the *audiencia*, were sold, giving access to power for those with funds.[10] The creation of a colonial militia, financed by the proceeds from the sale of commissions, established another source of prestige that would be converted into power in the revolutionary wars. When the Jesuits were expelled in 1767 (1759 in Brazil), their valuable lands were sold instead of being offered to the old families. When Church debts were consolidated in 1803 and all outstanding loans were called in, only those with a sufficient commercial base were strong enough to withstand or profit from the measure.

In these ways, traditional power lost support. Mid-eighteenth-century documents make faint appeals to the past to protect traditional practices held "since time immemorial," but these were unsuccessful. "Pure blood," no longer a means of maintaining power, devolved into a social usage. Legally, the status remained, but only as a vestigial obstruction that a few pesos could remove.

Money and commerce joined family traditions as sources of authority after the mid eighteenth century. The proliferation in the number of merchant guilds in the 1790s symbolized the new values, as did the enlightened "Societies of Friends" established among the new merchants.

People still attended church and new families gave their children to the cloth, but the Church no longer monopolized the culture. Newspapers proliferated and commented on colonial life as the pulpit once had.

Though the new prominent families transformed colonial values, they had to accept much of the old cultural system. Money became the principal source of power, but the family was still the critical vehicle for maintaining authority. The newcomers clearly knew this fact. They established large extended families with holdings in different parts of the empire: a merchant house in the capital, perhaps one or two cousins in other colonies, and preferably one in Cádiz with a source of capital. Such interconnections guaranteed and continued power. Political marriages reinforced power. Where love and blood failed, money succeeded: alliances based upon commercial affinities and credit were created.

From 1750 until the end of the century, the new members of the secular and ecclesiastical cabildos, cofradías, and merchant guilds illustrated the rise of these new families to wealth and prominence. Cabildos and other organizations lost their influence. Where they once created new power, they now ratified the power that already existed. For example, the cabildo license to import meat, previously controlled by the traditional family web, was now held by the member who had sufficient commercial allies. Labor that the cabildo previously controlled (through repartimiento) diminished in importance as free salaried labor took its place.

But the quasi-extended notable family remained the basis for power. Government positions, agricultural and commercial holdings, honors and prestige all were cornered and passed on through kinship ties. Marriage provided a critical means of advancement, and blood lines remained important for economic and social reasons. In the revolutionary era of the eighteenth century, when old economic, political, and bureaucratic structures faded, the social power of the ruling notable family remained, and it endured through the wars of independence and into the national period.

The "Bourbon" families established their American position, especially in colonies like Cuba or Buenos Aires where commercial expansion and bureaucratic measures created a new societal order. Elsewhere they merged with old families. In places where traditional resistance to outsiders was strong, they, in the words of Mary Lowenthal Felstiner, "manipulated institutions." Within the cabildos, the militias, the universities, and the Church, they fought for power. In some areas, the second generation (creoles) fought the first (peninsulares) for trade and position.

As the new arrivals conquered traditional society, their children—products of the eighteenth-century union of American and Iberian blood—led America toward independence. The new arrivals had been rebels, invaders who had spent their energy gaining acceptance and positions of authority. Their children, however, were natives, members of creole society. The new creoles (as distinguished from the descendants of the hijos de los conquistadores) created an ideology to replace the fading religiosity of the ruling families. It merged Bourbon and Enlightenment thought, attacking Church privilege and introducing the idea that money ought to be, according to the laws of nature, free to move without restrictions. The ideas varied from region to region, but they were all radical reactions against and departures from traditional thought.

The rivalries between old and new creole families, between creole and peninsular groups, between merchants, planters, and artisans were articulated in doctrinaire language. Those individuals with direct links to Spain allied themselves politically with the lower artisan classes. The alliance was mutually beneficial since it allowed both groups to combat those who traded contraband with the English, French, and Portuguese. These monopolists, or mercantilists, also found allies among creoles who were descended from the conquerors, had received titles and privileges from the crown, and had gradually lost some of their social and economic power over the past half century. The new merchants, with their sources of capital and their prestige enhanced by marriage with traditional families, fought in the cabildos for control of the meat and grain trade and in the empire for the right to trade in a free market. They discovered, translated, and frequently misinterpreted enlightened laissez-faire ideology to meet their own needs.

In most areas of Latin America, connections can be traced between the newly created ruling families that were formed in the late eighteenth century and the leaders of the political "parties" of the national epoch. After independence was gained, the families, by then interconnected into networks, became the parties. In areas as diverse as Buenos Aires, Chile, Lima, Bogotá, Quito, Guatemala, São Paulo, the Yucatán, and even in Spanish Cuba, family factions, family behavior, and attitudes from the earlier period were transferred to the later.

Postindependence Adjustment

The new ruling families perceived the implications of independence with limited vision. They had begun to form alliances with each other and had prospered markedly with the alterations the Bourbons fostered in colonial society. Now free to pursue their interests without royal restrictions or competition from peninsulares, they anticipated the continued expansion of their economic holdings and a significant increase in their political and social power. They assumed the changes in the rest of the society would serve their own ends as well.

Certain creoles, some notables among them, saw in independence the possibilities for the creation of a new national order, one patterned after the institutions taking shape in the industrial societies of the North Atlantic. They sought to graft republican institutions and enlightened ideas onto the existing colonial society and to encourage the new foreign contacts permeating the economy to serve as catalysts for the evolution of such a new order. But they were a distinct minority. Other sectors, including most notables, who supported the interests of traditional institutions and groups, overwhelmed them in numbers and influence and thwarted their political initiatives.

In some ways, the visions of each group were shattered. No new order was firmly in the making, yet notable families found the fundamental context of colonial society being altered. Independence had eradicated the imperial structure, which had provided established sources of authority and patterns for the organization of society and its institutions. Yet only weak nations emerged, and they were sovereign in name only. Below were provinces and states—formerly the focus of cultural patterns and economic activity, now invested with a complex political milieu—and the familiar district level of the colonial order, the locality.

Elements of a world market hovered along the edges of this emerging order, eager to penetrate. English textiles had entered the monopolistic Iberian trade network twenty years before independence. Now, unfettered by metropolitan intermediaries, English, French, North American, and other traders entered in earnest. British merchants, in particular, quickly established themselves in the ports, capitals, and important urban centers to compete with local businesspeople and formed sizable colonies in places like Buenos Aires, Rio de Janeiro, and Valparaiso. They offered the notables more favorable credit terms, better prices, and a wider selection of imported goods than local merchants could. Moreover, some of the resident foreign merchants cemented their mercantile ties by marrying into local notable families. Thus they repeated the pattern of the new Bourbon immigrants of the previous two generations.

The results of this "invasion," however, were not all positive. Along with the damage done during the war years, foreign contacts dislocated and destroyed both colonial patterns of interchange and local economies previously protected by the crown. They fostered the direct contact of each region with the international market, whether that region had attained nation status itself or was part of a larger national entity. For example, the complex economic network centered on the silver mines of Upper Peru fell apart. Chile was free from the virtual monopoly the Peruvians held on its trade. Increased demands for the livestock products of the littoral provinces of La Plata allowed those areas to finance imports. The interior provinces found their balanced economy unraveling. José Francia practically sealed off Paraguay from external economic activity.

Even when the restoration of these markets or the creation of new interdependent internal ones seemed feasible, other difficulties arose. Without a high protective customs barrier, geographical obstacles and internal tariffs made price competition virtually impossible. Goods manufactured abroad and transported across the ocean were still less expensive. Throughout the Americas, textile artisans and those who supplied their cloth especially suffered from the influx of cheap English garments. In addition, a large percentage of the population was reduced to self-subsistence. Through preference, impoverishment, or the destruction of their protected natural markets, they no longer participated in either the remote metropolitan economy of the dominant cities or the world economy.

Even the notable families who wanted to expand their holdings through interchange with the world economy faced serious difficulties. The war and independence had precipitated labor shortages, and service during the conflict uprooted many laborers. Many slaves were freed. Regions like coastal Peru, Colombia, Venezuela, and Nicaragua were especially affected. Without royal support, notables could not easily compel the laboring classes to perform regular salaried work. Stubborn, even violent, resistance often confronted their efforts to secure additional land and the labor of those working on it. In Mexico's Yucatán peninsula, such efforts led to a caste war.

Notables with a national perspective, generally those in the principal cities and ports, were thus trapped between the dismal outlook for interdependent, self-sufficient internal economies and the attraction of the international market. In Paraguay, Francia demonstrated that one could choose the former, though at considerable cost to prominent families. For notables in the localities, the prospects of stagnation were all too clear and immediate; those of dependency were only dimly perceived. Yet only in the latter part of the century did the notables systematically adopt a position that made them dependent upon the world economy.

The political context changed as well. In the colonial order, the crown had been the ultimate arbiter between sectors enmeshed in a continual, often bitter, struggle for predominance, prerogative, or autonomy. Colonial society respected the sovereignty of royal will. With independence, the source of legitimate authority quickly came into question. The monarchical mode of authority, developed through centuries, could not be passed on easily. The crown had respected a diversity of interests among regions and groups. The new national structures embodied a commitment to unity and uniformity, but they could not contain the regionalism, caste and class conflicts, and personal and familial rivalries developed in the colonial period. Some nation-states failed quickly, breaking down into national entities that corresponded closely to colonial regional societies: Uruguay, Paraguay, Ecuador, and the Central American Republics. Others divided into smaller groupings of regional societies. In Argentina, Peru, Colombia, and Venezuela, nearly a half century elapsed before national and regional interests were reconciled. Only Mexico and Brazil kept their colonial structure intact, but even there, regionalism and group conflict could not be avoided.

In this political vacuum, those endeavoring to consolidate power and establish their claims to authority faced two new facts of political life. The cessation of royal supervision brought with it both freedom and liability. Royal restrictions to colonial initiative had been removed, but also terminated were a variety of supports to colonial endeavors and relations. Moreover, the very nature of politics was altered. In the past, each sector had used the political institutions as petitioners fighting for their own prerogatives before the crown. With independence, they continued to use the new governmental structures almost solely as vehicles for the protection and promotion of private interests, even though mediation, compromise, and acquiescence to majority will were prime requisites in the new representative, republican structures, which lacked a final arbiter. Notable families held a distinct advantage in such a political milieu. Their advantage was circumscribed, however, by the fact that less-advantaged groups, the new military, and caudillos resorted to the use of armed force.

In this situation, each group had its own aims. Some had nationalist pretensions. Personalist caudillos, military commanders, and dominant groups in new metropolises like Buenos Aires and Bogotá (formerly colonial administrative centers) tried to establish centralized governments. While they had the power to achieve nationhood and to open their nations to trade with the international market, they lacked the authority that the king once possessed to enforce their sovereignty. The control of trade and of the centralization of its commercial and fiscal benefits was difficult at best. Localities frequently ignored edicts issued at the national centers since they wished to manage and profit from trade and taxes themselves. Even in Brazil, where monarchy successfully continued, autonomous tendencies threatened national unity for two decades.

At the local level, notable families faced similar problems while trying to expand their interests. They frequently found their authority over other groups questioned or resisted. The legitimacy they had derived from royal authority evaporated. Such families in the Northwest and the Yucatán in Mexico, in the interior of Argentina and Uruguay, and in Guatamala came to understand particularly well that authority now rested in military force, in personalist leadership, or in some fragile hold on tradition.

The situation at the provincial or state level was even more amorphous. As an intermediate level of the colonial government, its authority and actual power had always been nebulous. The Bourbon intendancy system, devised to correct this situation, had come too late and had operated too briefly to succeed. After independence, this intermediate level became a focal point of political contention. Those with extralocal interests set about creating institutional political structures through which they could impose their will downward to the localities. At the same time, local families sought to extend their domination upward to the provincial or state level through alliances with other families or through the sheer weight of their expanding economic domain.

Politics in nineteenth-century Latin America, while concerned with a number of conspicuous issues such as Church-state relations and corporate privilege, was primarily engaged in the problem of working out a governmental framework in which national, provincial, and local interests could coexist to mutual advantage. Each had its own problems, its own "visions" of what society should become. It is for this reason that politics after independence seems so wrought with geopolitical conflicts and with inconsistencies in the composition of political elements and in their responses to specific issues.

Ideological questions reflected these conflicts and inconsistencies. The ideological division at the national level was twofold. On one side were those who favored implanting the ideals of the Enlightenment, building upon the Bourbon reforms and the liberal peninsula constitutionalism of the late colonial period; the other side preferred the benefits and security of the traditional colonial order. For twenty-five years, the conflict continued between enlightened reform and traditionalism. By mid century, however, the influence from Europe was growing, especially after the revolutions of 1848. Reflection on the turmoil of the recent past in Latin America and European liberal and conservative philosophy combined to create a more coherently based and comprehensively drawn struggle.

At the local and provincial levels, the preoccupations of notable families were less ideological. Notables quickly took the initiative in their areas and became the focus of political elements and issues. To secure their dominance in the local society and economy, prominent families affiliated themselves with ideologies current at the national level. Local notables did share, often among themselves and at times with national interests, a common vision of what society should or could become. However, their ideals were often obfuscated by other realities: the practical means to realize or preserve their visions and the appropriate responses to often unfamiliar and unanticipated circumstances.

The location of government power was a prime consideration in determining ideological affiliations. In the Plata, the "centralists," who were the Unitarians and centered in Buenos Aires, desired an "enlightened" transformation of the former viceroyalty and wanted to concentrate economic and political influence in that port. The "federalists," notable families of the interior and littoral provinces, aligned themselves with other local elements to preserve their interests. In contrast, Mexican centralists were the chief defenders of the existing order, based in the former colonial power centers of the central core, the capital being the most prominent. Mexican federalists, dominated by the notable families of the provincial centers outside the central core, promoted reforms and sought a new societal order. In Colombia and Central America, "liberal" towns assumed their political pose against neighboring "conservative" ones as each allied with the enemy of the other to gain regional power.

The question of fiscal policy also helped determine ideological affiliations. During the independence years, the impoverishment of the treasury in most countries made the formulation of fiscal policy especially critical. National governments and institutions diverted revenues to themselves, leaving local notables with meager public funds to cover administrative and military expenses, to finance education and public improvements, and to subsidize private enterprises. Moreover, such revenue usually came at the expense of the private economic holdings of the local notables and were frequently used to undercut their influence: these funds subsidized centralized administrative structures, national police and military forces, and extralocal economic interests.

Free trade was both an ideological concept and a way to achieve power. Questions of monopolies and legal equality that had been decided earlier by the crown were reopened as privilege was challenged and taxes expanded. The Indian tribute, for example, became a direct or "voluntary" annual contribution that all sectors had to pay. The individuals or groups controlling the collection of revenue frequently determined who had to pay. Of course, those sectors that endured and were able to influence fiscal policy used the subsequent income to expand their authority.

One's position regarding the new and the old—what was to be done about the colonial past and the institutions that embodied and upheld it—was equally important in determining ideological affiliations. Some notables saw the Church, the Indian village corporate community, the military, the artisan guild, and slavery as obstacles (either individually or together) to the expansion of their families' economic activities and to their consolidation of political power. Others viewed them as necessary supports of local society and their own dominant position. Military garrisons could be a bane to those involved in contraband. They could also be a blessing to those facing hostile tribal Indians or slave insurrections. The Church could strongly reinforce the strict colonial hierarchical authority in the turmoil of the independence epoch. It could also impede wider contacts with the North Atlantic world in matters of trade, education, fashion, and thought. Frequently, the position of family members in each of these groups or institutions, or the family's relations with them, determined the notables' ideological stance in this matter.

After independence, society still revolved around the notables. Other local elements might challenge their dominance: caste rebellions in the Yucatán, Central America, or Northwest Mexico; gaucho or llanero revolts on the plains of South America. But notable families successfully countered these contentious elements or merged their interests with them. They controlled municipal politics, dominated local economic activities, and to a great extent determined the acceptable, refined modes of behavior of local society. Almost exclusively, they possessed the power to allow or block entrance to the new North Atlantic currents. They made arrangements with foreign merchants, banks, and governments and introduced improved modes of economic operation. They chose and then translated new ideas and fashions. They permitted or continued the ban on different religious thought and practice. They determined the type and extent of changes in schooling and public improvements. They established the criteria for the inclusion of foreign entrepreneurs into local society.

Some notable families remained totally loyal to the old colonial order, tolerating minimal republican alterations as the necessary price of securing independence. Others were open to the influences of the North Atlantic world and the new societal order such influences seem to foster. Most, however, fell somewhere in between. Alarmed by the instabilities arising in the wake of independence, they guarded many of the prerogatives of the colonial order to restore and maintain stability. Nevertheless, the possibilities for expanding their political and economic power through foreign contacts and republican government led them to tolerate, if not embrace, the North Atlantic influences.

These frequently contradictory tendencies coexisted within individual notables, their families, and in the family networks. Circumstances determined them, though personal inclinations were also important. The contradictions were further enlarged with the emergence of a new generation at mid century. This group was less tolerant of opposing inclinations than their elders and were more pronounced in their ideological commitments. They had no memory of Iberian rule and the wars of independence. They possessed an independent past on which they could pass judgment and had the advanced educations—greatly influenced by North Atlantic thought—that prepared them to so. As they came into power, the North Atlantic world began its great nineteenth-century investment and expansion in Latin America.

Generational and interfamily conflicts were mitigated by an awareness among notables that the basis of their local dominance and of the expansion of their interests rested, to a large degree, on family cohesion and cooperation. This understanding, above all, enabled them to overcome the threat to their power in the political struggles of the mid nineteenth century. These struggles extended beyond the internal conflicts of the notables to the issue of the widening of political participation that such disunity occasioned, impassioned by the marked infusion of ideology into politics. The 1850s and 1860s also saw political nationhood enforced, achieved, or confirmed through revolutions involving the new political participants, wars with neighbors, and resistance to foreign invaders. These struggles almost always left national governments with more effective influence, power, and authority. In Argentina, the Paraguayan War created the first national army and bureaucracy. In Mexico and most of Central America, civil war and foreign invasion led to the rise of strong, liberal, national regimes.

For the notables in the Dominican Republic who accepted recolonization by Spain, for those in Mexico who cooperated with the French intervention, for those in the interior of Argentina who supported the revolt opposing the war with Paraguay, family cohesion provided a haven from retribution and the mechanism for recovery. For those notables on the victorious side in such political struggles, the family network became the chief means for securing their interests.

By this time, most countries had a far more energetic and influential national government with which to deal, one becoming more prosperous and effective. Economic conditions had begun to change once again. Those with national pretensions would be in an increasingly favorable position to expand their power and interests into the political vacuum at the intermediate level of government and, eventually, down to the local level as well. Local notables had to contend with this potential threat. Notable family networks acquiring provincial and even national aspirations found it an opportunity from which they could profit.

The Late Nineteenth Century: Zenith of the Family Network

Latin America in the late nineteenth century witnessed the emergence of national political structures, though they varied in stability and centralization. National economies began to form; these linked regional activities, destroyed or transformed many local economic patterns, and uprooted and transformed various segments of the laboring classes. Almost always, however, these national economies were directed outward. New cultural patterns appeared that belittled traditional modes, but older expressions of national or indigenous culture remained visible and were preferred by large portions of the population. Social relations became less personal, less bound by obligation, more controlled by the public realm, yet the patronal and familial habits and sensitivities persisted.

Although these changes would seem to have threatened the notables' predominance, they prospered through their family networks, expanding their wealth and control in their localities. Many extended their hegemony to the provincial and regional levels; some even parlayed their wealth and power into control of the new national political and economic structures. At all levels—local, state, regional, and national—notable networks reached a consensus. They were still contentious, sniping for improved position and occasionally engaging in hostile, even armed, encounters. However, among these networks existed a common awareness, a tacit understanding, an accepted mode of operation. This enabled them to convert the potentially challenging circumstances of the late nineteenth century into opportunities to expand their power and preeminence until they dominated Latin American society at all levels.

These families endured and attained such power because of the strength and adaptability of the network structure. The intrusion of the industrial revolution set off political and economic expansion and specialization in late-nineteenth-century Latin America. It triggered the demand for specific raw materials in great quantities and spurred commercial agriculture in numerous commodities. Roads and railroads were built to move products to seaboard shipping points. The telegraph and then the telephone cable accompanied them, which produced a crucial transformation not only in communication but also in managerial structures initiated by the emerging national and state governments and business organizations. The family networks became the advocates and conveyors of centralized, technological modes of operation introduced by foreign capital. Adopting the new managerial principles, the family networks operated as quasi-public entities and often paralleled official governmental structures. By these means, notables generally solidified and extended their local control and worked out an agreeable compromise with the national and state political structures; and some families extended their influence, even hegemony, to those high political levels.

For most notables, this particular response was more a matter of necessity than choice. After a half century of periodic instability and general feebleness (Chile and Brazil being noteworthy exceptions), national and state governments were crystallizing into instruments of power and permanence. They could no longer be ignored, put off, or even finessed by notables with local or regional interests. Most striking was the rapidly expanding presence of the national and state governments.

In the last third of the nineteenth century, government bureaucracies appeared. They were increasingly specialized, with clearly defined lines of authority. Customs agents, ministerial and departmental secretaries, engineers, educational supervisors and inspectors, tax assessors and collectors, medical officers, armed forces and police personnel—their numbers steadily increased. Since better and more specific training was required of those holding bureaucratic positions, they performed managerial duties more effectively. Consequently, public education was firmly established and the number of professional and technical schools also increased as part of the enlargement of the sphere of higher education. Expertise became a requisite for educational and fiscal management, public works, and judicial administration. European military missions, particularly from Germany and France, were contracted to professionalize the armed forces and upgrade equipment and capabilities. National and state police forces, established on a permanent basis, received formal organization and logistical support and soon developed intelligence sections.

The technological revolution spreading throughout Latin America assisted the expansion of the bureaucratic presence, and both government and private enterprise turned that intrusion to advantage. National and state bureaucracies could maintain quick, direct contact with the localities because of improved communication and transportation. Rail, telegraph, and telephone lines largely overcame the difficulties of distance, delay, and isolation that faced government officials in earlier years. National and state offices, agencies, and troop detachments became widespread, permanent fixtures at the local level, working closely with one another.

Above all, the altered condition of the treasury made this improved training and technology possible. In the last third of the century, the struggle to make administrative ends meet and to head off the steady accumulation of public debt gave way to fiscal soundness and, in many cases, prosperity. The increased efficiency of the bureaucracy (a cyclical reinforcement) contributed to the rising revenues. Far more responsible was the accelerated expansion of economic activity, supported by the renewed accessibility of foreign capital after four decades of caution and lack of interest.

Pragmatically assisting the hands that now fed them, national and state governments placed their enlarged capabilities at the disposal of entrepreneurs whose activities entailed extralocal, national interests. These enterprises, an increasing number of which were foreign, both fostered and profited from the new technology, the more corporate forms of business organization, and the large concentrations of investment capital.

Both the extralocal enterprises and the national and state governments eventually understood that their interests paralleled one another. Through the notable family network, their mutual concerns became increasingly intertwined. Each reinforced the other's interest in breaking down local barriers and in extending power and influence over the localities. For example, in return for revenues, loans, and services, extralocal entrepreneurs received subsidies, generous concessions, profit and loan guarantees, judicial and diplomatic support, and security assistance. More specifically, this meant grants of land to help finance railroads, police to put down workers' strikes and peasant resistance, tax exemptions for new industry, and legal removal of local tariffs and trade restrictions. Every port work, every telegraph line, every railroad connection, every

surfaced road—whether governmentally, privately, or jointly financed—
furthered the position of those in the localities with extralocal interests
(whether political or economic).

In some countries, the interrelated power and presence of the representatives of national economic and political institutions appeared at
mid century. Peru shows a family network emerging in the guano trade;
it involved both national and foreign entrepreneurs, the importation of
Chinese laborers, the transfer of capital to coastal haciendas through the
liquidation of the domestic debt, the beginnings of a railroad infrastructure, and the creation of a strong national government. Chile offers another case, centering on the copper and nitrate mining industry. In Brazil, coffee and rails (as Richard Graham and Warren Dean have shown)
provided the initial bases for the process. Expansion was delayed a decade or two in other countries (especially Mexico, Colombia, and Central
America) until the serious conflicts of mid century were settled or dif-
fused and foreign investment became widespread.

A new sociopolitical philosophy helped cement the alliance of those
with national, extralocal interests. Positivism mitigated the ideological
divisions of the mid nineteenth century, offering a world view broad
enough to accommodate both liberals and conservatives. Consequently,
they could cooperate or at least compete within acceptable bounds. Liberals were promised the dissolution of the traditional colonial order,
though positivism also required a centralization of power and a restraint
on the exercise of freedom. Conservatives were offered an ordered society in which they could add to their wealth and position, but at the price
of abandoning the traditional modes of society. Family networks that
heretofore had been divided by ideological schisms found a way to unite
through the positivistic view.

Most important, positivism blessed the "progressive" activities of those
with extralocal interests (whatever their political bent) who wanted to
broaden governmental activity, make it more scientific in scope, and
prosper by it. After nearly a century, the power, wealth, and influence of
notable families could very well have been subordinated and diminished
in the process. But they employed the family networks they had been
constructing for three generations to permeate and then dominate the
new economic and political structures.

The family networks joined or integrated their economic interests
with those beyond the local level through a variety of arrangements:
partnerships, shareholding, branch operations, professional services, incorporation, and agency representation. In many cases, these were

made within and among family networks and, in growing instances, crossed local and even provincial boundaries. Connections were also made with newcomers, whether foreigners or nationals, with new wealth or political position. The notable networks increasingly adopted and spread the new managerial principles practiced by North Atlantic entrepreneurs in setting up business arrangements. Marriage sometimes gave permanence to these business ties.

Political connections were formed in similar fashion. Family members began political careers, office holding becoming a full-time responsibility. Through family politicians, political coalitions were formed between notable networks and with other influential elements at the local, state, and national levels. Many coalitions of notable networks secured ongoing control of state politics; some succeeded in dominating whole regions. A few (a group of families of Buenos Aires, for example) placed themselves at the center of national politics. The expansion of economic holdings and political power was mutually reinforcing, and the new managerial principles provided a common denominator in developing business and governmental structures.

Once political activities grew beyond the local level and stabilized and economic activities accelerated, profound geopolitical changes took place. The family networks that were successful in expanding their influence beyond their localities profited greatly from them. Even those that did not, found their local positions significantly strengthened. Relations between states (or regions) and the national government became predictable. They began to understand that their interests could be mutually beneficial rather than antagonistic. In return for cooperating with or at least deferring to the national government, those who dominated states and regions found they received support when consolidating their political power and promoting their public concerns through the local family network. Opposition circles could be muted, and middle- and lower-strata elements effectively excluded from the political process. Important concessions and subsidies could be secured to build the infrastructure necessary for economic expansion.

State control over the localities greatly increased as well. But here, too, prior adversary relations were increasingly turned to mutual advantage. Although local family networks encountered greater regulation and supervision of municipal government, they also received external backing to enhance their position and achieve their public and private aims. State security forces assisted in quelling political disturbances or protests against the notables' expanding enterprises. Financial aid from the government provided the essential economic base for the construction of new municipal buildings, jails, and power and light systems. Tax exemptions furnished additional incentive and profit for enterprises.

Accommodation of the foreigner—as immigrant and investor—was a corollary of the new political environment. Foreigners had open and equal access to all levels of the government and the economy, and they were soon present there in various capacities. The foreigner was regarded primarily as a source of capital and technical expertise. For example, North Americans and Europeans established packing plants in the La Plata estuary. Germans contracted to set up normal schools and to professionalize the armed forces in Chile. British mechanics installed machinery in new Brazilian factories, while North American engineers directed the construction of railroad lines at numerous places along the West Coast from Mexico to Chile.

Foreign entrepreneurs and family networks involved in state and national governments supported schemes to import labor. Chinese laborers built railroads in northern Mexico and worked on Peruvian haciendas; later, many entered business for themselves in urban centers. Immigrants from southern Europe worked in factories, on docks, and on farms in Brazil, Chile, and the La Plata area.

Local notables realized that the foreigners enhanced their own local power and interests. As a potentially large work force, they often could do the skilled and technical labor that local workers could not. As investors, they supplied the capital necessary to exploit undeveloped resources, and they made the public improvements necessary to promote such ventures. As commercial agents and shippers, they offered new lines of goods; as professionals, they provided improved or previously unavailable services in such areas as education, management, construction, and medicine.

The state and national political interests that increasingly subordinated local notables (and into which the more successful family networks blended) also furnished the backing and assistance these families needed to promote their expanding economic enterprises. Government provided access to resources like land, water, timber, and minerals. It granted loans, subsidies, or tax exemptions to ensure the success of family businesses and provided similar aid to improve transportation and communications to make them highly profitable. If other social elements resisted (gauchos, tribal Indians, communal villagers, or workers, for example), the government furnished security forces to stifle such resistance.

In the new political and economic environment, conflict remained but was increasingly diminished by the awareness that the benefits of accommodation and the costs of political defeat were steadily rising. In countries like Mexico, Venezuela, and Guatemala, where a strong national political machine or coalition had consolidated power, the family networks knew the consequences of pushing a political complaint too far. In countries such as Colombia and Chile, where more open competition among regional networks existed, the economic price of carrying opposition to the point of revolution was also understood.

Given the growing consensus among their networks and between them and the extralocal political and economic structures (which they increasingly influenced if not controlled), the notable families rapidly accumulated wealth and consolidated political power. In the process, they also altered their conception of themselves and their society. They had fulfilled the aspirations to hegemony for which the previous two generations had striven. But in the late nineteenth century, they began to view themselves as more than the locally prominent, more even than the nation's eminent. Their world view began to extend beyond national boundaries to include association with the North Atlantic world, a world of assured progress, the most successful of human societies, the direction of the whole world's future. Participation in that successful North Atlantic community, for themselves and for their countries, was, in their terms, the height of notability.

The countries of the notable families had been beset with difficulties for more than a half century. Now they were beginning to cohere, to gain a permanence of prosperity through their ties with the international market. The lesson for the notables seemed to be that as they "progressed," so did their societies. Moreover, they were progressing as they modeled themselves after the powerful of Europe and North America, who had brought their countries to such an advanced state of progress and civilization. In that way, Latin America's notables concluded, they, along with the societies they led, could take their place alongside the advanced societies of the North Atlantic.

To participate fully in that North Atlantic world, notable families increasingly adopted the manners, tastes, accoutrements, and attitudes of those successful societies. Things foreign, things "North Atlantic," became marks of distinction in the notables' own societies that signaled a new level of status and authority. The modes of imitation were varied and far-reaching.

As reflected in their newspapers and literary works, the notables began to think "foreign" more and more. Living foreign was equally important. From residences to household furnishings, from diet to fashion, the more foreign the better. Even burial caskets were imported; as one had lived in the latest style, so one went out in it. All of the latest techno-

logical improvements, planning, and architectural styles were introduced into urban life and on many country estates. Notable families
wanted their institutions and their gathering points to be North Atlantic
as well. They supported European military missions and educational administrators, and hired foreign-born professionals to staff medical facilities, lead bands, and design buildings and parks.

While ascending to the ranks of the successful in the North Atlantic
world, the notable families separated themselves from the rest of society.
They cut their ties of association and obligation with fellow countrypeo-
ple, who were far poorer, far less educated, and almost always, less
white. They employed a variety of means to separate themselves from
the rest of society. New residential neighborhoods physically isolated
them. The greatly enlarged residences allowed them to pursue many of
their activities in the privacy of the home. Exclusive schools served the
same purpose for their children. Lectures, concerts in extravagant halls,
grand balls became occasions for notables to isolate themselves from
those beneath them in their own society. At the same time, they could associate with distinguished foreigners in their midst and feel a part of that
desirable North Atlantic world.

The notable families, who had traditionally assumed social and economic obligations as part of the quid pro quo of their dominant position
in local society, began to neglect them, particularly in the cities. They
slighted client relations, affecting the middle strata (especially the families' poor relations) and the *clases populares*. Their focus increasingly
narrowed to business advantage. Competition intensified markedly as
protective local isolation broke down, and as resources became more usable and marketable, the population was increasingly uprooted, both
physically and culturally. Competition allowed a few to get very rich
precisely because they discarded traditional associations and obligations.[11]

In place of the patronal relations by which their dominant position
had been customarily maintained, notables turned to more impersonal
means to control society. This trend increased as family members assumed political careers. The family networks, influencing if not controlling all levels of government, more and more employed public resources
to meet minimum obligations to the middle and lower levels of society
and to thwart any resistance to their interests or position.

More and more, the government dispensed services, alleviating the
notables' traditional patronal obligations. Education, medical care, re-
lief, utilities, security, festivities all were subsidized and administered by
the public realm, particularly the local municipal government. Quasi-

public juntas (almost always directed by notables) often assisted in these tasks. When the consequences of the notables' expanding economic interests and political power led to resistance, the enlarged and more efficient governmental security forces were employed. They quelled workers' strikes and suppressed village uprisings. Individuals in trouble with the law (many of them as a result of the economic changes) were put away in new state penitentiaries and municipal jails or were organized into work crews and contract laborers.

The expansion of public services and institutions did more than serve as a buffer for the family networks controlling the rest of society. It also conferred benefits on the families themselves. Besides the supports to their private economic endeavors noted above, government (and the quasi-public juntas organized under its auspices) assisted them in attaining the new style of life they eagerly sought. Public funds turned dilapidated plazas into elegant gathering places, mirroring North Atlantic parks in material, furnishings, and styles. Government helped organize and sustain band concerts and elaborate festivities to honor notable accomplishments. It provided quality education, especially at advanced and professional levels, where private instruction was unavailable or unfeasible.

Enjoying a level of wealth and power never before achieved, linked to the successful North Atlantic world, distinctly set apart from those beneath their station, Latin America's notables in the early years of the new century could look back with a sense of accomplishment. For three generations, through family networks adapting to changing circumstances, they had steadily extended their dominance and authority beyond the Bourbon colonial districts and localities. After more than a century, they were the centers of power and authority at all levels of their national societies.

We now turn to specific case studies that illustrate this synthesis. In Latin America in the modern period, the conditions and circumstances of the cases vary. Guatemala's capital city was the metropolis for a colonial province that became a nation-state. Northwest Mexico was a colonial region that remained provincial through the nineteenth century. Buenos Aires was a province and capital city that established itself as the power center of a collection of regional entities that became the nation of Argentina.

2

Central America

The patriarch of the archetypal Central American notable family arrived in the middle of the eighteenth century. He linked up with traditional groups, forming strong commercial connections throughout the colony, to Spain, and eventually to Great Britain and the United States. The notable family he founded helped to shape the intellectual milieu that led to the liberal nineteenth century; its children took part in the independence movement. Subsequently, these links allowed the family to maintain its position despite political turmoil, lost battles, temporary exile, and severe economic fluctuations. Some branches of the family were able to preserve their influence into the mid twentieth century.

Central Americans utilized the notable family and many traditional "strategies" of holding status and power to weather the storms of market economies and industrial changes. Vulnerable to fluctuations in capital, in world markets, and to periodic political reversals, families created defenses through linkages or networks among themselves.

Although the notable family typified the nineteenth-century strategy, we trace the pattern to Iberia, to the long heritage of familial power in the Spanish colony and in preindustrial Spain. Of course, market fluctuations did not have the same impact then as they did in the nineteenth century. Neither were political changes as dramatic as with the comings and goings of caudillos, the civil wars between liberals and conservatives, and the intense regional tensions that characterized the later period. But though the forces it faced differed, the family was the major institution for the preservation of status and wealth.

In Latin America, Central America provides a good example of the force of the past on the nineteenth century. Unlike Buenos Aires and

Northwest Mexico—the other regions focused upon in this work—Central America was an old colony with a deep-seated tradition. Much like Mexico City and Lima, its families harked back to the early days of the conquest. Its institutions, labor, and land tenure patterns were two hundred years old when the new regions began to evolve.

Buenos Aires and Northwest Mexico were "new" regions. In neither area does the ritual tracing of origins to the conquerors, to the founding fathers of the sixteenth-century colony, compare with that of the regions of the Yucatán, Lima, and Central America. The Spanish presence in Buenos Aires may have dated from the sixteenth century, but in the late eighteenth century a swarm of immigrants overran the old settlement, demolishing the past and building an enlightened, mercantile society. A similar phenomenon occurred in Central America, but there traditional institutions, practices, and families remained strong. The force of the eighteenth-century invasion was not nearly as great in Central America, where there was a preponderance of Indian populations. Differing from both Central America and Buenos Aires, Northwest Mexico was actually opened up in the eighteenth century; its earlier history belonged to Indians and scattered *presidios* and Jesuit missions.

The First Two Hundred Years

As ancient as Mexico and Lima, Central America was quite different in the evolution of its economy. Minerals and boom-bust economies played an important role in creating and destroying status in Mexico and Lima. In the mining and agricultural centers of the empire's commercial network, new families came and established their wealth. The second generation exploited that wealth, and the third dissipated it.[1] The rags-to-rags-in-three-generations generalization that pervades Latin America does not fit here. The Central American economy was too stagnant, too distant from the major trade lanes to partake of the ups and downs of family fortunes that characterized Mexico and Lima.

Privilege, rather than economic fortune, was the critical element of familial authority in the first two hundred years of the Central American colony, although wealth could not be ignored. The privileged family controlled land both directly and indirectly through the Church; it held rights to Indian labor through custom, reinforced by cabildo authority; it controlled monopolies such as meat slaughtering, alcohol and meat sales, and tax collection through the cabildo; and it received government positions and pensions, that is, a guaranteed annual income as reward for and reinforcement of its loyalty to the state.[2]

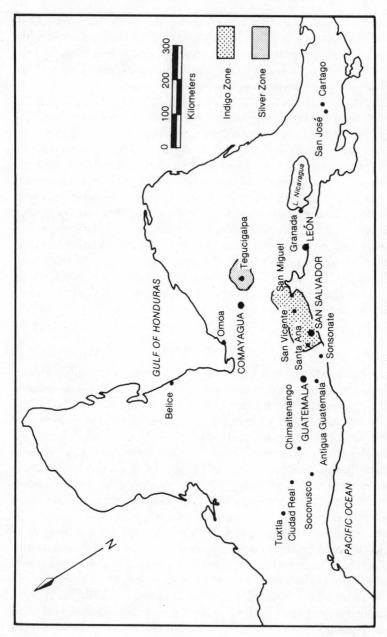

Central America about 1800.

In Central America, the family's authority was preserved through the Church. The Church provided access to finance in time of need, to clerical positions, to the fruits of its land, and to the Indian labor under its control, as well as to monopolies such as tithe collection and sale of tithe commodities.

The crown ensured the status of the family in return for its loyalty. But while privilege secured the family, its position could be weakened by a variety of causes. The family could not ignore its financial standing; impecuniousness could render it unable to pay the king his due in taxes and "voluntary" contributions, which would lead to reduced privilege. The family could lose its authority through division of resources among heirs over time. Overly pious men destroyed their families' position by giving their wealth, land, and labor to the Church to ensure their salvation. Family lines could end "naturally" by disease or a lack of heirs.

The small size of the Central American dominant group limited its ability to rejuvenate by restricting marriage choices. There were no more than 250 Spanish families (or vecinos) in each Spanish settlement, apart from Santiago de Guatemala, in 1620. In the capital city itself, there were only 1,000 families. As many as a fourth of their number entered the Church. Many never married.[3]

The pool for new blood was small. The family had to search for new "Spanish" families both to preserve the line and to increase its influence within Central America and the empire as a whole. New blood came from an erratic influx of people—officials and merchants, some from Spain and others from elsewhere in the New World, especially Mexico. These newcomers recognized that, although they might be wealthier or more powerful at court than the Central American ruling class, the power of wealth and office was fleeting. It could not be grounded in Central America without access to privilege, and that could only be achieved through marriage.

Fortunes could be made in Central America, but these did not ensure long-lasting status either there or, for that matter, anywhere in the Hispanic world. Newly made fortunes had to be linked to traditional privilege through marriage into "the families." The obverse was also true. Privilege did not require great wealth, but judicious use of privilege to preserve the family's economic position could maintain its status through centuries.

Thus, from the sixteenth to the eighteenth century, though society was not stagnant, the major source of status was traditional privilege. Beneath this principle, there was no discernable pattern of family survival. Some Spanish, like many of the early conquistadores, came for a brief

period and left. The new group that emerged in the second half of the
sixteenth century were the font of Central American privileged status.
(Succeeding generations would call their sons "hijos de los conquistadores," though they were, indeed, not.) From that time on, privileged families rose and declined according to no general rule other than recourse to
their somewhat dubious ancestry. Some survived a mere generation before the line died. Other notable families merged to survive the entire period. The most prominent example of the mid-sixteenth-century family
that maintained its status through the entire colonial period was the
Gálvez; the Montúfar family remained prominent for two hundred
years from its founding in the seventeenth century.[4]

The road to privileged status was a rocky one, and once established,
privilege was none too sure. Two seventeenth-century examples of rapid
rise and decline suffice: Juana de Osegueza was an impoverished Teguci-
galpa woman who came to Guatemala and married her daughter to
Gregorio Carillo, a peninsular *oidor* of the Guatemala audiencia and
later, of Mexico. The family rose overnight but fell just as quickly with
the daughter's early death. Josepha Inez de Asperilla, on the other hand,
derived from a prominent Salvadorean family. She married a man much
poorer than she. With her dowry, the husband purchased an indigo
farm, but when he died five years later, leaving her penniless, the farm
was seized for its encumbrances.[5] Josepha Inez lost her status in just a
few years' time. Other families lost their wealth and position more
gradually.

Nonetheless, in this early period privileged status was remarkable for
its permanence. Generally speaking, the great families—those with sufficient tradition, control over land and labor, power within the Church
and over cabildo membership—were able to maintain their status as
long as they were able to continue their line.

The Economic Revolution

The great change came in the early eighteenth century. It emerged, it
might be said, from the sea, in new currents of commerce, in the shape
of Bourbon bureaucrats and new merchants from Iberia, and in direct
response to the early industrial revolution. The change came in spurts or
jumps, restricted by the intermittent warfare of the eighteenth century,
irregular government regulations, and market forces. Warfare stunted
Latin American growth far more than it did European. Those colonies
bordering the Caribbean whose lands and commercial traffic were rav-
aged by the half-dozen wars during this century were affected more di-

rectly and immediately than England, France, or Prussia. The eighteenth-century social, economic, and intellectual revolution began fifteen years late in Latin America, after the War of the Spanish Succession. The next thirty-five years marked a slow evolution and adjustment to market forces within the stringent rules of Bourbon absolutism and to the slowly evolving Spanish industrial revolution. The influence of enlightened bureaucrats at the Madrid court took years to evolve, leading to major changes immediately after the War of Jenkins's Ear at mid century and then, after the Seven Years' War, leading to an expansion of trade within the Spanish empire.[6]

Within Central America, the commercial and legal changes were dramatic. In 1724, new government regulations stimulated mine production, which in turn attracted contraband traders along the coast. Two competitive markets were established for mineral production: one, illegal, at Río Tinto in 1729, controlled by the English, the other, a royal mint in Guatemala in 1733, by the Spanish royal authorities. Commerce expanded, and with it, attention to the colony's chief agricultural product, indigo.[7]

Central American indigo production had been limited by wars and economic fluctuations in Europe since its inception in the late sixteenth century. Throughout this period, indigo farmers in Salvador mastered the art of creating a product of a quality unparalleled anywhere in the world. For their part, the English had been attracted to the Caribbean coastline by contraband trade and by dyewoods (or Campeche wood) and were probably extracting more in true value from Central America in the late seventeenth and early eighteenth centuries than all the commodities exported from Spanish Central America combined.[8]

The commercial and industrial revolutions spurred the demand for dyes as English and European textile production rose. As textile producers learned the holding qualities of the dye and Central America's superior product, the region became a center of attention. During the War of Jenkins's Ear, demand increased further. The market boomed by 1749, and during the next decade, the price of indigo tripled on European markets.[9]

Demand for indigo brought new merchants with capital to invest from Cádiz to Central America, and in the third quarter of the eighteenth century, the structure of most of the economy changed. Before this grand reawakening, Central America had a weak commercial system, lying as it did outside the major routes of commerce. Most Spanish and Indian settlements, although involved in some trade from time to time, relied upon their individual regions for survival. In the second half of the century, what had been zones of semisubsistence became mono-culture economies. In Salvador, indigo was cultivated instead of food. All territory within the dye-producing region became extremely valu-able. Powerful groups forced poor farmers off their lands and seized In-dian common lands and cofradía properties. Money from the sale of the dye was used to purchase clothing from highland Guatemala, where food lands were converted for sheep and cotton cultivation, creating a supportive and export economy. Honduras and Nicaragua became the prime suppliers of cattle for the indigo-producing, food-hungry areas that had previously been food-producing zones. All regions became con-nected and dependent upon each other and, above all, upon the Guate-malan financiers.[10]

For the first time in the history of the colony, the capital, Santiago de Guatemala, truly became the heartland. Through its merchant houses, indigo was sent via the Caribbean port of Omoa to the outside world. Foodstuffs were sold either within the city itself or in agricultural re-gions in partial exchange for the dye. Each area became dependent upon the other for survival, and all upon the indigo markets in Europe. Gua-temalan financiers greased the commercial mechanism by extending credit for production and serving as the middlemen in trade between provinces and with other countries.

As the commercial revolution brought an unprecedented flow of cap-ital, people, and foreign intellectual influence to the New World, Bour-bon government reforms altered colonial rules and brought a new class of bureaucracy in large numbers. Population growth altered the dimen-sions of colonial society. Transportation and communication networks expanded more than at any time in the previous 150 years. New roads, ports, shipping methods, and post offices revolutionized the colonial landscape. Finally, at the end of the century, newspapers purveyed En-lightenment thought from the commercial center at Guatemala to the rest of the region.[11]

The Notable Family

The change in family authority and strategies was not as dramatic as the great watersheds in commercial and bureaucratic activity. It evolved slowly, imperceptibly, from the mid seventeenth century onward. We can appreciate how contemporaries accepted what appeared to be a continuation of old patterns and traditions from the histories of "new" families who arrived anytime from 1650 to 1750 and became prominent in the society. The eighteenth-century flow of new blood, we insist, was not a new phenomenon; the Atlantic migration had been going on since Columbus. But the influence, power, and eventually, the endurance of these groups were different. They shaped the commercial and ideological structure of the colony, and they formed the basis for the notable family strategy that endured through the nineteenth century.

The Vidaurre family provides an excellent example of the early colonial roots of the later strategy. José de Vidaurre came to the New World in the mid seventeenth century—the exact year we do not know. A Basque with commercial connections in Cádiz, he married the daughter of a Granada merchant and sister of the dean of León Cathedral. The union of peninsular and creole notables created a strong dynasty based upon tradition and extensive landholdings in León and Granada. The marriage of their son, Bartolomé, to Juana de Carrión y Mendoza, cemented an alliance with one of the most powerful families in Nicaragua. The Mendoza lineage in Central America dated back to the conquest, and the Carrión, to the late sixteenth century. The Carrión and Mendoza links yielded enormous privilege. The primogenitor and Juana's brother, Fernando, had been a *regidor* (councilman) of the León cabildo for an extraordinary sixty-six years. Another brother, Nicolas, was master of León Cathedral and head of the Office of the Inquisition in Nicaragua through the early eighteenth century.[12]

The power of the Vidaurre Carrión y Mendoza dynasty grew in the early eighteenth century. Bartolomé Vidaurre was a major Nicaraguan merchant, having the unusual privilege of serving as regidor and alcalde ordinario on both the Granada and León cabildos. The offspring of the unions spread this power throughout the colony: José studied in Guatemala before becoming bishop of León. His brother and the primogenitor, Francisco, was a dominant force in the royal government in Guatemala, serving as advisor to the audiencia and filling in as its fiscal officer in the absence of royal appointees. Francisco married the daughter of José de Medina, one of the leading lights of the Guatemalan enlightenment and the *protomedico* of Guatemala. Their children extended the dynasty's power. Diego became one of the leading officials in the Comayagua diocese and Felipe, a leader of the cabildo in the indigo zone of San Vicente. In the nineteenth century, the Vidaurre clan was a leading merchant family and a major force for loyalty to the crown and, after independence, conservatism in Central America.[13]

Thus, in 150 years, the Vidaurres expanded from their Granada base of privileged power, using clerical and secular bureaucracy and fortuitous marriages to establish links throughout Central America and to become a truly "national" Central American political and economic force.

The migration and dynastic evolution of the Vidaurre clan was not atypical. Regardless of economic fluctuations, the Central American ruling group changed over time. With the eighteenth century and the end of the War of the Spanish Succession, the pattern continued, but with a subtle shift. Spanish traders and ship captains arriving in Central America with finance from Cádiz established themselves in Santiago de Guatemala or Granada, married into dominant families, and allied themselves with other new families, strengthening their links with peninsular capital and the bureaucracy. The source of capital, the market, the numbers of newly arrived peninsulares were different and greater than heretofore, although the pattern of entry via marriage or family connection remained the same. In sheer numbers and in wealth, the immigrants overcame the old guard and the old traditions, leading to a new colonial structure with new institutions and eventually, a new and enlightened view of the world.[14]

Simón Larrazábal slightly modified the pattern of entry into the Guatemalan privileged class, using capital and commercial links in Spain to forge his way into the colonial hierarchy. Unlike the Vidaurres, who used privilege and position to attain membership in the ruling group, Larrazábal relied upon capital and trade. Arriving in 1725 as a ship captain—piloting one of the two vessels that had come from Cádiz to the Bay of Honduras in the past fifty years—Larrazábal was tied to the merchant Pedro Carrillo of Cádiz. Together the two entrepreneurs profited from the small but burgeoning trade in textiles and silver. Larrazábal remained and joined the ruling class through his marriage to Manuela Gálvez, the descendant of one of Central America's most prominent sixteenth-century families; his great-grandson would become a symbol of Central American liberalism, a hero to nineteenth-century liberals against the crown's persecution.[14]

The important transition in familial patterns came after the War of Jenkins's Ear as the demand for Guatemalan indigo increased in Britain and Europe. A new generation arrived from Spain, representing various commercial interests in Cádiz. Gaspar Juarros emigrated in 1752, Martín Barrundia and Gregorio Urruela in the 1770s. They each founded businesses that established their names by the time of independence.[15]

Two new families are particularly significant: the Piñoles and the Aycinenas. José Piñol, from Barcelona, migrated with two other brothers to Cádiz in 1720. With strong commercial connections to a Barcelona trading company and with Cádiz merchant houses, he went to Guatemala in 1752 as the factor of the Real Asiento de Negros. The slave trade revolved around the construction of the Fortress of Omoa, built to guard the indigo trade in the Bay of Honduras, and the Piñol family profited heavily from the government privilege. By 1760, it was sufficiently wealthy to bring its own vessel to Guatemala, trading slaves for indigo. The return voyage carried over 200,000 pesos of indigo—about a third of the annual export from Central America at that time—back to Cádiz. José's family continued to be a major power after his death in 1765.[16]

The Aycinena clan was the most important and enduring of the new families. Indeed, it is archetypal of the rise of Latin American notable families in this early period of the commercial revolution, of those newly arrived at Buenos Aires who sold hides for Europe's trade or beef jerky for Brazilian slaves, or the merchants of Mexico whose fresh capital allowed them to exploit old mines to find new veins, many of whom founded dynasties.

The Aycinenas were founded in Central America by Juan Fermín, who emigrated from Navarre to New Spain in 1748 with, it is said by friends and enemies alike, three hundred pesos. There he became involved in running mules before migrating to Guatemala in 1753 at the age of twenty-four. The next year, the Basque Aycinena married the daughter of the alcalde ordinario of the Guatemalan cabildo, Anna Carrillo y Gálvez, who was linked to the sixteenth-century Gálvez family, the seventeenth-century Basques Baron de Berrieza and Carrillo y Mencos, and the eighteenth-century Basque Micheo family. The union cemented peninsular dynamism with local privilege. Overnight, Aycinena took control of much of local commerce. As a result of his marriage, Aycinena became within three years of his arrival a síndico of the cabildo, and the following year, alcalde.[17]

This rapid acceptance was not atypical. Young, entrepreneurial Spaniards were always sought by creoles as new blood for their lines. The tendency of the children of the notables to become *rentiers*, members of an unproductive leisure class, or to join the Church, could be offset only by the energy of first-generation ambition and skill. We are reminded of Romero de Terrero, who also began in New Spain running mules but who, through good fortune, marriages, and business acumen, became the wealthiest man in Mexico within thirty years of his arrival. We can look to Chile where, a Chilean historian reminds us, the families of the conquistadores and encomenderos were replaced by new families and merchants in the same period.[18]

Well-established, Aycinena went on to expand his position after the fortuitous death of his first wife, another political marriage, another fortuitous death, and still a third marriage. The second wife came from a family that also had major interests in domestic trade. Micaela Majera y

Mencos was a direct descendant of the nephew of the seventeenth-century Guatemalan president, Martín de Mencos, whose notable service was rewarded with a large pension and other privileges with which the family established itself in Guatemala. That this second wife was a cousin of the first is not at all surprising. This was a small ruling group. Aycinena's marriage to two of its wings was politically auspicious.

The third marriage, to Micaela Piñol y Muñoz and into the Spanish Piñol family, crowned his rise to power, linking the internal trade of the two earlier marriages to the European market. Blood ties paralleled the invasion of the western economy. The network was formed.

Again the pattern of family ties linking commercial relations during this industrial revolution is typical. New money funded new production and trade from growing European populations; the best security for commercial dealings was blood; the best manner to gain new energy for commercial families was to attract young, entrepreneurial outsiders and bring them into the family. We see this same pattern in Cali, New Granada, in São Paulo, as well as in Mexico and Buenos Aires.[19]

Aycinena's family connections were not limited to auspicious marriages. There were other, more distant, connections to the Iberian peninsula, to Navarre in particular, the nature of which we are not sure but the significance of which we should not underestimate. Pedro José de Beltranena provides us with the key. His paternal uncle, Martín, was the husband of Anna María de Aycinena, sister of Juan Fermín. His maternal uncle, Manuel de Llano, came to Guatemala in the late 1740s—before Juan Fermín—as treasurer of the Real Hacienda. In other words, Juan Fermín had connections to the powerful fiscal administration when he first arrived, a factor that served him well when he gained the wealth and privilege of Guatemalan notables through his first marriage. Pedro José de Beltranena, the link in this extended network, came to Guatemala himself in the 1770s.[20]

In Guatemala, the network formed by Aycinena's three marriages and his fourteen offspring was further cemented. Aycinena's eldest son, Vicente, married the sister of his third wife, Juana Piñol y Muñoz (that is, another Piñol daughter), making father and son brothers-in-law but also uniting more completely the families' mercantile fortunes. Other sons and daughters married into families that controlled the trade of cattle into central Guatemala and of cloth from the highlands throughout the colony, the Batres, Marticorenas, and the Pavónes, as well as becoming members of the high clergy. José Aycinena was, at one time or another, regidor, síndico, and alcalde ordinario of the Guatemala cabildo, director of the Economic Society, intendant of Salvador, a member of the ruling Consejo de Indias in Spain, and an aguacil mayor of Mexico City. One daughter became a nun and experienced a number of miracles in 1815, or so it was testified. But the family network with God was short-circuited by the pope, and movements to have her canonized since have failed. Her brother, however, was named bishop of Trajanópolis, a titular position.[21]

In effect, marriage was the central bond in creating a powerful, colonywide network unequalled in Central America since the early days of the Alvarado conquest. But while marriages created the network, it was commerce that made it important. Through his ties, Juan Fermín Aycinena amassed control over more than 25 percent of all colonial commerce by 1781, his wealth was said to be over a million pesos. Aycinena controlled most of the trade in cloth into the interior and in indigo to Spain. With the Bourbon revolution in government that expanded taxation, government projects, and the flow of money, Aycinena and his network were used as agents for the transfer of funds for projects. Their names appear frequently on purchase orders for slaves who built fortresses on and populated the weak Caribbean coast. They were given large amounts of tax money by the government, which they converted into indigo and then shipped to Spain and sold at a profit before the funds were transferred back to the government's coffers.[22]

Political positioning counted for the family's prosperity as well. Now a very large mercantile house, with many children from many wives, Juan Fermín Aycinena became involved in a controversy that united the fortunes of the new families—those that had arrived around and after mid century—and the Bourbon reformist government in Guatemala and Madrid. When an earthquake destroyed a large part of the capital city in 1773, a seven-year fight ensued between the government and new merchants on one side and the clergy, artisans, old families, and general populace on the other over whether to move the capital to another site. The controversy went to the quick of the confrontation between old and new, traditional and enlightened, and Hapsburg and Bourbon. At issue was the control over land, food, and fuel provisions and the division of real estate in the capital. The new families had been unable to gain control of the land around or of housing plots in the old capital city. Although they were able to capture a considerable part of the colonial commerce, they were blocked from monopolizing the supply of food, wood, and labor to the capital by old families and Church organizations who maintained traditional authority over these provisions.[23]

Since mid century, the reformist monarchy had been attempting to erode these traditional privileges of Guatemala's creoles. It had first attacked the privileges held by the Guatemala cabildo, eliminating its monopoly on alcohol and card games, and then the important privilege held by the cabildo of gathering all royal taxes throughout Central America. In the 1773 earthquake controversy, the new merchants broke with the old group and allied themselves with the Bourbon bureaucrats. For six years, riots, bloodshed, and a general schism in the society disrupted the capital. In 1779, the government-merchant group emerged victorious.

As a supporter of the government, Aycinena was assigned the position of directing the acquisition of materiel and labor for constructing the new city. He was given the receipts from ten years of the sales tax, approximately a million and a half pesos. For a decade, he had immense power in determining which Indians were to be used to build which sections of the new capital, which land was to be exploited for construction materials, and which was to be farmed for food provisions.[24]

Aycinena's position gave him power over labor forces from Chiapas to Nicaragua as he ordered foodstuffs and construction materials from outlying provinces, much to the chagrin of interior families and clerics. We hear regionalist sentiment echoed fifty years later, after independence, in the complaints from Comayagua, itself damaged by earthquake, of insufficient labor and materials to rebuild its own city, or in the complaints from Chiapas clerics that Indians were being abused, forced to carry too heavy goods too far, in a time when an epidemic was decimating the Chiapas population.[25] Aycinena alienated both old families and more recent arrivals, through his control over the assignment of housing plots within the new city as well as his control over labor and land derived from his powerful influence on the cabildo.

Aycinena developed sufficient influence in Madrid and resources to purchase a *marquesado* from the crown in 1781, the only such title in Central America. He was granted the right to construct an imposing mansion on the central plaza. Geographical position is an important indication of status in the Iberian world. The central plaza in the new capital city had four major dwellings, each on a different side: the offices and fortress of the commander of arms, the presidential palace, the cathedral, and the Aycinena residence.[26]

As his wealth and power increased, Juan Fermín's domination expanded beyond international trade and local power in Guatemala City to the providing of credit throughout the colony. He advanced large amounts of money to producers (mostly miners and indigo farmers), using his control of capital as leverage to establish prices and control trade routes and, eventually, ownership of indigo plantations. One judicial matter concerning fiscal policy is typical of Aycinena's ability to control and eventually take over many indigo farms from 1780 until independence. This judicial matter determined whether the owners' property seized for failure to pay debts should be charged sales tax. A farmer in the San Miguel region of Salvador needed money to tide him over because the Seven Years' War was obstructing trade and he could not sell his produce. A subsequent infestation of locusts paralyzed production for a number of years. Aycinena lent him some 32,500 pesos, the producer to pay 3,000 pesos annually in time of war, and 4,000 all other times. Unable to repay any money for two consecutive years, the farmer was compelled to pay the next year the usual installment of 4,000 pesos plus some 5,000 pesos for three back years of interest. When he failed to pay, the Aycinenas took over the farm.[27]

This type of seizure occurred repeatedly and reached its peak during the bleak economic years immediately after the turn of the century. The Napoleonic Wars disrupted commerce; four years of locust infestation destroyed farms; there was a general decline in the quality of Guatemalan indigo; and finally, competition from East Asia wiped out most dye producers. Although the Aycinenas did not flourish during this period, they did survive, gaining control of much land through seizures. When the market for the dye expanded around 1819, the family owned about a sixth of all the indigo plantations in Central America.

Juan Fermín Aycinena held more power than any one man in the history of Central America. He profited and controlled much of the commerce of the region, dominated the capital, and was influential with the Bourbon bureaucracy. Through his credit relationships, he had economic power in most major producing areas. He died in 1795 and was succeeded by Vicente as marquis. The change was important. Juan Fermín was tied to the peninsula in his loyalty and trade connections. Vicente was American. Whereas the founder worked closely with the government to enhance the family position, the primogenitor was imbued with the ideology of the Enlightenment. The founder traded through Spain; his heir developed contacts with English and American traders. Juan Fermín was a peninsular who founded a dynasty in America. Vicente was a creole; he and his children would lead the ideological battle toward independence and beyond and would develop one of the two dominant political thoughts in nineteenth-century Central America.

But we should not overemphasize ideology, even during this ideological period of the early nineteenth century. The social power of the family was immense in Central America, Mexico, and Spain. It gave the grow-

ing family network entrée to the royal court in Madrid even while officials in Guatemala attacked the family's contraband trading and flirta-
tions with independence movements. When its power ebbed after independence, the family's extensive network gave it a certain degree of
protection against political attacks, even when its ideological enemy
ruled.

By 1820, the year for which we have the best data, the Aycinenas controlled a large portion of the indigo-producing lands and much of the internal marketing of goods. They had trade representatives in Peru,
Mexico, Cádiz, Belize, Havana, Jamaica, and Philadelphia. In Spain,
José Aycinena was a member of the supreme council of state that ruled in
1812 and 1820. Through the "liberal" party, the clan dominated the cabildo of Guatemala. Mariano Aycinena was alcalde ordinario (and
within a year would be a prime force behind the Act of Independence).
In the extended family of in-laws and cousins, the clan held important
positions in the archdiocese, the intendancies of León, Chiapas, San Salvador, and Verapaz, as well as being alcaldes mayores in many areas of
Central America and Mexico. An opposition, "conservative" newspaper
listed sixty-four members of the extended family holding positions that
brought almost 90,000 pesos in annual salaries.[28]

Thus when political attacks came, both under Spain and after independence, the family was partially protected by its enormous extension.
During the years of revolutionary tumult in Latin America, especially
between 1810 and 1817, a conservative Spanish president, José de Bustamante, attacked the Aycinena house, seeing it quite rightly as a center of
contraband trade and a supporter of independence. The Aycinena fortunes altered under this attack but did not collapse. In 1817, with an ebb
in the independence movement in Latin America, the house was restored through José Aycinena's successful political manipulations in Madrid. He used his influence at the court of Ferdinand VII to have the
Spanish official deposed from his position.[29]

Soon after, "the Family," as it was now called collectively, pressured
the next president of Guatemala to allow free trade with nearby Belize,
which led to free trade with Jamaica and the United States soon after.
The permission is a remarkable example of the authority of the clan during this violent period when Spain fought to maintain its monopolist
trade policies in an empire under seige. Where Caracas and Mexico
failed, and where Buenos Aires succeeded only through separation, the
Aycinenas were able to gain royal approbation.[30]

Free trade created an immediate boom in international commercial
traffic in Central America, with trade in indigo and silver for cheap,

English textiles profiting the Aycinenas while destroying the indigenous textile industry. It cemented the links between the family and the foreign, non-Spanish market while creating a political schism between merchants and domestic productive classes.

Finally, when Agustín de Iturbide led his successful rebellion against Spanish rule in Mexico, the Aycinenas allied themselves with him and led the movement for independence in Central America and the eventual union of Central America with Iturbide's empire.[31]

What had been politicking under the monarchy became, with independence, open political and military maneuvering in Central America. The hatred that interior groups held toward the Family in particular and centralized Guatemalan rule in general and the antagonism of the productive sectors toward the merchant class led to the internecine warfare and political anarchy that typified most of the century. The Aycinenas sought unsuccessfully a united Central America under their commercial and political control.

But despite bitter wars, feuds, and occasional political setbacks, the family was able to maintain its position. In the 1820s, as government collapsed, trade grew. English textiles flooded the Guatemalan market via Aycinena's house and in exchange for indigo. Only by 1826 did the market for English goods become saturated.[32]

An America visitor in Guatemala in 1825 described the families of the city and said, "that of the Marquis of Aycinena is both the most notable and numerous, it might perhaps, also be said that it is the richest." The visitor was invited to the Aycinena house where he was shown a string of pearls:

> I thought of course they could not be so from their extraordinary size. I found however that I was mistaken. I had hardly supposed it possible that such enormous pearls existed and wishing to ascertain their value, I guessed them at 10,000 pounds sterling. The Marquis, I understood, had given more for them: the necklace consisted of twenty-one pearls, the centre one being in the shape of, and as large as, a pigeon's egg, and the others large in proportion but round and decreasing in size, gradually, towards each end.[33]

During the postindependence period, the family became embroiled once more in politics, but this time it lost. As it had opposed the monopolistic tendencies of the Spanish empire, it sought to impose a centralized, Aycinena-dominated government upon the nation. As we have seen, immediately after independence, the Aycinenas linked their fortunes to the Mexican Iturbide government, supporting union between Central

America and Mexico in an effort to preserve their dominance. When
that government failed, the Aycinenas formed what became the "conservative" political faction whose ideology called back the old traditions of
the colony, including domination by the central city, effectively converting the family's ideology of opposition to Spanish mercantalist and absolutist policies to one advocating centralized rule from Guatemala. Mariano Aycinena was elected governor of the state of Guatemala and used
that position to influence the course of the national Central American
government. When regional wars erupted and the power of the Aycinenas was challenged, he assumed the presidency of the nation until interior regions drove him and his family from power. Most, but not all, of
the immediate Aycinena family went into exile. Some, like Mariano,
continued plotting from Mexico. Others, like the head of the family,
José, went to New York to continue the family business and publish
ideological tracts arguing for conservatism in Central America. The
liberal victors in Central America confiscated much of the family's
wealth.[34] But, and here is the significant point, despite political losses
the network held. The family was so large, so intertwined in the essential
social and economic structure of the region, that parts of it were able to
maintain their position until a new, more favorable political regime
came to power.

When, in 1839, Rafael Carrera stormed into the presidency over-
throwing the "liberal" government, the exiles returned home to their
strong position. The seized land was returned to their control, their
wealth recompensated. Mariano and Pedro Aycinena were named chief
counsels to Carrera. Pedro became interim president for a time (Pedro,
by the way, reached the epitome of networking in Guatemala: he married an Aycinena, his cousin, Dolores Aycinena y Micheo). José Aycinena
became archbishop of Guatemala. José Ignacio Aycinena was appointed
corregidor of the capital, giving him direct control over the distribution
of forced labor to the food and the valuable cochineal farms (He was
married to Antonía Piñol, further cementing ties to that family). Two
members of the Batres family, who were closely linked to the Aycinenas
through marriage, were prime ministers for most of the twenty-six years
Carrera ruled. The family itself continued to pursue its business, now
controlling much of the production and trade of the cochineal dye.[35]

The Aycinenas were driven from power with the liberal revolution of
1870. They returned to their lands. One, Juan Fermín, introduced coffee cultivation to his estate and made one of the first contacts with German traders who were so predominant in Guatemala at the end of the
last century. In the twentieth century, he withdrew into poetry, where

he received great acclaim, becoming known as the poet who upheld the "honor of religion" during this liberal epoch.

With the twentieth century, foreign investment, corporations, and new blood, the power of the Aycinenas was diluted. We see much the same phenomena all over Latin America. Still, today, the family is one of the most prominent in the country, with large landholdings and interest in banking. Although they no longer can rely upon networks to maintain their position in that turbulent land, they continue to serve in government and have held important financial ministries in recent military governments.

In sum, the Aycinenas were able to use marriage to establish their position and, in the nineteenth century, to use their extensive connections to maintain their political and economic authority regardless of political and economic fluctuations. Four times they lost power: in 1814 with the fall of liberal Spanish government, in 1823, with the collapse of the Iturbide empire, in 1829 with the military victory of liberal and interior Central American forces, and in 1870, again with the return of a liberal government. Each time, the family survived, maintaining its influence.

Certainly they were at the height of their authority in 1840, although this did not come about through their own political activity, but through the aegis of the caudillo and his mestizo and Indian fighters who drove the liberals from power and installed conservative government. After 1840, the family monopolized the ministries of the Carrera regime, dominated the economic life of Guatemala, controlled the Church through the archdiocese, and influenced intellectual life through José Aycinena's conservative writings and, later on, Juan Fermín's poetry.

Nevertheless, this direct political authority is not nearly as important as the informal authority that existed through the family networks. The position of the family pew in the cathedral, the position of the family house on the central plaza, the standing of the family in the city's nineteenth-century social clubs—all of these are evidence of the continued power of the group regardless of political reversals.

Notable Family Patterns

Clearly, the Aycinenas dominated Guatemala. But how much of the patterns described above can be seen in other notable families in Central America, both in the capital and in the interior? How much of the history of the Aycinena's was unique? How much was representative of the general trend?

There is a clear difference between family patterns in the rural interior and in urban Guatemala. In the Central American capital, the Aycinena pattern holds fairly true. The groups of families who came to Guatemala between 1750 and 1790 formed commercial and familial relations sufficiently strong to overcome traditional families and to fend off challenges from new groups through the next century. The new families brought with them a common ideological framework that distinguished them from the old colonial groups; this manner of expression and these values were used as the basis for political discussion in the nineteenth century.

A different pattern emerged in the interior, where families depended more upon the land than upon commerce. Old families were able to survive direct onslaughts from new by their ownership of land. They were less likely to survive mercantile onslaughts, that is, the takeover of their lands and produce through the Guatemalan merchants' control of credit and prices. While intellectual changes in the eighteenth century permeated the interior and influenced the leading families, it met more resistance, from the Church, old families, and Indian communities. Networking was not as extended as in urban areas. Indeed, the urban notable families' failure or inability to form extensive networks with the rural interior and the failure of rural families to establish networks beyond their immediate regions were two of the principal causes of the regional civil wars that plagued Central America through the nineteenth century.

Still, the pattern of notable families in interior Central America was more variable than in the city, more defined by economic function—the strongest traditional families were able to ward off invasion by new families; the weakest succumbed. In the city of Salvador, for example, when new Spanish came to purchase property and open up new lands in the mid eighteenth century, they were met with the opposition of the Salvadoran cabildo that maintained control over the area's valuable labor supply. The traditional families were close and well integrated; the city of Salvador had scarcely sixty vecinos in the previous decade. When the newcomers tried to force their way onto the cabildo in 1755, violent fights broke out with some bloodshed. Consequently, they had to go elsewhere to find their labor—to the Spanish alcaldes mayores whose jurisdiction lay outside the area.[36]

However, some new families did succeed, the most obvious example being the Herrera-Morazan clique that dominated Central American politics in the twenty years following independence.

We cannot categorize the growth of notable families in the interior by period nor can we identify the source of ideologies developed later, in the early nineteenth century. Most interior groups disliked Guatemala's notables, regardless of the politics they held. Some, like the old Arce-Gálvez family group and the Molinas or the Cañas in Salvador were fervent liberals, others, like the great Honduran savant, del Valle, were loyalists and later, conservative. Elsewhere, among the cattle barons of Honduras and Nicaragua, ideology was less important. The political positions held by these families were based more upon opposition to the ideology of rival families and towns and the establishment of alliances with distant, friendly settlements than upon liberal or conservative thought.

After independence, notable family networks became "political factions" in the towns of the interior; on the cattle ranches, however, the concept has little meaning. The Zelayas of Olancho, Honduras, typified the cattle barons of the nineteenth century. At mid century, the family paid no taxes to the Honduran government. All the "national" officials in Olancho were Zelayas: José Manuel was governor, and his brothers, alcalde primero, juez de primera instancia, and general of the army for the region. The residents of the area looked to the family for support, financial as well as protective. In sum, this notable family ruled with little challenge from any outside authority. Their power in the nineteenth century was as great as that of the cattle families in the colonial period.[37]

It was in the cities that the greatest political, economic, and intellectual changes took place, around the houses of the new Spanish merchants, around the government offices where enlightened bureaucrats allied with these merchants, at the University of San Carlos where the children of the merchants were schooled, and even at the cathedral. Families formed networks, strategic marriages, and commercial alliances, at best, to advance their positions, at worst, to guard them in time of economic travail. The fortunes of the Arrivillaga, Pavón, and Irisarri groups prove good examples of how networking protected some members and furthered the fortunes of others, laying the basis of a hemisphere-wide extended grouping.

The Guatemalan Arrivillaga clan derived from Domingo de Arrivillaga, a Basque who came in the mid seventeenth century and founded a mayorazgo in 1656. The family's economic power persisted through the next century. In the 1740s, the family joined with the Irisarris, another Basque family, to form a Guatemalan commercial company for commerce with Peru. The great expansion of trade to the Atlantic caught these families in the Pacific Ocean, it might be said. First the War of Jen-

kins's Ear slowed trade in the Americas, and then the commercial revolution stimulated demand in European markets for Guatemalan goods.
The Pacific group had little opportunity to reorient its operation, and
the Guatemala Company failed, almost stillborn.[38]

After the Guatemala Company's failure, the Arrivillagas declined
economically. Nevertheless, they remained as the fountainhead for
many other prominent groups. They turned to a son-in-law to protect
their interests. Manuela de Arrivillaga married a new immigrant, Cayetano Pavón, from Extremadura, bringing the mayorazgo to the union.
The remaining Arrivillagas were able to maintain their strong social position in Guatemala despite their economic decline. In 1793, the family
is listed as a minor contributor to the petition for the establishment of the
merchant guild. Antonio Arrivillaga was one of the chief officials of the
urban militia—a very prestigious position—in 1811. After independence, the family was still listed as one of the chief families of Guatemala despite its relatively minor wealth based solely on land.[39]

The Arrivillagas were bolstered by their close connections to the Pavónes and the Irisarris. The offspring of the Pavón-Arrivillaga marriage
became some of the most powerful political and economic forces in the
colony and in the postindependence period. Manuel Pavón was a major
figure in the plotting of the mid and late eighteenth century. His brother,
Bernardo, was bishop of Comayagua. José Ignacio Pavón was one of the
founders of the Conservative party in Mexico. He took part in the Iturbide uprising in Mexico and was a commander of Maximilian's army.[40]

The Irisarri family used its close connections in Spain to build a commercial empire that rivaled the Aycinenas. The Basque, Martín de Irisarri made the first commercial connection to Guatemala with the Arrivillagas in the Guatemalan Company, providing the capital for the
enterprise. His son, Juan Baptista, expanded the family business to the
Atlantic. He was closely associated with the move to establish a merchant guild in the colony and was named as a representative of the Guatemalan merchant community to Spain. At the turn of the century, the
Irisarris were the first merchant houses to trade to any major degree
with the English island of Jamaica.

Of Juan Baptista's two marriages, the second was the most significant:
1794 he joined with María Josepha de Arrivillaga, cementing his wealth
with privilege. When he died in 1806, the Banker Irisarri, as he was
called, left one of the greatest fortunes of the time. Of his twelve offspring, the first born, Antonio José Ramón, was most influential and became one of the chief figures of Latin American conservatism. Juan Baptista had allied with Vicente Aycinena, the marquis, in expanding

Central American commerce to England before independence. Antonio José was closely allied with Vicente's son Mariano de Aycinena in the push for Central American independence and the subsequent formation of the conservative movement. He served as minister of war under Aycinena and then was exiled after the defeat of Conservative forces. Irisarri went to Chile where he established a reputation as a prominent diplomat and conservative polemicist. He served briefly as Conservative president of Chile.[41]

Antonio Larrazábal, one of the most prominent names in Central America's history of the independence epoch, is another example of the use of networks to maintain position regardless of economic wellbeing. Antonio's bloodlines were excellent. He was great-grandson of Simón, the pioneering ship captain who came to Central America in 1725 and, through Simón's marriage into the Gálvez family, was a direct descendant of sixteenth-century notable families. His father also married into the Arrivillaga family. Although Antonio was deeply entwined with the Aycinena group and a leading spokesman and plotter in the 1812–14 Liberal movement in Central America and in the Cortes in Spain, he was quite poor. His entire income depended upon government positions and support from distant relatives. After his political role ended, he became a constant petitioner to the government for financial sustenance. Larrazábal is given a prominent position in nineteenth- and twentieth-century historical writings, in part because of his participation in the Liberal Cortes, and in part because of his extended family, whose descendants include most of Guatemala's prominent historians.

Old families, those that dated back to before the eighteenth century, also survived. But they no longer were the central factors in society. The most notable old family were the Montúfars, a prominent clan whose origins date back to the Madrid mayorazgo family. In the early seventeenth century, the founder of the Central American clan, Francisco, married the granddaughter of two conquistadores. A wave of Montúfars emigrated to Guatemala throughout the century, marrying into other traditional families and creating a creole dynasty. In the eighteenth century, they joined with the Batres family, itself closely tied to the Aycinenas through marriage. The Montúfars were a major force in the Guatemala cabildo through 1730. But as the new families became more important, the Montúfar name appears less and less frequently as a cabildo regidor. By the early nineteenth century, Montúfars were still described as one of the chief families of Guatemala City, but also as the poorest of the notables. Their wealth was said to derive chiefly from government positions.[42]

The reliance upon networks to gain government positions or to maintain social support is directly descended from the old, traditional practices of establishing family members in convents or with pensions to maintain their support. The distribution of favors and funds by the city's ruling class through the secular and ecclesiastical cabildos had become the appointment of government positions or the providing of a share in enlarged businesses.

Networking was a critical strategy in defending family privilege, but we must not oversimplify the concept. There was no one, unified network. In Central America, there was a series of family networks, some based upon blood, but others upon political or commercial needs, and the most important and powerful were established in the capital city.

The most important variation among the notable families was generational. Familial links, economic bases, and intellectual underpinnings were defined by the time in which they were founded. After all, the eighteenth century was a time of constant and enormous changes—the most dramatic since the early days of the colony. Changes were induced by the series of disasters that befell the capital: disease and earthquakes and enormous economic and intellectual fluctuations radically altered family fortunes. The names of city leaders who petitioned the crown to allow commerce between Guatemala and Peru in 1714 were quite different from those who joined to request the formation of a Guatemala commercial company thirty years later. These leaders in turn were overcome by the great migration that accompanied the commercial revolution after mid century.

The petition of Guatemala's seventy-three leading merchants in 1792 to form a merchant guild provides an indicator of the extent of the change. Of the 82 percent whose origin we can identify, 74 percent were new families. Of the twenty-four commercial houses listed as major, 84 percent were "new." I suspect that the unidentified 30 percent were recent Spanish merchants who had had little success; I have not seen their names either before mid century or in post-independence political or fiscal documents. Of all the names, I identify 16 percent as having close family or commercial connections with the Aycinena faction.[43]

The Aycinena success at forming a large, commercial extended family was repeated to a smaller degree by others. There were, of course, the Piñoles, the commercial family upon whom Juan Fermín built his empire. Gaspar Juarros came in 1752 to found what became one of Guatemala's most entrenched eighteenth-century clans. Manuel Batres linked his fortunes through marriage into the Barrutias, an old Guatemala family that controlled much of the textile trade in the colony as well as holding a huge sheep ranch, by far the largest in Central America, in Guëguëtenango. The Batres, Barrutias, and Aycinenas were all connected through marriage into the Naxeras and Muñozes, both traditional families. Cayetano Pavón, who profited from the mining boom of the 1740s, was also linked to the Muñoz family through marriage, and one of his children married an Aycinena. By 1770, the foundation for the new order was firmly settled.

After these *nouveaux arrivés* merged into colonial life, after they married into old families and formed commercial alliances both in Spain and in the New World, they created an establishment difficult for additional newcomers to enter. In the 1770s, any newcomer could become extremely powerful in business affairs, but he still remained outside the new dominant group, part of a different generation, a different network, removed from the founding of the modern, enlightened Guatemala, and, most important, detached from the circle that by now had twenty years of development.

The split between the two generations of immigrants can be seen clearly in the case of the Urruela family. Gregorio Urruela came to Guatemala in 1770 with strong connections to the Cinco Gremios de Madrid, a commercial and productive enterprise under royal patronage. Urruela served as the Cinco Gremios agent for sending indigo back to its textile factories. His position was sufficiently strong to have him mentioned as one of the four leading merchants in Guatemala twenty years later. When the urban militia was formed in 1811, Gregorio Urruela commanded the second unit—Vicente Aycinena commanded the first.[44]

Although their initial success may have been similar, there were profound differences between the Urruelas and the Aycinenas. Juan Fermín Aycinena died in 1795, Gregorio Urruela lived into the independence epoch. As the split between the Spaniard Juan Fermín and his son, the American Vicente, was great, so too was the schism between Vicente and Gregorio. Vicente played a major role in opening up trade to Jamaica and the United States. Gregorio continued his trade links with Spain. Vicente was trained in the enlightened age, a part of a generation of Guatemalans who gained their schooling under Fra José Antonio Goicochea at the University of San Carlos. Gregorio was a businessman, influenced by the Enlightenment to be sure, but neither by age nor inclination tied to the evolving thought that became Spanish liberalism.

After the turn of the century, still another group of Spaniards arrived, and if the Urruelas and their kind were frozen out by the strong social position of the Aycinena group, the newest Spaniards found themselves under economic attack by those established before them who traded illegally with foreign countries and who held almost a complete monopoly over internal trade.

Thus, when the Spanish liberal epoch was at its height in Central America in 1820, the political party network was formed around family networks. The one, a liberal Aycinena in-group linked in one way or another to the immigrants of the 1750s, and the other, conservative, composed of late arrivals, old families who had been shunted aside by the mid-century commercial revolution, and artisan groups hurt by the invasion of English textiles into local markets. It was Gregorio Urruela who as part of a group composed of his generation of Spaniards—men like Mariano de Larrave, newly arrived merchants as well as old Guatemalans (Díaz, Lopez, Flores, and Espada)—complained to the crown about the immense influence of and the overwhelming number of political positions held by allies and members of the Aycinena family:

> The attached list manifests the number of jobs that one family has been able to take over because of its relations and alliances. Most have received their work since Sres. José Aycinena and Antonio Larrazábal had influence in the Madrid government. . . . There are other meritorious members of other families of this capital, but they do not receive employment for not being united to this one family.[45]

Three groups formed the basis for opposition against Spanish liberalism, free trade, and then independence: the well-established families of Urruela's generation, the newly arrived Spanish merchants, and the old traditional families. Indeed, traditional historiography which poses creole against peninsular as one of the bases for the schism that led to independence does not apply, at least in Central America. The liberal movement, or that which was to earn the name after 1812, was championed in Central America through 1808 as much by peninsular bureaucrats as by the urban creole merchants. But more important, the liberal movement that pushed first for free trade and a greater voice in the political affairs in Spain and then for independence forced the creation of an opposing alliance between the old, diminished creole families those who came after 1770. They were outside the entrenched merchant authority headed by the Aycinenas; they championed the maintenance of Spanish monopolist practices for their own purposes. The "creole" families of the independence movement, be they Aycinena or Barrundia, had arrived in the past eighty years; the families of Antigua Guatemala who opposed the liberal drift dated back to the seventeenth and even to the sixteenth centuries. True, there were notable exceptions to this as well. Manuel Montúfar is the most obvious.

Just as I deny the creole versus peninsular origin of Latin American liberalism, I do not argue that nineteenth-century Latin American political parties are extensions of families and their networks. Clearly, the ideological schism runs deeper than that, in many cases across blood lines. As the century progressed, different groups gained access to the political theater. Nevertheless, in this microcosm of the Latin American region, we can trace the origins of the liberal thought of the period to the intellectual and blood descendants of the group that arrived in the mid eighteenth century. In the period that followed independence, notable families of this group were able to use this heritage to their advantage: to secure the leadership of political movements or to secure protection from political persecution through a call to a higher responsibility (as a priest might have done in an earlier period). Thus a José Aycinena would be exiled by his cousins whereas a mestizo soldier, Fulano de Tal, would be shot.

With independence, the old conservative and loyalist faction was defeated. Some of its members left for Spain, others removed themselves from politics, and still others submerged themselves in the camp of the victorious Aycinena faction. As we have seen, the Aycinenas, liberal in the mold of the 1812 Liberals and opposed to centrist and absolutist rule from Madrid, were themselves converted into conservatives after independence as they sought Guatemalan political and economic hegemony over Central America. But their victory was short lived; its assumptions—of a centralized Guatemala rule and of Guatemalan privileges in the interior—were questioned in the interior and the capital alike. After independence and the brief union with Agustín Iturbide's Mexican empire, Central America collapsed as a nation, and an epoch of internecine warfare and liberal-conservative political disputes began that lasted through the century.

The question is: How did the notable eighteenth-century families survive through all the bloodshed and political turmoil of the epoch, the constant civil wars, forced exiles, and expropriation of land and wealth? How did they maintain their position into the twentieth century with the political fluctuations, the revolts, and the accessions to power of the various Central American caudillos—of whom Carrera, the mestizo caudillo, with his hatred of liberal ideology and of most whites, was the most famous—and the late-nineteenth-century movement of liberal reaction that drove out those notables who supported the caudillos?

The answer is: The family, the cousin, the brother-in-law, or the son, in sum, the network too entrenched to be removed by political turmoil, too powerful socially to be discounted, and sufficiently flexible to bend with political change, to guard the cousins' holdings, or to save the brother-in-law from execution.

The Montúfars, the old, seventeenth-century family, is merely one example of a notable clan defeated and able to return to power in the next generation with a new ideology. Manuel Montúfar played a major role in support of the centrist Aycinena faction during the wars of the federation. He was driven into exile by the Liberal victory in the 1830s, to return to favor briefly under the Carrera interim. His son, Lorenzo, was a leading member of the 1870 Barrios liberal faction, the direct ideological descendant of his father's opponents.

There are others who came and went from one faction to the other, the Molinas and the García Granados are two of the most prominent. Perhaps most important is the survival of those who lost: the Barrundias who were driven out in the 1830s or the Aycinenas who were defeated in 1870. They survived, first in exile and then, after their cousins pardoned them, on their lands or in their urban houses, away from politics, at least for a time. Here the network was most important. Total political defeat was not sufficient to end the families' influence. Even economic setbacks were temporary in a land where labor was cheap and power fluctuating.

The Central American experience is archetypal of the formation of the Latin American notable family. The second- and third-generation patterns are best illustrated elsewhere in Latin America.

3

Northwest Mexico

Hispanic society in Northwest Mexico lay on the far edges of Mexican history.[1] Tenuously emerging in the sixteenth century, haltingly proceeding through the seventeenth and most of the eighteenth century, firmly implanted only at the end of the colonial period, there it remained until the second decade of the twentieth century, on the periphery. Through the course of that century and a half between late colonial embedment and national emergence, the notable family networks that formed in the Northwest did not move beyond the region in their scope and influence. The vast majority did not even extend beyond their locality. When the region did move into the center of Mexican history during the Revolution of 1910–20 and its aftermath, the apogee of the notable family networks had already passed. Nevertheless, the Northwest's claim to a share of national life derived in great part from the region's notable networks. Members of these families, and in particular their more humble relations, permeated the Sonoran dynasty that dominated Mexican politics from 1920–34.

The peripheral context of the region's history profoundly affected notable network formation. In a sense, one could say that the Northwest (along with the other regions on the edges of Mexico) was twice-removed from the core of such a large and complex historical entity as Mexico. Moreover, that peripherality is more than simply a matter of geographical isolation, of a lack of communication with the center. It involves as well such questions as identity, expectations for the future, and access to outsiders. Taken together, then, the late colonial implantation of Hispanic society, the general weakness of connections with the powers-that-be in Mexico City, and the relative ease of foreign contact resulted in the

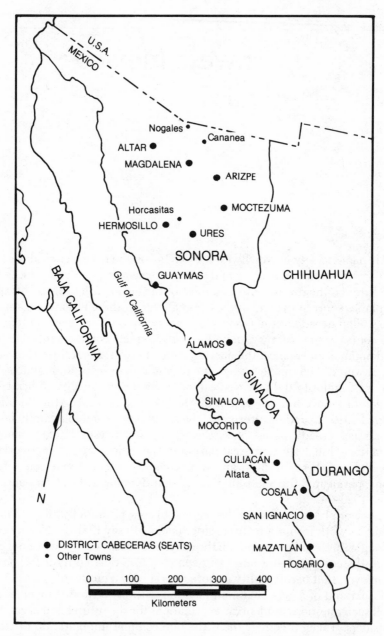

U.S.A.

MEXICO

Nogales
Cananea
ALTAR
MAGDALENA
ARIZPE
MOCTEZUMA
Horcasitas
HERMOSILLO
URES
SONORA
BAJA CALIFORNIA
Gulf of California
GUAYMAS
CHIHUAHUA
ÁLAMOS
SINALOA
SINALOA
MOCORITO
CULIACÁN
Altata
DURANGO
N
COSALÁ
SAN IGNACIO
MAZATLÁN
ROSARIO

● DISTRICT CABECERAS (SEATS)
• Other Towns

0   100   200   300   400
Kilometers

Northwest Mexico, with principal towns and cities in the states of Sonora and Sinaloa.

region's marked distance from the strong, long-established currents of Mexican society and life. Varying patterns of opportunity for and sources of power and wealth were a second consequence of these fundamental historical circumstances.

The response of those who became notables in Northwest Mexico reflected the continuity and discontinuity possible in these conditions. With the first generation seems to have come a well-established social model to which to aspire (if not already assumed for nurturing to maturity): that of becoming, or being, notable. In a local or regional society in the process of formation, that meant those families who gained prominence by coming to dominate its economic activities, to direct its public affairs, and to set and maintain a significant level of cultural refinement. Such first-generation notables shared a common world view about the future course of their society. They envisioned, indeed expected, a future in which the economic activity begun under the late Bourbons would continue to expand, in which social and political relations would crystallize and mature around their families, in which the level of cultural sophistication would rise in step with economic prosperity.[2]

This vision of progress runs through four generations of notable families between the late eighteenth century and the turn of the twentieth. Yet this common world view tended to fragment as notables faced the task of adjusting to historical circumstances and turning them to their own advantage: the need for outside assistance (from whom and on what terms?); the need to reduce isolation (in what way and to what effect upon their sense of themselves beyond their family networks?); the need to convert tribal Indians into subordinate laborers (at what cost?). There was general agreement that external contact should be promoted, though with a gradual realization of the need to channel it in acceptable directions, and that forces hostile to their vision (in particular, the tribal Indians) should be subdued and integrated into society through a mix of force and acceptance. There was less consensus on the terms and conditions of outside assistance, especially that of extralocal levels of government.

If the historical circumstances of the Mexican periphery permitted (if not encouraged) a fairly uniform world view among the Northwest's notables, at the same time they put a premium on flexibility in the formation of networks among notable families. The intrinsic structure of the networks themselves suited this demand for a high degree of flexibility. The families, in the choice of certain strategies, demonstrated their willingness to adapt in furtherance of their common vision.

Economic and occupational diversification was a principal means for achieving greater flexibility. The pattern, which clearly established itself in the first generation, accelerated in the second. Successful families learned that postindependence conditions would not guarantee security, prosperity, or a high probability of long-term growth in any one economic sector. By the third generation, it was less necessity than a clear realization among notable families that diversification was an essential ingredient to the expansion of their interests and authority as opportunities proliferated in the late nineteenth century.

Complementarity made occupational and business diversity an even greater asset, while fostering, rather than frustrating, family unity and cohesion. Complementary economic activities enhanced the possibilities of each individual enterprise and reinforced family ties and associations as well. Political posts and professional positions in particular provided the connections and expertise to diversify most profitably and the requisite linkages to synchronize the entire mix of family businesses for the whole network's benefit. Education, then a most scarce resource on the Mexican periphery, proved crucial in enabling notable families to expand into new endeavors and to integrate existing ones more tightly.

Given the fluctuating conditions, Northwest notables found marriage more important as a potential for addition, through affinal ties with outsiders, than as a protection for solid, well-grounded interests. Network families had to be ready to secure new political alliances, to seize upon new economic opportunities, since existing ones could prove unreliable, even fleeting. Exogamous marriages thus proved a generally more advantageous strategy than endogamous ties for coping with such circumstances.

There was a spatial context to these strategies that constituted a strategy in and of itself. The relative power and fortunes of the various districts within the region varied considerably during the nineteenth century. Spatial mobility reduced the liabilities and maximized the possibilities inherent in fluctuating circumstances. Successful families shifted their bases of operation when necessary and broadened those bases through the extension of branches, which enabled their networks to project their interests and influence with greater range.

The choices made through such strategies enabled notable families in the Northwest to expand their economic interests and sociopolitical authority through the course of the nineteenth century, though with difficulty in the middle third of the century. The most successful among them reached the state level. Above all, these families found in the networks they established the most effective device for adjusting to conditions on the periphery and for realizing their vision of progress and notability.

The First Generation: Urbane and Enterprising

The arrival of the Bourbon "revolution" to the Northwest periphery in the late eighteenth century resulted in transformation, not merely reformation. It did not create fissures in an existing colonial establishment into which newcomers could slip and, with the support of Bourbon reforms, steadily drive wedges that in time would alter vested interests and set that society in a new direction. Rather, the revolution cleared and decisively shaped the region so that a permanent, stable colonial society could be implanted for the first time. For an ambitious immigrant, this meant a world to mold, not one to wrest control of and reorient. Mexico City and Lima were places where the new Bourbon families of prominence merged with entrenched families and their institutional allies after considerable resistance; Guatemala and Buenos Aires, locales where newcomers more easily absorbed the more limited establishment. Northwest Mexico—like other areas on the edges of the expanding Iberian colonial world after 1750—was a setting in which newcomers began the creation of familial networks almost from scratch.

Prior to 1770, Northwest New Spain constituted only a transient frontier, with but bare outcroppings of the bedrock of colonial establishment that generally prevailed elsewhere in Ibero-America. The basis of Hispanic settlement was largely patrimonial, centered around Jesuit missions and a small number of presidial garrison communities. Market activities were meager and played only a supplemental role. There was little of substance or permanence upon which familial vested interests could build. The accepted, simplified description of society found in documents until the late eighteenth century manifests these societal conditions. The basis for stratification was almost wholly cultural: *indios* and *gente de razón*. Though among the "people of reason" one could find Spaniards (generally the vecinos of the few settlements), mestizos, and mulattoes, they were customarily discussed as a common cultural entity vis-à-vis the Indians, the predominate population element.[4]

To this transient frontier, the Bourbon revolution brought a comprehensive administrative framework that promised permanence, stability, and cohesion. These conditions stimulated an economic transformation and attracted large numbers of immigrants, the non-Indian population quadrupling during the last four decades of the colonial period. A distinctive settlement pattern resulted: a scattered chain of potential urban nuclei that ran the length of the region, between the Sierra Madre Occidental and the coast, almost all connected by a royal road. In the population centers that emerged as towns during these years, one encounters the first generation of notables in Northwest Mexico.[5]

The Formative Pattern

Those who became notables (some claimed notability upon arrival) encountered little in the way of institutions or prior familial power bases to which to defer, as was the case in so many other colonial regions.[6] With the expulsion of the Jesuits, the Church was weak. Its secular hierarchy was only in its infancy, while the wealth of its former missions (even much of those remaining in northern Sonora) was soon all but dissipated. Cabildos were apparently nonexistent until the last few years before independence. There were no guilds. Militia units seem to have been organized only after independence. Only in the expanded presidial companies could one find an ongoing social interest group, and it had emerged only within the previous generation. For those with notable aspirations, there were thus fewer encumbrances to overcome, but also fewer resources upon which to draw.

In such fluid societal conditions, those who began constructing strong, close-knit families held a distinct advantage in the accumulation of wealth and influence. Their intertwining into networks of shared interests would enhance that advantage even more. However, these close-knit, extended families were the fundamental basis of social organization for only a small minority in the Iberian colonial order.[7] This was particularly true in Northwest New Spain, with its legacy of frontier transience. Those who became the first generation of notables in the region seemed to have had the economic wherewithall, the will, and the understanding of the social reality to create such families and use them to their fullest advantage.

Predominant among these first-generation notables were immigrants who had come directly from the peninsula. The large majority of them were from the small towns and cities of northern and eastern Spain, where Bourbon efforts to infuse Spanish society and economy with the spirit of the Enlightenment had met their most favorable response. They came with an entrepreneurial bent, which meshed with the economic conditions they encountered.[8] On the Northwest periphery, there were not the established local political posts, the clerical hierarchy, or the large landed estates into which to sink the accumulated capital they brought with them. This, combined with a chain of market and mining centers in proximity to one another, fostered economic diversification among the would-be notables. With increasing frequency, they began to combine agricultural operations with mining ventures and commercial trades.[9]

The social and cultural background of the peninsulares also proved advantageous in a society where social credentials and cultural endowments were limited. There were very few, perhaps only the presidial officers, who could lay any significant claim to prestige from their experience in the region itself. The recent arrivals from the peninsula had leverage if they were of respectable families, better still, important ones. Some of them were already immersed in such a family orientation, as indicated by the complexity of their names: Elías González de Zayas and Baltazar de la Vega Colón y Portugal, for example. These immigrants carried with them a vigorous urban tradition. And if they had not yet already acquired the cultural endowments that were an important part of that tradition, they possessed an acute sense of their importance. One finds evidence of this in the rapidity with which goods reflecting refined tastes were acquired, with which the emerging towns took on more than a simple, rustic appearance, with which children began to obtain schooling—not only in the primary schools established in the urban nuclei, but in educational institutions in the far away provincial cities of Mexico's central core, and even in Europe.[10] The comments of the few foreign travelers who reached the region by the end of the first generation of notables, in the 1820s, are more often admiring than condescending. There is definite surprise that such a level of refinement in residences, attire, and accoutrements had been attained in such circumstances.[11]

These immigrants were among the thousands of peninsulares who migrated to America during the late colonial era. But in Northwest Mexico, there were considerably more of them in proportion to the population, and there were few established institutions and competing social groups to compromise their intentions. It was thus easier for them to make the region their own, and to do so more thoroughly in the first generation, than it generally was for their counterparts elsewhere in late colonial society. Above all, the construction of close-knit families, with linkages to one another, quickly began to set apart this first generation of notables in the Northwest from the rest of the Hispanic society that was beginning to take root. Within a couple of decades, in the most important of the region's communities, the loose distinctions of gente de razón and indios had given way to *notables*, a layer of *gente decente* (those of respectable origins, generally white, and with a modicum of wealth), *clases populares* (the remaining people of reason), and the tribal Indians.[12]

Marriage was foremost among strategies available in the founding of the first notable families and in initiating the linkages that grew into familial networks. With such a large proportion of the population composed of new arrivals, most of whom came alone or with one sibling, and with so few existing families of prominence, exogamous marriages were central to the formation of these families. Their prevalence continued in the nuptial choices of the second generation.[13] Such choices were based far less on calculating the best avenues to linkages with the interests and personages of the existing few families of prominence and far more on appraising the future prominence of other families like their own. Here the peninsulares had a decided advantage.

The formation of the first notable families, and the networks arising among them, can best be seen in the most well-developed of the region's urban nuclei—the mining and commercial center of Álamos in southern Sonora. Antonio de los Reyes, the Northwest's first bishop, stopped there in 1783 on his way to establish the see in Arizpe, the province's administrative center to the north. He went no farther. He had told well-wishers at a leavetaking in his home town of Aspe (in eastern Spain) of his expectations of seeing such examples of urbanity and refinement as the town's old church spring up on the northwestern frontier of New Spain. In Álamos, he recognized the resources and attitude for such endeavors. His chief welcomer, Bartolomé Salido y Exodar, an arrival to the region himself about a decade before, was then head of the royal treasury office and custodian of the crown-owned mercury that was dispensed to miners. His residence, occupying a whole block in the center of town, had a colonnaded front patio, which gave way to several high-ceilinged salons with red tile floors, carved wooden doors, and white-washed walls and ceilings interrupted by dark beams and crystal chandeliers. Guests dined with silverware, hand-painted porcelain, and crystal. Salido donated another commodious residence (formerly occupied by a niece and ward) to serve as the bishop's residence and organized a committee to raise funds for a large stone basilica at the bishop's urging.

Bishop de los Reyes was accompanied by two nephews. José Almada, a fellow cleric, became the town's parish priest and instructor at the primary school set up by his uncle. The second, Antonio Almada, married Salido's other niece and ward, whose father had been Salido's predecessor in the treasury office, as well as a miner and hacendado. The young Almada immediately employed his peninsular schooling in metallurgy to turn his wife's inheritance into the largest, wealthiest operation in So-

Alamos' main plaza, surrounded by the porticoed residences of the town's most prominent families and the basilica, constructed during the late eighteenth and early nineteenth centuries. Photograph by Stuart F. Voss, 1974.

nora, acquiring new mines in the process. He built upon his wife's land holdings in a similar manner.

Through Salido and his niece, the Almadas became associated with one of the most influential families in the region. The Elías González de Zayas, originally from Álamos, were in the process of relocating to the northern frontier of Sonora. They were among the relatively few existing families who could lay claim to prominence, and they had come to it largely through service in the presidios. The offspring of Salido, Almada, and some of the Elías González family became the core into which those who became the notable families of Álamos, most new arrivals from the peninsula, married: Ortiz, Gil, Cevallos, Quiros, Palomares, Zavala, Gómez Lamadríd, and Urrea.[14]

Bishop de los Reyes and the presidial officers of the Elías González family represented the essential patrimonial orientation in Northwest Mexico up until the nineteenth century. Such practitioners of the cloth or sword had often been the focal points for political, social, and economic organization. However, their part in the formation of an urban center led by a network of notable families in Álamos was surpassed by those of more varied occupation who quickly established a refined life style. Salido had mining and land interests as well as a bureaucratic post. The Almadas not only acquired diverse economic interests, but claimed descent from Portugeuse counts and family connections with a high noble family in Murcia. The other families acquired considerable interests in mining and commerce, many adding to these holdings by building up large haciendas in neighboring valleys.

By the early nineteenth century, the population of Álamos had grown to nearly five thousand inhabitants, with an equal number scattered in the surrounding mining camps and outlying settlements. The cultural endowments of the town's aspiring notables soon bore fruit. Their flat-roofed, proticoed residences were situated wall-to-wall along clean, cobblestone streets leading off the main plaza, which was attractively laid out in flower beds and palms. Seated in their handsome carriages in the broad alameda lined with spired poplars (*álamos*) from which the town took its name, they displayed their finery. In their homes, a growing accumulation of costly goods and furnishings reflected their growing wealth and refinement.[15]

The interlinkage of aspiring notables in Álamos was characteristic of what was happening in the other urban centers then beginning to take root in what became after 1786 the intendancy of Arizpe: Arizpe, San Miguel de Horcasitas, Pitic, Culiacán, and Rosario. It occurred most saliently in Álamos because of the numerous and substantial mining discoveries there. However, in the early nineteenth century, a transition in the process of family network formation took place. New circumstances arose that slowed some elements of the process and accelerated others. The transition overlapped generations, centering in the latecomers of the first generation and the early segments of the second. Frequently, this overlapping was manifested in marriage.

The Independence Transition

Independence—the long struggle to achieve it in Mexico and the new conditions it spawned—heightened the peripheral character of society in the Northwest. The region became more isolated from the rest of Mexico as lines of communication broke down and extralocal political influence began to steadily decline. Simultaneously, foreign contact appeared for the first time. It began in the form of permission to trade with neutrals during the war (and in growing contraband) and expanded with the opening of designated coastal landings to international and coastal commerce after independence.[16] In marked contrast to many other colonial regions, where the insurgent struggle led to significant, at

The front portico of the colonial residence of one of Alamos' most notable families, the Gomez Lamadrid.

times even severe, social dislocations, in Northwest Mexico social relations continued as before.[17] The strong peninsular base remained. The
recent immigrants from Spain had no cause to leave, and peninsulares
continued to arrive, though in reduced numbers because of the war in
the interior of the viceroyalty. As a result, the peninsular component
continued to play an important role in the formation of notable families,
especially through its reinforcement of urbanity and enterprise.

Independence "happened" to this first generation of notables. They
neither sought nor resisted it. Perhaps that best explains their naiveté as
to the ultimate consequences of separation from Spain. Foremost, it
meant the withdrawal of the essential supports of the society at whose
center they had come to reside. This was a long-term consequence of the
early-nineteenth-century transition that they neither clearly discerned
nor for which they were prepared.

Though they failed to perceive the underlying reality of the break-
down in external support until its full consequences were upon them by
the 1830s, the region's notables nonetheless began to react to its outward
manifestations in the preceding decade. Mining had become a sure,
prosperous investment only in the wealthy preindependence centers:
Rosario, Cosalá, and Álamos. Elsewhere the combination of increased
isolation from the interior and growing contact with the exterior produced marked shifts in the lines and focuses of commerce. The river valleys in northern and central Sonora found external markets for livestock
(and its by-products) and wheat down the Pacific coast as far south as
Panama and around the Sierra Madre to New Mexico and Chihuahua.
Ures, Pitic (renamed Hermosillo in 1828), Álamos, Culiacán, and Rosario became the inland commercial depots for the collection of agricultural products and silver, which were funneled through the infant ports
of Guaymas (Sonora) and Mazatlán (Sinaloa), formerly only landings.[18]

The most successful notable families adjusted accordingly. If a mining
strike could be found, so be it (and they usually kept their ears to the
ground and their pocketbooks open for such a happenstance). But increasingly they began to concentrate their accumulated interests in diverse agricultural and commercial activities. Those who had begun in
commerce acquired land, and vice versa. The pattern of economic diversification that had appeared before independence was solidified.
Shifts in business activity were accompanied by shifts in location, either
by transfer or expansion of one's economic base. Few first-generation notable families, even latecomers, joined the numerous foreign merchants
who began settling in Guaymas and Mazatlán. In the 1820s, the pressures (whether incentives or threats) were not so intense as to clearly in-

dicate the logic of the move. The two ports were still little more than entrepots for the commerce generated by the inland towns, which had become the focal points of refinement, education, social position, and new political power as well. The movement, then, came within the inland towns as notables began concentrating in the principal commercial centers.[19]

Families originally based in Horcasitas illustrate well this spatial and business flexibility during the transition period. The founder of the Iñigo Ruiz family, a peninsular, had settled in San Miguel do Horcasitas in the late eighteenth century, when it was still the most prestigious center of Hispanic settlement north of Álamos. Fernando Iñigo Ruiz had become one of the most prosperous hacendados in that productive agricultural community. His daughters married late-arriving peninsulares, who also established large landholdings: Manuel Rodríguez; Joaquín Astiazarán; and José Cubillas. Rodríguez had then moved to Pitic, becoming one of its most prominent merchants by independence. Astiazarán followed in time, as did one of Iñigo's sons, Pascual. His eldest son, Manuel, subdelegado in Horcasitas before independence, engaged in commerce there until 1830, when he moved to Guaymas, forming a commercial firm with branches in Hermosillo (supervised by Pascual) and in Horcasitas. The firm included the young Iñigo's cousin (Fernando Cubillas) and a son and daughter, respectively, of the Aguilar and Gándara families, two of the other wealthy hacendados in the Horcasitas area by the early nineteenth century. The Aguilars and Gándaras were also connected through marriage. Their children were beginning to establish themselves in Hermosillo, Ures, and to a lesser extent Guaymas.[20]

The early nineteenth century was also marked by a shift in the occupations of notable families. They increasingly moved away from patrimonial professions and posts toward those that complemented their business activities more. The most influential branch of the Elías González family continued the long-established pattern of profession and political position as presidial officers and priests who also held office.[21] However, after independence the Church became a marginal factor, and with it, the clerical profession and its influence in politics. The presidios, with the disappearance of adequate external support, rapidly began to deteriorate.

In contrast to the Elías Gonzálezes, the Almadas of Álamos were moving with the new circumstances. None of Antonio Almada's four sons entered the priesthood, though their uncle, who gave them their primary education, fervently wished that one of them would. None became professional soldiers, though each would take up arms temporarily as militia officers during civil and tribal Indian conflicts. After completing secondary schooling in Guadalajara (a trend that emerged in the postindependence generation), the Almada brothers learned practical mining from their father's mine superintendant. Upon their father's death in 1810, they entered into a joint mining venture, with the advice of Bartolomé Salido, their great-uncle and executor of the estate. They each pursued separate mining or landholding ventures as well, those of the youngest (José María) being the most extensive and profitable. He also branched out into commerce.

Like the Elías González brothers, the Almadas too assumed public office, but far less as professional keepers of the peace or of moral order than as amateur defenders of expanding private enterprises like their own. As militia officers, district prefects, municipal presidents, state legislators, commissioners (and in José María's case, governor), they protected their haciendas, mines, and trade (and those of fellow notables) from tribal Indian raids and from the retribution of political opponents.[22] Early second-generation notables like the Almadas were joined by the late arrivals of the first generation in seeking professions and political posts more complementary to their growing private interests.

The occupational shifts stemmed not only from changing economic conditions. Politics, too, had been profoundly altered. It had had little institutional expression even in the late colonial period. At the local level, cabildos had yet to appear. Royal administration had been represented by a governor or intendant and a handful of subordinates. Higher bureaucratic levels had been too removed to be an integral part of local political life. Nor did the independence struggle give politics form and character, as it did in so many regions of Latin America, for example, in Chile, as revealed in Mary Lowenthal Felsteiner's study of kinship politics in the independence movement there. Nevertheless, her contention that in the postindependence years prominent families had a vision of society in which family networks could thrive, in which "political relations had the security and intimacy of family relations," is manifested in the politics of the 1820s in the new state of Occidente, which combined Sonora and Sinaloa.[23]

Almost immediately, Occidente's politics came to revolve around family bonds identified with particular localities, not around class, specific issues, or nationality. The family networks then forming linked their futures to the urban centers in which they resided and from which they sought to extend their interests. With few solid institutions in the Northwest periphery, family alliances quickly came to serve as the principal political integrating mechanisms. Only the Yaqui and Mayo Indians of southern Sonora proved to be a sociopolitical group with enough cohesion to challenge the notable families. Nevertheless, the two tribes were only obstacles to notable expansion, desiring merely to be left alone. The Northwest's relative isolation left its notables without any serious challenges from competing regions or from powerful revolutionary, military, or political figures. Consequently, in office-holding disputes, in the composition of political factions, in the determination of a direction for the region, the notable family networks quickly became the dynamic core, the protagonists of Occidente politics.[24]

With little, if any, practical experience in the political intricacies of colonial society or the independence struggle, Northwest Mexico's prominent families were not testing and adapting familiar political mechanisms to the new republican environment. Rather, they were devising mechanisms and strategies to mold new institutions to suit family interests. Municipal govenment (appearing between 1810 and 1830 in the towns) proved easy to adapt to. The increasingly complementary occupational roles that had come to predominate among notables during the transition period readily included office-holding in the *ayuntamiento* (republican Mexico's nomenclature for the colonial cabildo). Particularly as alcaldes and síndicos, these enterprising merchants-miners-hacendados assumed direction over their locality's resources and gave official or legal sanction to business transactions.[25]

Beyond their localities, Sonora and Sinaloa's notables groped their way through the uncharted territory of republican government at the state and, indirectly, the national level. They latched on to territorial representation as the means to protect or extend the interests of the locality they dominated. Thus the number and boundaries of judicial, administrative, and legislative districts and the location of their cabeceras were of utmost concern. The introduction of competitive, electoral politics required the broadening of the family network if notables were to secure control locally and expand family interest beyond the locality. This translated ultimately into domination of state government, from which the families could promote the network's holdings and influence. Those families who best adapted to this new political reality taking root in the 1820s became the most notable core of the family networks in the second generation.

The Second Generation: Frustrated but Flexible

After 1830, when Occidente was divided into the states of Sonora and Sinaloa, the changes of the early nineteenth century intensified, with new challenges and complications that the region's notable families came to understand only slowly. Isolation from the rest of the country became acute. Nothing of any semblance took the place of the firm, supportive, centralized direction of the crown. National governments in Mexico City, which came and went over the next three decades, proved too penniless and unconcerned to assist. At the same time, they were unwilling to curtail restrictions on provincial prerogative. The result was a degree of instability greater than the norm in Latin America (which was none too stable in itself). The tenuousness of their society's footing was a major problem with which the Northwest's notables had to contend.[26]

The support structure inherited from the late colonial period gradually crumbled. The presidios rapidly disappeared. By mid century, the remnants of the missions on the far northern frontier too had vanished. Apache raiding resumed, converting much of northern Sonora into a deserted countryside, punctuated by cowering communities with fortress mentalities. Tribal Indians, faced with white intentions to encroach upon their lands, to control their labor, and to replace semiautonomous relations with strict territorial government, were driven to numerous revolts. The Yaquis and Mayos in particular achieved virtual autonomy. Aggravating these mounting insecurities was the growing civil struggle for state political power with its linkages to the federalist-centralist (and later liberal-conservative) struggles at the national level.[27]

Given these accumulating insecurities, sustaining economic activity was difficult at best. Trade links to the interior became increasingly irregular for Sonora and much of Sinaloa. Interregional contact was curtailed. Commercial economic activity was spotty, usually determined by relative security, access to the coast, and contact with foreign markets and credit. The continuing security problems markedly restricted the positive potential of foreign contact, especially in Sonora. Foreign merchants hung cautiously along the coast for easy departure, eager to trade with those who could deliver products to them, but rarely willing to invest in production itself.[28]

Another complication to the initiation of foreign contact after independence was the temptation for foreign elements to claim the resources of the region for themselves, even to steer the region toward another national society. Public insecurities fed the ambitions of foreign adventurers—in particular, North Americans, but also the French, by way of California—and of political circles in the United States and France, who employed various schemes of filibustering, colonization, or purchase. A far more complex response was required of second-generation notables to sift through the increasingly complex nature of foreign contact: to contain it where it proved threatening to their local dominance and to incorporate it to their advantage where possible.

The first generation of Northwest Mexico's notable families had caught the crest of the wave of the early nineteenth century transition, which followed decades of growing stability, certainty, and prosperity. It seemed an added blessing to their world. The second generation, which began to come of age in the 1820s, soon fell from the crest into the undertow, in which they floundered through their young adulthood and better part of middle age. Their world, until late in life, was one of growing adversity. For them, adjustment was not so much an enhancement of opportunity as a fact of life. Flexibility was not so much an attitude of advantage (though some in this generation used it profitably) as of survival. Only for prominent families in locales where foreign contact and economic opportunity achieved a fair degree of regularity, where public insecurities were minimal, was there the chance to amplify their notability. Elsewhere the option was narrowed to preserving the family's status. Whether success was measured in preservation or amplification, the family networks achieved it through their willingness and their ability to adjust. In so doing, they had the example of their own parents' strategies for responding to the independence transition.

Network Strategies: Flexibility

Continued economic diversification was crucial in this charge of flexibility. The steadily expanding foreign contact (and the growing, though still limited, travels and education of notables abroad) reinforced the existing entrepreneurial mentality among the second generation that had led their parents toward diversification. This was especially true in their attitude toward land; it was viewed less as a source of prestige and more as one of profit. The widespread insecurities (particularly in Sonora) discouraged landholding as a permanent, all-encompassing option, as did irregular, limited markets and the relative scarcity of available, willing labor. In contrast, there was an incentive to invest in urban property, given the greater risks in the countryside and the urban orientation of the notable families themselves.

Changes in business activity reflected this enterprising attitude and the requisite of being flexible. Merchants began branching out extensively into financial speculation, using disposable capital to diversify. They bought up promising agricultural holdings in the surrounding area. They purchased, and frequently resold, urban properties for residences, for additions or new locations for their commercial houses, and for small industrial pursuits (principally craft shops and mills). They arranged loans and mortgages at usurous interest—real estate generally was required as collateral—and acquired considerable property in the process. Ties with the public sector were cultivated as well. Though public treasuries were going through hard times and there were definite risks, they could make money as bondholders for public officials, as tax farmers, and as lenders at very high interest. They also developed credit alliances with foreign merchants (and some nationals) in ports along the Pacific coast and overseas, looking after one another's transactions.[29]

The Iñigo brothers offer one of the best examples of the varied activities in which second-generation merchants engaged. Manuel and Pascual both acquired large rural estates around Hermosillo, one of the few prospering agricultural districts in the region. They also invested heavily in commercial and residential real estate in the town itself. They engaged in moneylending, including a loan to the state government in 1839 (along with seven other merchants) for the *reducción* of copper money. They were partners in many of these commercial and agricultural ventures, including two transport operations: a stage coach line between Hermosillo and Guaymas and a freight line to New Mexico. Manuel also established the state's first textile factory in 1839 near Horcasitas, using cotton from his family's and other haciendas in the area. The textiles were marketed through the family's stores in Hermosillo and Guaymas. In that port, the third brother, Cayetano, served as receiver of the port's federal customs duties in the early 1830s (a position of no little help to the family commercial house). He was bonded by his brother-in-law, Joaquín Astiazarán. Cayetano also apparently handled family commercial business down the coast.[30]

The Iñigo brothers and other merchants also speculated in mining. Here one finds another flexible adjustment in the families' economic activity, one that would expand in the third generation: the use of more corporate association. Early in the generation, partnerships had begun to replace the more customary individual mining ventures (linking prospector and merchant creditor). After mid century, larger associations began to be formed, some taking on corporate structures. The Companía Explotadora of the La Brisca mine in north-central Sonora, formed in 1863 with a capital of 210,000 pesos at 100 pesos a share, comprised the principal businesspeople of Hermosillo and some from other towns, many of them interrelated: Camou, Ortiz, González, Serna, Noriega, Aguilar.[31]

One important result of the changes in business activity was large transfers of property and enterprises. For all of those who employed diversification successfully, there were those who failed to diversify enough or at the right time or with sufficient funds. In Hermosillo, whose notary archives included transactions not only from the immediate area but from a great part of central Sonora as well, the great majority of transfers seem to have taken place from those with more narrow interests, centered in agriculture, to those who expanded their interests from a commercial base. Feliciano Arvizu, scion of one of Hermosillo's prominent first-generation families, found himself so overextended in 1840 that he was forced to liquidate all of his properties to pay off his debts, including a farm worth 8,000 pesos and a mill of equal value.

The Arvizu family's principal creditor was Manuel Iñigo, who himself would encounter formidable indebtedness in the years following.[32] Iñigo's family commercial firm had to liquidate in 1850, and his textile mill be sold, to pay off the mortgage on his principal estate near Hermosillo. In 1863, having helped finance the losing gandarista side in the political struggle for control of the state over the preceding decade, Iñigo was able to borrow more than 80,000 pesos—at that time a very substantial sum—from Dionisio González, who through meteoric business success and marriage of his children was becoming incorporated into the same network. Through all of their ups and downs in the political and business arenas, the Iñigos, and the powerful family network to which they belonged, maintained their substantial wealth and influence and passed it on to the following generation.[33] The stronger, more diverse network links they had forged enabled them to secure the advantage in shifting circumstances and to weather the adversities faced by the second generation.

The strength and flexibility of successful family networks were reflected in occupational as well as business diversity. Principally, the second generation saw the consummation of the transition from cleric-professional soldier-officeholder to secular professional-amateur soldier-politician. In most secular parishes in the Northwest, priests barely had enough to live on. In Sonora, they could be counted on one's fingers.[34] In the main towns, sons of prominent families who staffed the parish churches (and who all came of age in the early nineteenth-century transition) also attained legislative posts, both state and national. After the 1830s, however, no new priests from second-generation families appear in public office. Indeed, in Sinaloa, beginning with state's first constitution, they were banned from public office.[35]

The military also ceased to be attractive as a professional career. The few who did become professionals, such as José Urrea and Alejo and Pedro García Conde, were increasingly sent elsewhere in the country. By

1840, the accustomed arena for career soldiering in the Northwest—the presidial garrisons—existed only on paper, starved of financial support. The continuing security problems necessitated a continuation of military service nevertheless. Now, however, young sons from notable families engaged in it as amateurs, leading militia units or voluntary forces. After 1850, with the limited resurrection of federal military colonies on the frontier and the establishment of a loose national guard structure at the state level, such service became more formalized for some. The few national command posts were usually filled by the permanent appointment of career soldiers from outside the region. The sole federal garrison, stationed at Mazatlán, was composed of units recruited in the interior and changed periodically.[36]

The second generation's choice of professional careers was far more diverse than their parents' and complemented well the more varied economic ventures into which their families were moving. But these professions were the fruit of their parents' stress on cultural endowment as an important criterion of notability. In surprisingly large numbers, they had received formal education, particularly secondary and professional education. The advanced training was acquired largely in interior provincial cities or abroad. Most of the sons of Manuel Monteverde—in postindependence years one of Hermosillo's leading merchant-hacendados, with investments in mining as well—received secondary and professional schooling in Mexico City: Manuel and Florencio in mine engineering and assaying; Pedro and José in law; Gabriel in medicine.[37] In Sinaloa, the establishment of a colegio in Culiacán in 1838 helped train that state's second generation of notables even more extensively, especially those in the northern district towns.[38] Law, now secularized, lent vital assistance in the growing complexities of business and republican politics. Engineering enlarged the capability for absorbing technology. Medicine and education were experiencing a rise in respectability and enhanced the notables' life style.[39]

These more varied professions did more than augment family economic activities and cultural prestige. Along with amateur soldiering, they also expanded the network's political influence. During the second generation, there was a steady push to increase local prerogatives through the municipal government. The ayuntamientos' general impoverishment during this period nevertheless limited the notables' ability to exercise the prerogatives they gradually acquired. Simultaneously, there was competition among families based in the principal towns for control of state power, especially the executive branch. The legislature was a middle ground from which district towns could protect or extend their local prerogatives, or a single urban family network, or a coalition of them, could secure control over the state government. In the political competition between networks, political posts acquired growing importance. It was as military veterans, lawyers, and other professionals that second-generation notables began to fill them.

Military amateurs could supply the physical force that frequently determined the power of family political coalitions. Moreover, given the prevailing insecurities, notable officers, with reputations acquired among the general populace from part-time soldiering, could accumulate considerable political capital for parlaying into important public offices, particularly the district executive post of prefect. The creation of the national guard in the 1850s provided a mechanism to build larger alliances among these amateurs through which state offices could be secured. Analogous experiences were influential in the growing political involvement of professionals, who offered expertise and conceptualizing skills at a time when government had increasing need, but possessed very little, of either. The colegio in Culiacán provided a meeting ground for many of Sinaloa's professionals. But even for those who left the region for their education, similar perceptions and experiences facilitated the ease of their interaction upon their return. This occupational commonality complemented and reinforced the growing linkages among the notable families as they dealt in politics.[40]

The politics of the region, occupational diversity, and economic diversification were increasingly intertwined. Growing foreign contact—although localized and irregular in Sonora because of continuing insecurities and concentrated in Sinaloa owing to problems of access and available capital—provided new opportunities for private gain. The spread of ayuntamientos at the local level and the nature of republican government had led to a proliferation of political office, which enabled more individuals to exploit those avenues to personal and family gain.

Locally, the newly created municipal governments had little monies to disperse. Nevertheless, in their judicial functions, they had considerable impact on private interests: the care and adjudication of municipal land; the supervision of the distribution of water; the notarization of business transactions, wills, guardianships, grants of powers of attorney, and bonding agreements. Notarial archives reveal the full extent to which members of second-generation notable families came to predominate in the offices that performed these functions: the *alcalde* or *juez de paz* (local judge and executive combined), *síndico procurador* (municipal attorney), and the *juez de primera instancia* (state district judge).[41]

In offices beyond the local level, one increasingly finds those with part-time military service or professional training, which they usually combined with entrepreneurial activities (if not initially, then not long after). Political posts at the state level (which included appointed district officers) determined the amount and kinds of taxes, the conduct of internal customs operations, the award of tax-farming concessions and monopoly contracts, and the securing of loans to the state treasury (which often had to rely on large loans at high interest). Residence in the state capital made those links between private opportunity and public office more probable and secure. Location of the capital had been the paramount issue in the state of Occidente in the 1820s. It was a bone of contention between the notable networks of Arizpe, Hermosillo, and Ures in Sonora until the late 1840s. In Sinaloa, it was the cause (along with commercial competition) of an embittered rivalry between Culiacán and Mazatlán until the late 1870s.[42]

When a site other than their town was chosen as state capital, the more successful notable families either moved or extended a branch of the family there. This practice was only part of a larger spatial strategy among the second generation in response to the region's fluctuating, often adverse circumstances, intensifying a trend initiated earlier in the century. Moreover, as the requirements of notability rose, geographical adjustment became a principal determinant in fulfilling them.

In Sonora, the recurring insecurities narrowed the potential for economic prosperity to the commercial and agricultural centers in the middle of the state and to Álamos and its immediate environs in the south. Children of prominent families established before 1830 in the communities on the northern frontier or bordering the Yaqui and Mayo valleys who now chose to remain found their fortunes stagnating or in decline. Those who moved to Hermosillo, Guaymas, Ures (and to a lesser extent Álamos)—or at least established economic activities in or around these towns—generally found their family interests expanding. In Guaymas, which had no first-generation legacy, the pattern can be seen most clearly. Second-generation members of the Maytorena, Iberri, Aguilar, Astiazarán, Montijo, and Bustamante families, among others, left their increasingly tenuous ranching, farming, and mining interests on the northern frontier to invest in the commercial growth of the state's only port. There they were joined by a number of foreign merchants—Robinson, Spence, Alzua, Espriu, and Camou among them—with whom they and their children intermarried, creating the first network linkages in Guaymas. In time, they began diversifying their commercial interests into mining in the sierra foothills to the east and into agriculture in the unsettled valleys near the port.[43]

In Sinaloa, spatial flexibility among notable families was more confined. With agricultural production largely limited to local consumption and with mining in decline, commercial activities were weighted heavily toward markets outside the state (principally in the interior) and became concentrated around the burgeoning port of Mazatlán and the initially designated capital, Culiacán. Families outside these two prospering commercial centers, not faced with the more severe insecurities of their Sonoran neighbors, felt less pressure to move. Moreover, foreign merchants of importance, who congregated almost exclusively in Mazatlán, were far less willing to be incorporated into the family networks than their counterparts in Sonora. Available evidence does not reveal why. That left Culiacán as the principal focus of family movement. The colegio was one of the strong magnets, as was the location of the capital there (except for brief periods) until 1852. For example, Eustaquio Buelna of Mocorito attended the colegio and, after legal training in Guadalajara, settled in Culiacán, where he became one of the town's leading liberal politicans.[44]

Marriage strategy, and to a lesser extent clientage, were important in the construction of family networks, in the expansion of their interests, and in the necessity of flexibility. Client relations generally linked the networks to other segments of society, whereas marriage was the keystone in associations of notables themselves. Matrimonial ties solidified the increasingly interwoven character of business association and family. The two partners in what was one of Hermosillo's principal commercial houses by mid century had both married into the prominent Salazar family of Horcasitas before coming to Hermosillo. When his second wife (Ambrosia Salazar) died, Dionisio González married a daughter of his partner, Pedro de la Serna. Her brother Francisco became first a clerk, then member, eventually his brother-in-law's full partner after the death of the elder Serna.[45]

Marital and client ties were also employed to expand network interests. To facilitate the extension of their business connections beyond Guaymas, the Iñigo family was aided by several marriages. Cayetano's wife (Luisa Ascona) was the daughter of a Tepic merchant, and at least one of their sons was born in that town. Manuel's daughter (Jesús) married Matias Alzua, whose father, an immigrant from Ecuador, was one of Guaymas's wealthiest merchants and whose uncle was the consul of Ecuador in Mazatlán. Iñigo's eldest son (Juan) married the granddaughter of another foreign merchant, the North American John Johnson, who settled in Moctezuma. Johnson, his son Ricardo (the girl's father), and later the younger Alzua acquired some of the most valuable properties in the mining districts south of Hermosillo and east of Guaymas.[46]

Such bonds could also amplify a family network's political influence. They could add the physical force of amateur soldiers, the expertise of professionals (especially lawyers), the financial capital of merchant entrepreneurs, and the cooperation (or at least neutrality) of a rival town's network. The Vega family, which formed the core of a network emerging in Culiacán, dominated state government in Sinaloa from the mid 1830s through the mid 1850s mainly on the strength of its family and client ties.[47]

In using marriage strategy to expand their networks and to adapt flexibly to the varying circumstances, the second generation accelerated their parents' tendency toward exogamy. Elsewhere in Latin America during these years—in Northeast Brazil, for example, as Linda Lewin's study of notables reveals—the logic of circumstances often dictated consolidation through endogamous marriages. However, in the middle third of the nineteenth century, Northwest Mexico's notables generally found marriages to those outside the family, and frequently to those outside the network, of most advantage. Indeed, marriage incorporated those non-notables—especially newcomers to the state—who had acquired political or economic influence: foreigners, the professionally educated, those of humble origins with "rags-to-riches" stories. (Dionisio González in his meteoric rise from Opata Indian prospector to Hermosillo notable exemplifies the latter kind of newcomer.) As a consequence, brothers-in-law, rather than cousins, often formed the critical bonds of political and economic association. Cuñados provided a more fluid and far more numerous pool than did primos in securing the immediate needs of the family, at a time when flexibility was at a premium. Furthermore, if the needs proved of long duration or trust were established, further bonding could be achieved through their children. Thus, Joaquín Astiazarán and José Cubillas, who both married into the Iñigo family, each married a son and a daughter to one another, consolidating their move to Guaymas.[48]

State-Level Networks Prove Unsuccessful

The operation of the most successful of the region's family networks can be seen to its fullest and most integrated extent in the often violent struggle for power at the state level through all of the second generation. In both Sonora and Sinaloa, despite the families' strategies—or perhaps because of their tendencies toward expansion at the expense of consolidation—accommodating one segment of the network as well as the interests of the others proved a difficult and often unsuccessful task. However, if the network failed to achieve general success in forging lasting predominance in state politics during these years, it did make recovery after political failure a fairly probable bet for most of its families.

The notable networks centered around the Almadas in Álamos and the Elías González family in Arizpe had enjoyed the greatest measure of political success byond the local level through the 1820s and into the 1830s. They allied with federalism in order to gain more prerogatives in dealing with their two major concerns: Apache raiding and submission of the tribal Indians. During the course of the second generation, they lost control of these hostile forces, became increasingly isolated by them, and generally failed to seize upon the strategies of flexibility to retain their position. They tended to remain in their original locales, limit their marriage pool, and live off their accumulated wealth until a better day.

In marked contrast were the family linkages being formed in central Sonora, based in Hermosillo, Guaymas, and Ures (the capital after 1837). The most successful of these interlocking networks—that gravitating around the Iñigo, Gándara, and Aguilar families—dominated state politics from the late 1830s through the mid 1850s, integrating political office and family interests to a formidable level. Their diverse economic activities (many of which have been noted above) were frequently in partnership with relatives, either the result of intermarriage among the second generation or of marriage to other prominent families establishing themselves in the central part of the state.[49] Moreover, the preponderance of these families and their in-laws in state officeholding was skillfully, though not always tactfully, employed in furthering those enterprises. Among the Gándaras, Manuel María was governor nine years, and two of his four brothers figured prominently in the legislature. During the two decades, the Iñigo brothers assumed revenue posts and were intimately involved in financing the state treasury as well as a sizable portion of the military forces led by the Gándaras when political conflict turned violent. José de Aguilar and Fernando Cubillas (a cuñado of the Iñigos) were state judges and local officials before becoming governors. Other members of the Aguilar, Cubillas, and Astizazarán families held judicial and revenue posts.[50]

Much of the gandarista armed force consisted of tribal Indians, with whom the Iñigo-Gándara-Aguilar network was far more willing to coexist than their federalist opponents in Álamos and Arizpe. In return, the Indians were their clients in the struggle for state power. As the ugliness of the violence grew, Manuel Iñigo and the Gándaras were discredited politically on charges of fostering a caste war. In addition, the bonds within the network steadily weakened as the Gándaras favored Ures, as the private interests of the Gándaras and Iñigos outran those of other network families (especially the in-laws), and as their predeliction for alliance with centralism proved a growing embarrassment (given its inattention to the state's needs and its restrictions on regional initiative). In the late 1850s, the Aguilars broke ranks over the question of the degree of cooperation with the new liberal government in Mexico City. By then, disgruntled in-laws in Guaymas and Hermosillo did likewise. They fell in behind the political coalition forming around an amateur soldier and entrepreneur of notable origins from the Arizpe district, Ignacio Pesqueira.

The Álamos network had been among the first to support Pesqueira as he turned back the gandaristas' attempt to retain power in defiance of Mexico City's preferences. However, the pesqueirista circle was not a restoration of the old federalist coalition anchored in Álamos and Arizpe. True, for three generations before Ignacio, Pesqueiras had served as professional soldiers in the presidios. But he himself had been sent to Spain and France for schooling in commerce and upon his return had pursued various enterprises and acquired a statewide reputation as a militia officer on the frontier. One of his bases was among fellow militia officers scattered over the state, who made up the nucleus of the new national guard's officer corps. He married the sister of one of the most influential of these officers, Jesús García Morales, member of one of northeast Sonora's most prominent families.[51] For a decade, this alliance of brothers-in-law controlled governmental and military operations. Pesqueira's other base was among the business circles of Hermosillo and Guaymas, including some in-laws of the Iñigo-Gándara network. He was an entrepreneur like themselves and willing to branch out beyond Arizpe in his interests. From 1859 to 1864, his vigorous policies to promote economic activity—making clear to foreign interests (especially from the United States) that investment would be welcomed but no form of political intervention tolerated—brought the first widespread prosperity to the state since 1830.

Nevertheless, Pesqueira's hold on the state steadily eroded over the next decade. His failure to honor the political bargain with alamense notables and harsh repression of those who dared resist (most conspicuously, the Almadas) converted the Álamos family network into the lightning rod of a growing opposition movement. Even more telling, he had failed to be spatially flexible enough and to amplify family connections sufficiently to secure his other base of support in central Sonora. After Ignacio's wife died, his brother-in-law drifted into the position of chief military arm of the federal government, with which Pesqueira increasingly quarreled, and of figurehead of the opposition. Pesqueira fell back upon his own family, marrying a cousin. Some militia officers, merchant entrepreneurs, and politicos stuck by him (as did much of his popular and client support). But they increasingly did so as individuals, not as representatives of their family's network. It became a vicious circle. The more personalist the pesqueiristas became, the more network centered the opposition became, the more arbitrarily and repressively the Pesqueira government responded.[52]

In Sinaloa, the struggle for political power at the state level was more narrowly focused. By the mid 1830s, the contest was between an emerging family network, headed by the Vegas and rooted in Culiacán, and the cosmopolitan merchant community in Mazatlán. The foreign merchants who dominated the port sought a commercial monopoly and even semiautonomy from governmental interference in their affairs. Control of state government for the Vega network and their clients soon became vital to ensure that the advantages of the lines of trade (both legal and contraband) were bestowed upon themselves and denied their rivals.

The Vega network was led by the most prominent grandchildren of the family's founder, the five sons of José María de la Vega. In the mid 1830s, with the backing of their notable relations (principally the Martínez and Verdugo families), the clique dispensed with rival claims from the declining mining center of Cosalá to the capital and to state leadership. Their family filled many state offices (in particular the revenue posts), joined by numerous clients, both in Culiacán and in the smaller district cabeceras, who had come to depend upon the Vegas for access to lines of trade. Through control over the state government apparatus, the Vega network opened the nearby port of Altata to coastal trading, imported large shipments of contraband goods (while cracking down on the illegal activities of their rivals in Mazatlán), and employed the judicial branch to enforce repayment from their debtors and to elude their own creditors.

In the struggle for political power that ran through most of the second generation, client relations came to take precedence over family relations. With commerce so concentrated in the two competing commercial centers and with considerably more public security than Sonora until the late 1850s, notables in other district towns had less opportunity and less incentive to avoid dependence upon commercial activity emanating from Culiacán and Mazatlán. Nor do the two political factions seem to have cultivated family ties to any significant degree. The foreign merchants in Mazatlán developed few such ties in the port itself, and rarely with the prominent families in the southern district towns who were their clients. The Vega network had some family ties with notables in the communities of the center and north of Sinaloa, but they seem to have been narrow in their selection, opting for numerous linkages with fewer families. This limitation in family connections hurt both the Pesqueira and Vega political cliques when the decade of the Reform War and French intervention (1857–67) altered circumstances markedly.

The Vega clique gave way to a wider network of family interests centered in Culiacán. Some were notable families who had been left out or on the margins of the Vega network. Others were newcomers from district towns. Both groups included those who had been educated professionally (and, most, "liberally"). The second generation of Vegas and their kin had not been flexible enough to accommodate and incorporate them. They were increasingly resentful clients, and when external political forces intruded, they seized upon the opportunity. During the course of the armed struggle of 1857 to 1867, liberal officers from notable families in other district towns acquired military prominence and political office. The foreign merchants had scant family connections to draw upon in the face of new political elements in their part of the state: refugees from neighboring Tepic; veteran officers, most of whom, along with their soldiers, were from outside the state; and aspiring entrepreneurs migrating from elsewhere in Sinaloa and the country. Having only wealth as a resource, the foreign merchants, with declining success, were forced to bargain with these new elements to protect their interests.[53]

Rising Standards of Notability

Through the whole of Northwest Mexico, a changing geopolitical reality was ushered in in the late 1850s, spurred by the Reform War and the French intervention. For nearly three decades, regional, national, and foreign political currents had evolved in a disjointed fashion, though often overlapping. They constituted an accumulating mix of political challenges that had generally frustrated the family networks and had often divided them from one another and sometimes within themselves. With the decade of national conflagration, these various challenges to notable predominance were more synchronized; and the second generation, late in their years, at last began sorting them out: solving some, coming to satisfactory terms with others, failing to reach a consensus on still others.

There had also been a sorting out among the notable families themselves by the latter years of the second generation, with a large number of newcomers added in the process. The alterations were far less the result of political failures than of errors in the selection of family strategies that could cope with the fluctuating and often adverse circumstances. It was not so much that the less or unsuccessful fell from notability, though some did. Rather, they fell short of the rising expectations of notability in the region. They had remained prominent in their locales. But either their localities had stagnated or declined or the level of wealth, prestige, and political influence in their towns had ascended beyond their ability to keep pace.[54]

In the transition years between the second and third generations—the years in Mexican historiography referred to as the Restored Republic (1867–77)—a new political (and to a lesser extent economic) challenge appeared that would serve as the prime criterion in establishing new levels of notability in the third generation. A regional political framework, upon which the notable families held a steady if not yet unchallenged hand, had finally emerged. This construct now operated within a strong national (and almost exclusively liberal) context. The boundaries (political, cultural, and psychological) between the region and the nation (and between the region and the world beyond) were far more fixed and clarified. The Northwest's notables were committed to this new political reality and thought they understood it.

What all but a few of the second generation overlooked, however, was the fact that the two political worlds (regional and national), once firmly established, would increasingly interact and affect one another. Herein lay the new challenge. The national political sector was no longer weak and ineffectual, unable to penetrate significantly the periphery. In parallel fashion, state political power within the region, was no longer impoverished, fleeting, and fragmented among competing localities. Accompanying these new political realities, and closely intertwined with them, were new economic structures and conditions. Those in the third generation who understood the challenge and accommodated themselves to it—cementing connections with the political and economic levels above them that increasingly began to penetrate their world— were those who kept pace with the rising standards of notability.

The Third Generation: Fulfilled yet Finessed

For two generations, notables in Northwest Mexico had pursued a vision of progress. They had sought a world in which families of prominence might prosper through a steady expansion of their private holdings and form a core of urbanity and public responsibility around which the region's society would take shape and move. Inaugurated in promise, the vision had met with mixed results at best. Conditions ushered in by independence had given these families more leverage in realizing their vision of progress—they found themselves with fewer rivals to their predominance. Their familial networks, as organizing and integrating mechanisms, far surpassed limited institutional and extralocal structures. Yet postindependence conditions had also left them with a sense of growing frustration, with a seeming inability to turn things fully, or even adequately, to their advantage. The notables had the societal arena to themselves, and yet they could not successfully master either the social elements with which they coexisted or the new circumstances that arose. Flexibility had brought a measure of progress (which varied among the families). It had minimized the frustration. Nevertheless, a sense of unmet expectations remained.

For the third generation, coming to adulthood in the last third of the nineteenth century, those expectations of progress were fulfilled. Circumstances once again coincided with the view of the world their families had held for nearly a century. They prospered economically as never before. They attained a level of social refinement and prestige that, most likely, surprised even themselves. They achieved a degree of control over public life unprecedented in the region. But notability on such a grand scale had not been achieved without a price. Northwest Mexico was no longer theirs exclusively to mold and shape. They increasingly felt the influence of extralocal political and economic forces. Cooperation with these external elements brought them notability on an enlarged scale, brought them fulfillment of their vision of progress. Yet it also compromised their direction of the region more and more, left them with a feeling of being finessed.

During the last third of the nineteenth century, Mexican politics gradually stabilized. Political power was greatly centralized. The process was initiated with limited success by Presidents Benito Júarez and Sebastían Lerdo de Tejada and then carried to fruition by Porfirio Díaz, in alliance with state political machines that arose for the first time on a long-term basis. Politics also were increasingly bureaucratized; public offices proliferated. National political presence in the states, and that of the state in the localities, was greatly amplified. Both the national and state political machines sought satellites in the states and localities, to which they delivered economic benefits and a dependent share in the cornering of political power and the direction of public life.[55]

In the Northwest, that arrangement meant a resolution of the security problems that had plagued the region since independence. Contingents of the federal army and the new national rural police force (the *rurales*), with the periodic support of national guard forces, provided the princi-

pal means to overcome the long-standing insecurities. The public sectors
at the national and state levels were also the principal agents through
which infrastructure was greatly expanded. Through direct funding,
subsidies, loan guarantees, tax exemptions, and other favors, they
brought (or stimulated) rail lines, regular shipping, telephone and telegraph communications, port works, and an improved, enlarged road
network. Parks, prisons, electric lighting, streetcars, hospitals, and libraries also became a regular part of life in the towns.[56]

This profound change in the whole technological context of life was
also the result of a foreign presence that became constant and accelerated rapidly between 1870 and 1910, bringing capital, markets, machines, skills, and training. In particular for Northwest Mexico, this
meant contact with the rapidly developing economy and society of California. The newspaper advertisements, commercial directories, government memorias, and foreign consular reports, among other sources, reveal the extent to which foreign interests penetrated the various sectors
of the economy. The foreigners were joined by a significant number of
internal migrants.[57]

The combination of these extralocal elements—the national and state
public sectors and the foreign presence—stimulated an unprecedented
level of economic activity and growth in the region. The economy expanded in both complexity and scope, and opportunities proliferated at
a rate previously unknown. Notable families could ignore them and try
to continue as before, indirectly benefiting from their general stimulus.
But those who tapped the resources of the foreign and public sectors
were the families whose networks strengthened and flourished. Accompanying this economic boom was a demographic spurt, which saw Sonora's population rise by 131 percent and Sinaloa's 74 percent between
1880 and 1910.[58]

The distribution of population, economic activity, and political power
was profoundly altered in both states by the new circumstances.
Throughout the region, the countryside was invaded by enterprise in a
manner and on a scale that made pale by comparison all previous endeavors. In Sonora, it was in part a return of economic activity, especially along the northern frontier and on the edges of the Yaqui and Mayo
valleys, though large areas were opened to market production for the
first time. In Sinaloa, it was far more an initial commercialization of the
countryside, where largely subsistence activity had been maintained
with the gradual expansion of the rural population. Previous pockets of
commercial agriculture and mining rapidly expanded, engulfing most of
the subsistence activity and opening new areas as well.

The benefits of the economic invasion of the countryside, however, largely went to the district towns and principal urban centers. Rural products were managed from, marketed through, processed by, and consumed in the towns. Rural profits, while frequently reinvested for increased production, more often financed the expansion and refinement of town activity and living. In Sonora, the commercial border town of Nogales, the booming mining center of Cananea, and the agricultural and marketing town of Magdalena joined Hermosillo and Guaymas as principal urban centers. With the loss of the state capital in 1879, Ures fell to the second rank, while Álamos fought a losing battle to keep pace. Mazatlán and Culiacán continued their preeminence in Sinaloa, but the other district towns in the north and center finally emerged as more than simple local market communities. The mining centers of Cosalá in the center and Rosario in the south experienced recovery. Families of prominence in these towns began to acquire a level of notability that only their counterparts in the two principal urban centers had attained in the second generation.[59]

The notability of Northwest Mexico's family networks in the third generation, at whatever level—district town, principal urban center, or for some, statewide—rested narrowly on the paradox of more control and less autonomy. The price of accelerating progress, power, and prestige was the increasing surrender of their prerogative in determining their fate. In the concentration of political power, their options could be restricted or even closed. In the growing foreign penetration of the economy, they could lose access to resources. One finds murmurs of discontent among notables before the mid 1890s, but the tradeoff between control and prerogative seems to have been generally rewarding enough to quell their doubts. However, around the turn of the century, questioning among the Northwest's prominent families began to rise, especially in Sonora. Those families who obtained the largest degree of control while surrendering the least amount of prerogative were the most successful and least disgruntled.

The foremost task of the region's third generation was, then, to strike deals with those above them (in political power) and beyond them (in economic access). Continued flexibility remained important, but above all it was upon the new connections that third-generation notability rested. The most successful families went a step further by privatizing those connections as incarnate links in their familial networks. To convert a wealthy foreign entrepreneur partner or important politico ally into a trusted son- or father-in-law, that was the trick. And once those connections were obtained, it was encumbent upon the family network to expand itself into the enterprise, governmental branch, or institution as much as possible or necessary to secure its interests firmly.

Network Strategies: Making Connections

To make these connections, third-generation notables employed the strategies developed by their families for two generations, adapting them to the circumstances. They found that continued economic diversification was essential. Political and economic conditions were rapidly changing and diversification was necessary to link up with them, and to avoid being subjected by and to them. In mining, for example, which revived markedly during the period, joint-stock ventures between notables continued. But by the late nineteenth century, its greatly enlarged and technically more sophisticated scale translated into huge capital requirements. Families increasingly found it more profitable to sell off previously worked mines, or ones newly claimed, to foreign entrepreneurs. Often they retained shares in the new company's operation. The proceeds from such sales then provided sufficent capital to branch out into other economic activities opening up.[60]

Increasing capital requirements and the need for expanded dealings with foreign suppliers and domestic producers led to more formalized and concentrated mercantile endeavors. Former moneylenders became part of banking institutions as shareholders, directors, or agents. Families thus acquired access to greater amounts of capital, as well as profitable returns. Merchants also specialized as agents for other business firms, especially foreign manufacturers and financial companies. Exclusive agency provided an effective method for securing control over goods. Another technique was to specialize in lines of goods for which there was a new or growing demand: agricultural equipment, mining supplies, and naval stores, for example. Frequently, these specialized trades and agencies with foreign manufacturers were linked.

Notables also continued established patterns of diversification in commerce. Commercial houses expanded and tightened their connections with agricultural production. Families who had merged the two operations in the preceding generation were now able to take full advantage of the possibilities, often adding to their holdings. They were joined by many third-generation merchants—particularly newcomers to the state or to a given district in the state—who had acquired land extensively for the first time. Another avenue in commerce was the growing number of commercial houses (many of them foreign owned). There a family member could learn the business as a clerk and then either use the accumulat-

Early twentieth-century office/residence of the Clouthier family, who were part of the Culiacán network, and who combined interests in commerce, mining, and agriculture.

ed savings and business connections to start a firm of his own or rise within the commercial house to become a partner or even successor.[61]

Industry became more than a token venture for the first time. Improved transportation and the rapid demographic growth assured expanding markets, while technological introductions made large-scale production possible. Commercial capital and connections with foreign equipment suppliers were often the stimulus for manufacturing enterprises. Notable families joined the many new and existing foreign commercial houses—especially those based in Mazatlán and Guaymas—in diversifying into industry, sometimes in partnership with them. Profits from agricultural holdings also went into the establishment of factories. Both Alberto de la Vega and his cousin Luciano operated commercial houses in Culiacán, worked several large estates, and established cigarette factories.[62]

Another new field of enterprise was the public service sector. As public revenues rose dramatically and technological innovations were introduced, contracts, subsidies, and concessions became available. The acceleration of economic activity gave towns sufficient revenues to invest heavily in public improvements.[63] Even more rewarding were the opportunities resulting from the state government's steadily increasing involvement in the economy: concessions for the use and acquisition of natural resources, in particular water and land; subsidies and tax exemptions for the initiation of new enterprises, especially public services; and public security assistance.

Numerous foreigners made their start in the region by the experience, professional training, and capital they could provide such public service ventures.[64] Nevertheless, notable families were equally, if not more, involved in such undertakings. Alejandro Loubet, whose father, a French immigrant, had established a foundry in Mazatlán, received a contract with the port's ayuntamiento to build a new public market. A subsidy of 100,000 pesos accompanied the contract, obtained from leading commercial houses there at 15 percent interest. Loubet also secured contracts to introduce piped water and manufactured ice into Rasario, with a twenty-year exemption from all state contributions. Needless to say, the foundry's products played an integral role in these ventures.[65]

The complementarity exemplified by Loubet's public service ventues was to a significant degree the basis for the extended diversification of notable family interests. A growing number of families, for example, added company stores to their hacienda operatons or retail outlets in neighboring towns and installed processing plants. Jorge and Jesús Almada (originally from Álamos), who established near Culiacán the largest sugar hacienda in Sinaloa in the late nineteenth century, added distilleries, tram lines, a box factory and planing mill, and an electric light plant, as well as laying out the new community of Navolato, which sprung up around the sugar refinery. Foodstuffs grown on the hacienda were sold to the community of nearly three thousand. The brothers' in-

vestment of more than two million dollars in these operations was assisted by state government subsidies of three hundred thousand pesos and
by important tax exemptions.[66]

Occupational diversity and complementarity were also important in
securing connections to the public and foreign sectors. Building upon the
experience of the second generation, an ever-growing number of notables recieved professional training, with special emphasis on mining and
civil engineering, business administration and accounting, corporate
law, and educational administration. Europe remained the training
ground for some. Alejandro Loubet had studied for ten years in France
before returning to Mazatlán to enlarge and incorporate his father's
foundry business.[67] The professional schools of Mexico City and Guadalajara still attracted a large number of third-generation notables. In Sinaloa, the state-run Colegio Rosales continued to stress law and letters,
though medicine, pharmacy, agronomy, and accounting were also introduced. A state-run secondary and professional school was at last inaugurated in Sonora, but an even more important new source for professional
education were the colleges and universities of California. There family
members acquired modes of training familiar to North Americans, as
well as language skills that helped smooth business relations.[68]

Foreign entrepreneurs often brought with them a variety of necessary
occupational skills. But many also understood the added advantage of
having a member of a notable family in their employ. Ignacio L. Almada
began as the bookkeeper for one of the most important foreign mining
companies in Álamos district (the firm having acquired the most important of his family's mining properties). Notables with professional training also served as doctors for large foreign companies as well as for new
public hospitals, as legal and technical counsels, and as intermediaries or
partners in securing concessions. Some, like attorney Guillermo Robinson of Guaymas, who represented the Sonora Railroad Company and
the Sonora and Sinaloa Irrigation Company, made such services their
principal focus. Others, like Almada, used it as an important stepping
stone to expand their interests.[69]

Almada and Robinson were also heavily involved in local government, both serving as municipal president, a new, wholly executive office that reflected the expansion of local political offices in number and
differentiation of function. Under the liberal constitutional reforms of
the Reforma and the Restored Republic, municipios assumed more responsibilities. The ayuntamientos awarded contracts for public improvements, granted concessions for the operation of improved or new
services, determined a wider range of taxes and exemptions, and im-

posed greater regulations on economic activity.[70] Notable families, especially those with the most important local business concerns and with members possessing advanced education, filled the enlarged town councils. Some families monopolized a council post for many years: for example, the Morales in Ures and the Osuna and Bernal families in San Ignacio, Sinaloa.[71] Such political posts guarded their interests and secured access to new opportunities presented through the local public sector.

For many notables, municipal posts were stepping stones to the more coveted state offices. Celedonio Ortiz, who studied commerce and English in San Francisco and returned to use his professional skills in his family's commercial business in Hermosillo, soon began working his way up the bureaucratic ladder. He was regidor on the town council in the late 1880s, then rose steadily in the state government as legislator, deputy to the secretary of government, secretary of government, vice-governor, acting governor, and thereafter (1900–1913), secretary to the legislature. Notables with professional training, such as Ortiz, increasingly filled the higher posts of the bureaucracy.[72] This was particularly true among Sinaloa's third generation (and among their children by the turn of the century) trained in law, medicine, letters, and engineering.[73]

The rewards of salary were attractive, especially for those just initiating their careers. Moreover, the proliferation of public offices provided posts for the expanding number of family members. But it was in the burgeoning opportunities resulting from the public sector's growing role in the economy—and the important connections with the foreign sector that often accrued—that the family networks found the principal incentive in having members become full-time politicos and bureaucrats or in marrying their daughters to them.

The connection between enterprising ventures and political office in Sonora was perhaps most extensive in the Monteverde family, into which two of the state's political triumvirate married. Two family members were state legislators, each for more than twenty years. Another directed the state press and served on the supreme tribunal for a decade, while two others were assistants in the office of the secretary of government. Among the numerous and varied economic activities of the family in the third generation were contracts to clean and repair the streets of the state capital, concessions to introduce streetcar and telephone service there (the latter was sold to state treasurer Víctor Aguilar), and the organization of a mining operation for a North American company.[74]

Marriage strategy secured or reinforced the necessary linkages with the public and foreign sectors. Nuptial ties solidified the Monteverde family's position in the political circle that dominated Sonora. Through marriage, successful outsiders were woven into the fabric of the family network: military veterans and politicos, especially those who had obtained political influence with, or were part of, the state and national political cliques forming; migrants to the state, of varying social origins, who had acquired economic wealth or the benefits of advanced education; foreign immigrants, who possessed capital, technical skills, and external contacts. Intermarriage bound families more closely to one another, giving the networks in the various towns more cohesion and delineation. The previous importance of brothers-in-law, while remaining strong, was somewhat moderated in favor of cousins.

The primary task of the family networks was to solidify their control at the local level and, if possible, to establish ties with the state political machine. Sometimes, particularly in areas where newcomers with economic power or political connections with the state machine were numerous, that objective dictated more exogamous marriages. In locales where newcomers were less prevalent, intermarriage among the prominent families was the more effective strategy. The most successful networks achieved a balance between the two strategies that met the circumstances confronting them.[75]

Where marital ties with important outsiders were unobtainable or less available, clientage often provided a productive, though less optimal, substitute. As the scope and complexity of the economy and government increased, prominent families in smaller towns in particular found client relations their most practical option. The foreign and large national entrepreneurs in their midst, along with the district-level bureaucrats, were almost always from the main urban centers, where more advantageous marriages could be secured. Thus, becoming clients of these outsiders was the next best thing to being their in-laws. This alternative was also taken by many notables in urban centers where foreign economic presence was most prevalent. The owners of large foreign firms were more often than not as reluctant as their predecessors to sink their roots permanently into the towns in which they based their enterprises.[76] In Cananea—the coppermining center that practically overnight at the turn of the century became Sonora's largest town—notables succeeded largely to the extent they made themselves clients of William C. Greene and his associates. They provided professional services, managed the local government apparatus, and pursued the entrepreneurial scraps from Mr. Greene's table.[77]

Linkages with the foreign sector also required spatial flexibility. Cananea was the most important of the new communities that became centers of new economic endeavors along the northern border of Sonora, in the Yaqui and Mayo valleys, and in the river valleys of northern Sinaloa. Several important mining centers revived, especially Cosalá and Rosario in Sinaloa. Some families moved their base to these new or reinvigorated localities. Most extended branches to them. Where not previously established, family branches were also moved to the older principal towns, which shared disproportionately in the economic boom. As a consequence, ties of business association and marriage were fostered among these urban centers to an extent never previously attained.[78]

A Triad of Notability

In the context described above, the economic, matrimonial, and spatial interrelation of the notable networks can be broken down into three arenas. On one level were those networks of families in the various localities (usually district seats), whose extension of interests during the late nineteenth century was largely restricted to their districts. On another level were the state political machine and the network of prominent families closely associated with it, based in the state capital. These families had branches and interests that extended to other districts: the branches, generally in the other principal urban centers; the interests (and family members representing them), wherever the economic and political opportunities of the moment seemed most profitable. In between were notable families who bridged both levels. They were not part of the state network, but their ties to it—economic, marital, client—enabled them to extend their interests beyond their districts and predominate in their localities.

In the preceding generation, the Álamos network had been the initial support base for the Pesqueira clique that attained state power, only to see its own aspirations to expand interests beyond the district level spurned. The third generation of the network fared no better with the political circle that dominated Sonora from 1879 to 1911. Two of the original four leaders (cousins Rafael Izabal Salido and Carlos R. Ortiz) were part of the town's notable network, and a third (Ramón Corral) was linked to it through client and marital ties. Nevertheless, the circle, headed by outsider Luis E. Torres, once securing a foothold in the state government, moved its base to Hermosillo, to which the capital was transferred in 1879.[79]

The Álamos notables were left as clients of the Torres circle, which had slipped out of their grasp. Granted, the continuing Yaqui-Mayo conflict until 1900 restricted their opportunities. However, following the tendencies of the preceding generation, few families branched out elsewhere to compensate for those impediments. And while most had sold their mines to foreigners between 1860 and 1880, they failed to diversify their interests significantly with the capital obtained. Emphasis on accustomed hacienda production (foodstuffs) and commerce remained, both circumscribed by the tribal Indian conflict and the want of transportation improvements. Manufacturing was limited to a handful of small enterprises. The Almada brothers who moved to Culiacán and established diverse interests centered around their sugar refinery were farsighted exceptions to the alamense rule. With the exception of the Salido family (relations of Izabal), the notability of families in the Álamos network extended no farther than their locality, though they shared in the general increase in local prosperity and refinement.[80]

The beneficiaries of the alamense network's loss were the notable families of Hermosillo, in particular the Iñigo-Gándara-Aguilar network that had lost its predominance in state politics late in the second generation. Each of the three politicos who came to direct state politics (commonly referred to as the triumvirate) sealed their growing economic and political ties with the emerging Hermosillo network through marriages with its leading families. In 1884, Torres married a daughter of the Monteverdes. The following year, Izabal did likewise. Three years later, Corral married the daughter of Vicente V. Escalante, grandson of an Iñigo. After 1891, only a single non-hermosillense served in the legislature: Bartolomé A. Salido, a cousin of Izabal's, who served twenty consecutive years. Three Monteverdes each served fifteen years or more in state office between 1890 and 1910. They were joined by names familiar around the capital for more than a half century: Ortiz, Cubillas, Muñoz, Aguilar, Camou, Velez Escalante, Noriega, Díaz, Gándara Bojorquez, Rodríguez, González, Loustaunau. Francisco M. Aguilar was the district prefect, and Victor Aguilar the state treasurer all of those years.

Marriages among the third generation were integrating the Iñigo-Gándara-Aguilar network more closely with other Hermosillo notable families, locating it more firmly in Hermosillo, and creating an enlarged network whose interests attained a statewide level. Members of the network filled state offices, increasingly serving in district posts outside the capital. Family enterprises became more and more intertwined as mining ventures, public service contracts, and other business deals were exploited with government encouragement and often direct government assistance. Added to the arrival of the railroad in 1882 and the spurt in foreign investment were the blessings the state government showered on the city: state funds to assist education, municipal services, and public improvements. The Hermosillo district was the leading center of economic activity into the 1890s. When other areas quickly rose to prominence thereafter, the capital network's families extended their interest to them, often building upon acquisitions already made but only minimally pursued. In doing so, they readily employed their connections to the state political machine, as well as branches of their families in other important economic centers.[81]

In Nogales, which sprung up in the 1880s where the new Sonoran Railroad bound for Guaymas crossed the border with Arizona, one finds representatives of notable families who bridged the district and state levels of notability. Though several foreign businesses were established there in time, from the beginning the border town was dominated by three large business firms—those of Manuel Mascareñas, Cirilo Ramírez, and Prospero and Aurelio Sandoval. The Sandoval brothers specialized in organizing companies and in buying and selling properties for foreign investors. Ramírez became the largest commission agent in the state, in 1901 acquiring the agency for the Greene enterprises in Cananea. Macareñas, who did considerable business with members of the triumvirate and many of Hermosillo's and Guaymas's leading families, was named Mexican consul for Nogales, Arizona, in 1894.[82]

Control of the municipal government was a point of contention among the three business firms for two decades. Apparently because all three had important interests that extended outside their localities and had important links to the state political machine, the latter could not settle on a permanent deal with any one of them and arranged a truce in 1897. Marriage seems to have provided a more lasting resolution to the conflict. In 1900, one of Mascareñas's sons married Ramírez's only daughter. Thereafter, the Sandovals led the municipal government.[83]

The three levels of notability were somewhat more clearly defined in Sinaloa due to the earlier concentration of urban development and certain constitutional changes. In 1880, constitutional reforms reduced the thirty-six existing municipios to ten, to coincide with the number of districts. This enabled the family networks in the district cabeceras to control their localities more fully. As new opportunities developed in the surrounding countryside, families sent members there to establish or expand their enterprises. They often secured the appointment of family representatives in the local executive offices that governed small communities and the rural population.[84]

The constitutional reforms also transferred the executive power of the district ayuntamiento to the prefect. In most districts, the families who occupied that office generally filled the intermediary level of notability in Sinaloa. The Inzunza family of Mocorito provides one of the best examples. They occupied the prefectura all but four years between 1877 and 1895, thereafter serving several years as alternate, as well as filling a slot on the ayuntamiento most years. Pedro Inzunza and in-law Víctor A. Aviles served as diputados or alternates for the district twenty years. The Inzunza and Aviles families, in addition to their agricultural and commercial interests in the district, entered into several business ventures with prominent members of the state regime in neighboring districts.[85] The Colegio Rosales also served as a bridge through which some local notables established close relations with the state network, attaining important state and district offices and expanding their interests beyond their localities.[86]

As in Sonora, the notable network that exercised hegemony at the state level in Sinaloa owed its elevation to its linkage with the politicos upon whom Porfirio Díaz had settled as his principal clients: in this case a single individual, rather than a triumvirate. Though a client of the Vegas in his early years, Francisco Cañedo's political loyalties had drifted back and forth between Culiacán and Mazatlán. Once having struck a deal with Don Porfirio, however, he settled on Culiacán's notables as his principal associates. Four families formed the core of the state network that solidified around Cañedo: Vega, Martínez de Castro, Izabal, and Batiz. Cañedo himself had married in to the Batiz family. Members of these families figured most prominently as state bureaucrats and diputados, joined by their in-laws.[87] Those with affinal ties included members of the state capital's other notable families, but many were newcomers, like Cañedo, who had achieved positions of economic or political power.[88]

The business community of Mazatlán, which previously had tried to undermine a state regime based in Culiacán (often successfully), still grumbled. Cañedo understood the necessity for moderating the urban rivalry, and the state-level family network played a significant role in his ability to do so. Above all, this was accomplished through the marriage of enterprising newcomers to the port into Culiacán's notable families. Some, like Joaquín Redo and Agustín Haas, established business ventures in and around the capital. Others, like the Pelaez brothers, remained in Mazatlán, occupying important bureaucratic posts.[89]

The moderation of the long-standing conflict between Culiacán and Mazatlán was part of a larger consensus attained among third-generation notables in Northwest Mexico. It took place within the framework of the hierarchy of notability noted above, which emerged in the 1880s and endured until the Revolution of 1910. There were some political and

economic challenges stemming from the growing influx of foreign entrepreneurs and companies and of nationals who migrated to the region or
from localities within the region to important urban centers. In most
cases the various strategies employed by the family networks either absorbed these challenges or adjusted to them. The great amplification of
economic opportunity and bureaucratic office afforded room within
which a consensus among the notables could be reached. The extension
of effective, enduring political machines downward from Mexico City
through the state capitals also fostered consensus. Equally important
was the rising degree of social integration of notable families in the third
generation, the increasing intertwining of their networks.[90]

An elaborate series of public functions and semipublic occasions arose
to trace more definitively the boundaries of notable society and the several degrees of notability among the region's networks of prominent
families. These social observances provided the opportunity for apprais-
al and comparison of family status—welcomings and leave-takings of
leading officials, national holidays, inauguration of public improvements, and annual fiestas such as the carnival before Lent. Attendance,
special seating, or responsibilities at special activities surrounding such
occasions were marks of social distinction. At public functions, verbal
testimonials to notability were often given. Entrepreneurs were touted
for their contributions to progress. Professionals were lauded for their
additions to the standards of refined living. Students were reminded of
their future public opportunities and responsibilities.[91]

Participation on the junta that planned and supervised such occasions
carried the highest prestige. Steadily proliferating in number, the juntas
provided the means by which the notables managed the public social
calendar and endowed it with ever more refined standards. The juntas,
of course, were not only supervisors of celebrations but also agents of enterprise, which improved the quality of urban life (particularly for network families), and agents of service, attending to basic amenities and
emergencies for the general public (relieving individual families of that
burden).[92]

Special occasions in more private settings also fostered the delineation
of, and between, notable families. The wedding of a daughter of Vice-
Governor Alberto Cubillas to a leading North American merchant of
Cananea in Hermosillo's cathedral—celebrated with a profusion of electric lights and two orchestras—was attended by all of the Sonoran capital's upper crust. A fishing party in honor of Governor Corral brought
together members of the state network with notables in Sonora's capital
and main port.[93] In the principal urban centers, the meeting of notables

The state capitol, as seen from the bandstand on Hermosillo's main plaza. Built at the end of the nineteenth century, both served as principal sites for public functions that showcased the town's notables.

became narrowly focused and institutionalized through the establishment of clubs. The plush Casino Club in Hermosillo became the center
of recreation for "all the most elegant and aristocratic gentlemen" of the
capital.[94]

Turn-of-the-Century Disgruntlement

The outward signs of notability—in their various degrees—reinforced
a growing sense of fulfillment among third-generation network families
in the Northwest. The evidence of notability accumulating all around
this third generation demonstrated the realization of their families' century-long vision of progress to levels their grandparents most likely
would not have anticipated. And yet by the turn of the century, there
was also emerging among them a gnawing feeling of being finessed.
From this perspective, the bargain with the political cliques above them
and the foreign sector beyond them looked less and less equitable.

The state political machines, and the family network associated with
each (particularly in Sonora), became the chief repositories of the resent-
ment that began to build in the first decade of the twentieth century.
They were the main intermediaries in the bargain that had been struck
with extralocal elements. They were the guarantors for the interests of
the region's notables vis-à-vis those above and outside. They were also
the guarantors in the consensus reached between the various levels of notability within the region itself.

The cornering of resources by outsiders or a select few in power was
beginning to exceed acceptable limits for an increasing number of notable families. Foreign influence was rising dramatically. In Sonora, more
than half of the large commercial establishments were owned by foreigners. The pattern was similar, though not as prevalent in industrial
concerns. Their domination of the mining sector was overwhelming.
Immense acquisitions of land by foreign investors for resale to individuals or groups of colonists (many foreign immigrants) began to occur in
the last years of the decade. Víctor Aguilar and members of the Monteverde families were among those in the state network cut in on such land
deals.[95] In Sinaloa, well over half the mining companies were owned by
North Americans. In 1910, the Sinaloa Land Company acquired the La
Primavera sugar hacienda from the Almada brothers and, with the assistance of the federal courts, set aside the claims by notables in the Culiacán Valley against expropriation of their lands for the company's canal
network.[96]

Notables in Sonora united with less prosperous farmers to send protests all the way to President Díaz against the huge land acquisitions and
water concessions, but to no avail. Members of prominent families
joined others with intentions of starting out on their own after appren-
ticeship as a clerk in decrying the inroads of the Chinese into the expanding markets for goods and services among urban and mine laborers.
Families who had come to depend upon the labor of Yaquis, who had
been scattered throughout most of the state after the conquest of their
homeland, protested vociferously when the triumvirate acquiesced in
the Díaz regime's final solution of deportation to ferret out the rebels and
their accomplices. In the notables' judgment, the limits of centralized
power in the pursuit of progress were being exceeded. Moreover, a few
selected employers—principally members of the state network—were
being given squads of Yaqui laborers.[97]

Not only were the state networks losing sight of the acceptable limits
of outside economic interests—as well as beginning to corner an undue
share for themselves. From the view of the rest of the region's notables,
they were instigators, as well as accomplices, in the squeezing of political options beyond what was tolerable (again, especially in Sonora). To
extend their political hegemony firmly into the municipalities, the state
machines had begun promoting small cliques, fully obedient and in
complete control of the ayuntamientos. Often prefects with local power
bases were the principal instrument in this political manipulation.
Worse still for networks at the local level was the imposition of outsiders
as such agents. Representatives of notable families (particularly those
previously neutral or in political opposition) were dropped from official
slates. In the important urban centers, especially, one finds after 1900 a
decided change in personnel, with the ayuntamientos staffed by the
most successful of recent arrivals (businesspeople and professionals, both
foreign and national), who had few connections to the family networks.[98]

For an increasing number of notables, entire families as well as individual branches, the political deference of the state machines toward
Mexico City after the turn of the century had passed acceptable boundaries. The Sonoran triumvirate's response to the violent Cananea copper
mine strike in 1906 epitomized it. When Governor Izabal employed
North American "volunteers" to repress and contain the strike and then
replaced the municipal president who objected to the move with a recently naturalized North American, notable families were shocked and
ashamed. Ironically, in their zeal to protect unconditionally the vast interests of William Greene in Cananea, Izabal and Torres exceeded what

even the president's agents thought prudent.[99] This excess made the suppleness of the Sonoran regime's mind-set toward Mexico City all the more telling.

The Fourth Generation: The Bequest

The opposition to the Porfirian regime in the wake of the Creelman interview in 1908 became the channel for the growing discontent among Northwest Mexico's notable families. Representatives of the networks at the local and middle levels of notability—and even some from the state network in Sonora—began affiliating with, and in most cases assuming the leadership of, the series of opposition movements that culminated in the Revolution of 1910. Their presence, though not their predominance, continued through the decade of armed struggle and the establishment of a "revolutionary" politics and society in the years that followed.

As we have seen, the families came to opposition having concluded that the foreign sector had penetrated the economy to an unacceptable degree, that the public sector at the federal and state levels had begun to corner political opportunity beyond forebearance. Moreover, unrest was building below the notables. Incidents such as the Cananea strike and policies such as deportation of the Yaquis made notables question whether extralocal elements could maintain the social and economic stability under which they had so prospered for three decades. The bargain struck by the third generation no longer appeared reasonable, especially to its offspring.

Network family members in the various opposition movements were overwhelmingly from the fourth generation. They could not put aside political ambitions for economic success as easily as their parents. Indeed, they seriously doubted whether the Porfirian system could any longer guarantee even their economic success. They fell back on the ideals, the far more open politics, of a liberal world they had learned about in school and celebrated on commemorative days: effective suffrage; independent courts; municipios free from subservience to state authorities; above all, an open competition between families of prominence in a given town or in the state as a whole. They found in the movement of Francisco Madero a program for the nation in which these aspirations could comfortably reside.

Representatives from notable families began by organizing public meetings and opposition clubs. In Sinaloa, Cañedo's death in 1909 prompted an opposition candidacy for governor—that of Lic. José Ferrel, supported vigorously by his cousin, Francisco Valadés, whose family had recently acquired the important *El Correo de la Tarde* in Mazatlán. Valadés's wife was from the Lafarga and Maldonado families, both among San Ignacio's most prominent and closely linked to the Cañedo machine. A brother had married into the Urrea family, one of the wealthiest in the Culiacán network. Candido Aviles also ran against the official grain. Though his father managed the large textile mill owned by the leading members of the state network, though his in-laws were the most powerful family in Mocorito district, Aviles nonetheless led the organizaton of the ferrelista clubs in that district and their affiliation with Madero's anti-reelectionist movement.[100]

With the outbreak of the armed maderista struggle (in the winter of 1910–11), some notables joined secret revolutionary cells. Both states machines recognized the accelerating alienation of the family networks. In Sonora, the triumvirate decided to resurrect the *Junta de Notables*, which had been used to choose candidates in the 1870s and early 1880s. In return for the promise of free elections, a majority endorsed the official slate for the state executive (General Lorenzo Torres and Dr. Fernando Aguilar). In Sinaloa, Cañedo's successor, Diego Redo, offered constitutional reforms to reinstitute a policy of no reelection, restore municipios suppressed in 1880, and require the approval of a majority of municipios in any future constitutional changes. But in both states, there was little trust or respect remaining among most notables upon which to base such concessions, especially in light of the growing maderista strength.[101] During the Madero government (1911–13), representatives from network families figured prominently at both local and state levels, particularly in Sonora.[102]

Madero's revolution was able to open up the closed politics of the Porfiriato. It could not, however, reconcile the notables' liberal political world with the rising political manifestations of the profound socioeconomic changes and dislocations engendered by the rapid development of the Porfirian era. A politics based upon relatives, friends, clients, and employees was giving way to one far more group oriented and interest based: organized workers, campesinos, professional groups, business associations. A political structure that merely permitted individuals with education and opportunity (and, one might add, family connections) to rise above their former station was no longer adequate to rectify popular grievances.

After Madero's fall in 1913, political power increasingly settled in the hands of those who had come to know the popular classes as mineworkers, villagers, millworkers, farm laborers, craftspeople, small ranch-ers—each with their own list of grievances against the Porfirian system. The new politicians were young men of modest or limited means who had previously found opportunity restricted or closed to them. They confidently sought to enlist popular interest groups under their leadership. They offered to redress grievances through structural changes in the economic and social system—in promise and ideology, if not always in reality—in return for political support.

In Northwest Mexico, among the most influential of these new politicos were the poor relations of the family networks. Many had known personal or family misfortune, some failure, almost all the frustration of thwarted ambition. Alvaro Obregón and Benjamin Hill were in-laws of the Salidos. Plutarco Elías Calles was a generally unsuccessful offshoot of a branch of the Elías family.[103] These three, along with Adolfo de la Huerta, whose family also had recently known hardship, eventually formed the core of the revolutionary group from the Northwest that came to be known as the Sonoran dynasty. The group consolidated power at the national level after 1920, initiated the first broad revolutionary program, and directed the government until the rise of Lázaro Cárdenas in 1934.

These poor relations seem to have been the mediators through which the family networks (representatives of which affiliated with the various revolutionary factions) adjusted to the new revolutionary realities. When one examines the lists of officeholders after 1920, one finds network families prominently represented. Indeed, of the eleven Sonoran governors who served between 1920 and 1973, at least eight were from notable families (including sons of Obregón and Calles). Notable family names appear frequently in the legislative rosters.[104] Institutionalized political parties and interest-group politics were responsible for their elevation to power, but fourth-generation notables and their children still adapted to the new realities by using their family connections to the fullest to secure influence in institutional structures. They preserved much of their economic position in the wake of revolutionary dislocations and have generally prospered. Perhaps above all, they have guarded safely the social prestige, the reputation of their family's name. In that alone has been considerable influence and the basis for retaining their positions of prominence.

Today the family networks and the direction of society no longer seem to coincide to a marked degree (the extent of their influence and interests in postrevolutionary Mexico has not been studied in detail). Yet notability achieved over a century, with a familial mechanism that proved so flexible, does not appear to have decayed so readily. Thumbing through the telephone directory, observing store and office signs, catching a notice of a coming recital for young musicians, one familiar with the nineteenth-century world of notable families in Northwest Mexico feels to a certain degree at home. Though hegemony is now clearly a memory, and being notable perhaps a bit outdated, a link to one of the nineteenth-century networks is still an asset to be desired.

4

Buenos Aires

Historian Tulio Halperín, discussing Argentina after independence, wrote that "distinguished families from the colonial period seemed to recover a position which higher officials and corporation members did not."[1] Individuals, no matter how great their economic or institutional power, did not retain their positions; the families did. Thus families were crucial in Argentina's transition from the colonial-mercantile to the estancia-based society. They survived because they were part of a *network* that interwove groups of families through marriage, business, politics, professions, and government posts. It allowed them to work as a group; through concerted action, they could gain control of a region, a town, or a country. In Latin America during this period, the families formed the microstructure and the network became the macrostructure of society. By the first decades of the twentieth century, institutions such as clubs, corporations, and professional groups formalized the links of the network in the areas of greatest development; in other more marginal areas, links were formalized later.

This chapter focuses on a group of families in Buenos Aires over a period of three generations. It covers a period of one hundred years between the late eighteenth and nineteenth centuries, examining the creation and development of such a network. Among its members, clear and distinct patterns emerge in the family business, their professions and posts, and their marriages.

Eighteen families, chosen from lists of members of the Sociedad Rural (1866) and the Jockey Club (1882), were originally studied. Then the study was extended to comprise the total membership of both clubs, or 198 individuals. Of these, 154 were traced.[2] These two clubs were the most important in the city and made the network visible as its members emerged in positions of power in Buenos Aires in the 1870s. The families, whose third generation appeared on the rosters of the Sociedad Rural or Jockey Club, will be called the "Club families" or the "154 families." (A list of the founding members of the clubs appears in the Appendix.)

The formation of the family network in Argentina began in the late eighteenth century and took three generations to complete. During this time, a definite occupational sequence evolved: the members of the first generation were traders; the second estancieros with cattle and sheep ranches; and the third financiers, bankers, and politicians. Each change in occupation signified a rise in social and economic position and an increase in power. By their second and third generation, the families in the network had become "notable."

The groundwork for the emergence of the networks was laid before 1800. The males of the first generation were mostly immigrants who arrived in Buenos Aires in two waves, the first between 1780 and 1810 and the second between 1820 and 1840. From 1780 to 1810, they came from Spain, and many established their economic base in trade. From 1820 to 1840, most came from other European countries. Only 16 of the 154 were in the city in 1778 when the census was taken. Thus most of the males of the first generation were newcomers, not local or established individuals.

Because of the difference in time between the two waves of immigration, naming the generations as "first," "second," and "third" is difficult. Members of the first group were in their second generation when the first generation of the second group arrived. The decision to call those who came from abroad, whenever they came, the first generation has, therefore, a certain amount of arbitrariness. The term is consistent only in that these individuals are the first generation in Buenos Aires and share many first-generation characteristics. So although the main body of families in this study spans three generations, some cover four (the early arrivals, i.e., those arriving before 1780; their number totals 16 out of 154) and some cover only two (the late arrivals, i.e., those arriving after 1820, a total of 32 out of 154).

Arrival between 1780 and 1800, however, initiated a pattern so pervasive and dominant that it pulled early and late arrivals into step with it. In other words, a specific coetaneous group seemed to prevail over the period. It set up a way of doing things that persisted beyond its own era. But we do not have a true opposition between the generational sequence and the general march of events. Rather, the general march of events from 1780 is the generational sequence, and it is so strong that it pulls the early and late arrivals into its own sequence. Thus, we can call the generational sequence beginning in the late eighteenth century "mainstream."

By and large, the first generation were not the *comerciantes* (major merchants) described by Susan Socolow in her work on late-eighteenth-century Buenos Aires.[3] They were *mercaderes* (traders) and *pulperos* (shopkeepers), who occupied a much less important level of trade. However, the two groups overlap slightly in that twelve first-generation families were part of the group of 178 studied by Socolow and formed part of the dominant group of important merchants of the late colonial period (referred to hereafter as the colonial merchant families or the 178 merchant families). In addition, by 1821, twenty-two of the 154 families were members of the Consulado del Comercio, the corporation that gathered and represented the merchants of substance (it was dissolved in 1821).

Though most of the males in the first generation were newcomers, those in Buenos Aires prior to 1778 also are important to this study. Those who were part of the highly visible mercantile community that dominated the city in the 1770s and 1780s supplied brides for many of the new immigrants and thus contributed to the foundation of the network. These marriages provided the newcomers with the assets of the established families, which they used to found the estancias that dominated *porteño* (from the port city, that is, Buenos Aires) society after 1800.

The first generation bought land on which the second generation created and managed estancias. They began by capturing wild cattle and ended by breeding cattle and sheep. In general, the fathers and sons jointly held the ranch. The father provided capital, and the son—usually a second or third son rather than the eldest—provided labor. These estancia ventures also established an important pattern. The son created the estancia and lived on it for a few years. Later, though usually before he was thirty, he returned to the city.

During this period, however, the father's shop or retail outlet in the city was not left to flounder. The oldest son, an uncle, or a son-in-law would manage the store and handle the hides, tallow, hooves, horns, or cattle-on-the-hoof from the estancia. At all times, the estancia depended on its urban connection. Without initial capital or a commercial outlet, the rural business could not prosper. This financial connection between rural and urban areas was reinforced socially by the family linkage be-

tween the young man on the estancia and his older relative in the city.
When the son returned to the city from the estancia, he took over some
branch of the trade, either expanding what was already there or specializing in one area.

By 1826, the families in this study had shifted their economic base
from the city to the country. Nevertheless, they maintained residences
and participated in the politics of the city. Buenos Aires supplied the
needed capital for the estancia and was the place where all political and
economic decisions were made. The family's social and political base
would always remain urban, though by the second generation its economic base had become rural.

The second generation merged the cattle estancia and the urban trading post. During its life span, the second generation captured wild cattle, then crossbred sheep, and eventually crossbred cattle. Wool became
an important item in the family trade. By the third generation, agriculture was incorporated into the estancia. Wheat and other grains joined
wool as important trading commodities, and the trading outlet often became a successful export business. Activities on the estancia were handled by *mayordomos* (overseers) and *capataces* (foremen) who lived
there. The third generation added a professional manager or administrator who resided in the city.

Members of the third generation were professional people and therefore did not live on the estancias or run them. Nearly all of the members
of the third generation occupied urban posts, either public ones in government or private ones in banking, insurance, or investment companies. By the third generation, the families concentrated on financial and
political ventures and developed new opportunitites to expand and control the products of their estates. The movement was always from retail
or wholesale trade to development of a large rural estate, and then to international trade, government, finance, and railroad transportation.
Strong connections were built between the rural and urban enterprises,
between economic ventures, and between the different occupations and
posts held by family members.

Though the generational differences may be explained in terms of responses to changes in the economy, one must add that the families
seemed to respond quickly and in concert to the changes. In addition, by
the third generation, they themselves had something to do with the direction of the economy. In a way, the third generation summarizes the
economic strategy that was most successful for each of the three generations.

In terms of political and economic events, the generational timetable covers the transition of Buenos Aires from capital of a Spanish viceroyalty to capital of the new nation, Argentina. The first generation started in a society dominated by merchants, mainly large exporters, and in an economy dependent on silver. But they also lived in a climate of change heralded first by the beginning of free trade and followed by the rise of power of dealers in hides and by the appearance of British merchants dealing in cash.

Many changes affected this distant and modest outpost. Industrialization created a demand for raw materials. Technological innovations, for example, the construction of much larger holds in ships, made feasible the exportation of building materials, such as hides, or of barrels of salted meat.

These changes and the lack of strong colonial traditions attracted new immigrants from northern Spain. Because an important Spanish establishment of officials did not exist before the eighteenth century, Buenos Aires became the first area to break with Spain (1810–16). The first generation, therefore, participated in the area's transition from a Spanish colony dominated by large export merchants dependent on silver to a mixed and unstable economy gradually shifting from silver to exporting hides and salted meat. This generation would, toward the end of its life, invest in land. Consequently, the period after independence witnessed a rise in land prices.

The second generation, however, became the first estancieros. The main thrust of the second generation's activities was the creation and settlement of large estates, which often included pieces of land in different parts of the province (consolidation occurred in the third generation). The economy of the estancia, based at first on grazing cattle used for hides or salted meat, shifted in the second generation's time to include crossbred sheep and the production of wool, until wool predominated in the export market in the 1860s. The second generation, though an estanciero generation, was also active in politics and in the military.

From 1830 to 1852, Buenos Aires was dominated by Governor Juan Manuel de Rosas. More than the tyrant usually portrayed, he represented the regime of estancias. Rosas boasted of governing the province like an estancia (but then, so did General Julio Roca, president of Argentina in the 1880s). His government dramatized the unsettled and brutal period during a major economic shift and a structuring of a new social order.

The second generation fought the battles to determine which regional economy would prevail as the national one. This was the period of the conservative-liberal and of unitarian-federal battles throughout the whole territory (and familiar to us in every area of Latin America). In what was to become Argentina in the period of the second generation (the 1820s–1860s), the battle became one for the receipts of the custom house of the city of Buenos Aires, the main source of currency for financing a government or, alternatively, for the preservation or elimination of the city's monopoly. One provincial union attempted to challenge Buenos Aires. Urquiza, the most powerful estanciero of Entre Ríos, used his estancia headquarters as government house. His attempt shows the estancia economy, based on cattle and sheep, was the only one to present a viable alternative to Buenos Aires. (But how the benefits from this economy were to be distributed regionally was not to be resolved until the 1860s with the final defeat of Urquiza and the provinces by Mitre's army, financed by the proceeds of the custom house of Buenos Aires.)

The third generation spans the 1860s to the 1900s, the period of so-called national integration. This period saw both the consolidation of a network of families in Buenos Aires and the extension of their power to national matters through political and military intervention in the provinces and through pacts and deals with regional family networks. With them, they brought peace and cooperation and submission to Buenos Aires. The political system inaugurated by Roca in the 1880s represented the installation of this system, which lasted until 1914. During this period, thousands of acres of estancia lands passed into the hands of the 154 families. The wealthy families, by backing the so-called Conquista del Desierto, benefited from the last plentiful land market for large estancias.

Also during this period, a political shift occurred from the Buenos Aires legislature, in which most of the notable families concentrated their activity when Buenos Aires was a separate state, to national politics (not to the national legislature but to the national ministries). Buenos Aires was established as the capital of the nation (which meant a battle with Buenos Aires's province and the province's loss of the income from customs), and a major new port and national railway system were created, concentrating in the center of the city of Buenos Aires.

To conclude, the complex interconnections between families in the social and political realms bolstered economic enterprises in subtle and overt ways. Covering a range of activities and showing strong generational patterns, they merit more detailed examination. We will trace the patterns of the families' activities over three generations in the following areas: first, the family business; second, their professions, posts, and politics; and third, their marriages.

The Family Business

The First and Second Generations

In the 1866 and 1881 membership lists of the Sociedad Rural and the Jockey Club, only twelve names appear that belong to the old wholesale merchant families of the colonial era. The rest belong to the newer immigrant families that formed the network. The 1778 census shows only 16 of the 154 families in Buenos Aires. Eight came from other parts of the viceroyalty (later Argentine provinces) and from other parts of Spanish America. In half of these cases, the heads of families were born in Spain and went first to another place in Spanish America before coming to Buenos Aires; the other half were born in Buenos Aires of Spanish fathers. Twenty-two of the 154 reached the upper level of the mercantile community by 1821. But most of the new immigrants were involved in commerce at a lower level: they were not comerciantes, rather mercaderes or pulperos. These new immigrants were the first to direct their commercial interest to the pampa and its cattle products.

During the late eighteenth and early nineteenth centuries, then, a major shift occurred that caused the dominant families of the colonial period to lose their power. This change took place in the world of business and, as historian Halperín-Donghi explains, relates to the battle in the post-1810 period between *mayoristas* (wholesalers in international trade) and *minoristas* (retailers in local trade, or the *frutos del país*.)

> Although from 1813 onwards the Consulado [the Corporation of the important wholesale merchants] had given up hope of obtaining for them the legal monopoly of any sector of the market, they did, nevertheless, enjoy certain tax concessions which . . . they were prepared to defend tenaciously against the foreigners (n.b. mainly British merchants). Through them expression was given, not only to the sentiments of hostility to the foreign merchants, but also to the desire . . . to place severe limitations on the opportunities of the *local* small merchants. Both the solutions proposed in the Consulado in 1815 and the proposal for a mercantile company made by J. J. C. Anchorena in 1818 evince the same tendency. The former proposed to prohibit all trade with overseas to merchants who did not possess a comparatively large minimum capital and the latter proposal envisaged making such trade the privilege of a company which,

formed as a corporation by the local merchants, would be dominated by the most powerful among them. Such reforms were an attempt to shut out the foreign competitors from contact with those small local merchants who had been too ready to act as their associates and 'front men.'[4]

By 1818, the last attempt to control the local traders had failed, not because of the Consulado group's power, but because of the revolution in trade. Initiated by the British merchants' cash payments for products, the trade revolution allowed the small trader to survive and subsequently prosper by eliminating a twofold dependency on the letters of credit issued by large merchants and on a trade based on a shrinking and uncertain source, the precious metals of Upper Peru. These small traders, who dealt mostly with frutos del país and the gathering of local goods from rural areas, slowly moved to the forefront of the commercial sector, which the merchant dealing in *efectos de Castilla* (Spanish or Castilian imports) had formerly occupied.

Between 1796 and 1802, trading in Castilian goods still provided the basis for economic prominence, even for the families that began the network. The 12 of the 154 families who reached the highest levels of the mercantile hierarchy in the colonial period did so in the wholesale trade of Castilian goods. They appear in the *Almanaque* (Commercial Guides of Buenos Aires), which reflects their importance in the mercantile community. In the 1796 *Almanaque*, 2 of the 154 families appeared as members of the Consulado, 2 as mercaderes, and 4 as comerciantes de la Plaza de Cádiz (merchants involved in international trade based in Cádiz, Spain). In 1802, 1 other family of the 154 joined the Consulado, 10 were classified as important merchants, or principales comerciantes, and 2 (possibly 3) as mercaderes. Thus by 1802, 14 of the 154 families had reached a high commercial level. But they were not doing anything new; they traded in Castilian goods.

But by 1800, several indications of change appeared. In 1798, a royal order decreed that hacendados should gain representation in the Consulado.[5] The 1802 *Almanaque* reveals other innovations. After listing the different levels of commerce, it mentions pulperos as a category of trade for the first time. This listing is surprising because in the Hispanic world, the term *pulpero* indicates the very lowest level of trade. To appear in the guide, the pulperos must have risen in importance. The newness of the listing is highlighted further by the *Almanaque* editor's explanation for their inclusion:

Independientemente de los comerciantes referidos hay otro gremio que se compone de 400 a 500 individuos conocidos con el nombre de pulperos porque las oficinas que manejan se llaman así; y son en las que se menudea todo género de bebidas y de comestibles con otras menudencias propias de su mecanismo; sin embargo, el manejo de ellas es de mucha consideración por su entidad, y de mucha conveniencia al público por las circunstancias con que se gobiernan con respecto a la costumbre del país.

Besides the merchants listed, there is another group which consists of 400 to 500 individuals called "pulperos," taking their name from their places of trade. These stores sell retail all kinds of foodstuffs and drinks. But their trade is quite large in volume and of great convenience to the public because they work in accordance with local custom.[6]

Clearly, by the onset of the nineteenth century, pulperías were growing in importance in the commercial hierarchy. However, a careful study would be required to ascertain the importance of pulperías among the 154 families. At least 20 of the 154 families had them, mostly the young males of the second generation and in the rural areas rather than the city. Although pulperos are listed as selling foodstuffs and drinks locally, they also sent hides to the city from the surrounding areas. But the economic importance of such local products should not be overstressed; in the first decade, they made up only between a fifth and a third of the total value of Buenos Aires exports. The old colonial trade in precious metals from Upper Peru still dominated and would continue to do so for another decade, until 1821.[7]

Despite these indications, no substantial changes took place until 1826. At that time, the *Almanaque* further stressed the importance of the pulperos by listing all of them. It also redefined the different trade categories. Instead of first listing members of the Consulado de Comercio, then comerciantes, and then mercaderes, the directory lists *negociantes* (commercial agents representing foreign commercial houses) first, comerciantes second, and owners of *barracas* (warehouses) third. The last it lists in one category only: hide warehouses. Seventeen *barracas de cuero* are given, four of which belong to members of the 154 families. Fourth and last in the guide are the pulperos.

By 1826, negociantes, comerciantes, barraqueros, and pulperos also dealt in goods from the area where the new estancias were being settled. While the family's urban outlet for the estancia products grew in importance, city goods also found a ready market in the estancia's hinterland. Sugar, yerba mate (the local tea), and cheap British cloth and clothing became important trade commodities. Sometimes the traders and the new estancieros of the 1820s were one and the same, or they were different members of the same family: one gathering goods in the countryside and the other managing the commercial outlet in the city.

By 1828, the list of subscribers of the Banco de Provincia, the first joint stock bank, reflected these new developments by including several new names. It shows fourteen names from the powerful colonial merchant group of 178, but thirty from the group of 154 families. Like the earlier list of the Consulado del Comercio, this list identified those with a strong economic position or capital.

The Second Generation and the Estancia

Land seems not to have been valuable until the 1820s, though speeches given in the 1820s legislature indicate that the new wealth was based on cattle.[8] Thus the families needed land for settling cattle. In 1826, the enfiteusis or land lease law, of Rivadavia allowed the lease (and sometimes the eventual sale) of vast areas of public land at very low prices. But this move indicates a need to create an immediate source of revenue for the debt-ridden government more than an increase in the relative value of the land.[9]

During this period, the second generation acquired its land and became the estancia generation. In some instances, first-generation merchants purchased land for their second sons. Most frequently, they received land through government grant or lease in return for active military service or aid in military provisioning (cattle or horses for the troops, food, money, etc.). The 1833 Indian expedition of Governor Juan Manuel de Rosas, for example, not only established forts south of the province but also provided estancia lands for many of the families; supporters of the expedition received land or gained a first choice in land leases in return for their help. Land speculation also started in the 1820s. For instance, Capdevila, a merchant, founder, and part owner of the famous sheep estancia "Los Sajones," bought bordering lands at one price during one year and sold them at a higher rate the next.[10]

During the second generation, the estancias developed rapidly. Land for grazing wild cattle was used to crossbreed sheep. The estancias acquired wire fences, machinery, and buildings. The economic activities that accompanied this change were also varied: exporting hides, exporting meat for the salted meat market, or acquiring meat-salting plants (*saladeros*). Eighteen of our families had a saladero at one time or another (seven of them in their first generation, nine in their second, two in the third generation).

Saladeros were important in a few of the family businesses in the first and second generation, but wool from the sheep that were crossbred on the estancia became the important item of the business in the second and third; the introduction of cattle crossbred for the meat export market followed. Only toward the end of the mainstream third generation did crops become an important part of some families' businesses, but this did not diminish the importance of cattle and meat in most of the enterprises.

The estancias of 106 of the 154 families have been found on county maps. Many families had more than one estancia: ninety-three of the 154 families in their second generation were considered hacendados, whatever other occupation they might have had. So the estancia was the main business of the second generation and, if not the main occupation, at least the most important one in early adulthood.

The growth and change in the estancia's line of business encouraged the second generation to engage in complementary activities. Because of the need for major capital investment, several members of the group markedly increased their banking activities: twenty-eight of the families joined bank boards or became bank directors. Several also developed related land businesses, such as founding towns, colonies, or resorts in new areas, which enhanced the value of family lands.[11] Seven families in the first generation and nine in the second founded towns in open country (only two in the third generation); eleven families in the second generation and six in the third developed important colonies or resort towns (only one in the first generation). These colonies and resort towns, clearly very ambitious development schemes, were possible because the second and third generations wielded greater political power and control than their fathers and grandfathers.

Finally, a few families began to industrialize estancia products (milk, meat, and wool, for example), creating the basis of the Argentine Industrial Union. In this area, the marked effect of the second wave of European immigrants (first-generation, non-Hispanic immigrants in the time of the mainstream second generation) was felt: Cambaceres changed the meat-salting plant into assembly line production and invented a new steam process for more efficient removal of usable materials from the cattle carcass, and Billinghurst started the first industrial textile mill.

Thirty families began new ventures or introduced new or more efficient processing methods. Of these entrepreneurs and industrialists, nine belonged to the first generation, all from the second wave of non-Hispanic immigrants. Fifteen in the second and five in the third generation formed some kind of industrial entrepreneurship in their businesses, most having to do with new methods, machines, or processes for some estancia product. However, the data indicates that the fundamental changes, the railroad, for example, came during the lifetime of the mainstream's second generation. The third generation mainly built upon them.

The Third Generation

The third generation did not change the direction or makeup of the family business as drastically as the second, though it did diversify its interests. The group continued to use the estancia as its economic base, albeit a more complex one requiring very large capital investment. It also invested in companies: mainly insurance, some banks and real estate, a smattering of utilities, and for a short period, railroads. The third generation, however, eventually left the railroad business.

The period of maximum change and activity in the family businesses continued through the late 1870s, particularly on the estancias. The third generation completed the transition to raising cross-bred cattle and supplied the new European meat market that opened with the introduction of refrigerated shipping. They also added grain cultivation to the list of family business activities. With railroad access, the third generation further transformed the estancia. They built large mansions where they conducted the family's social life in the country.

The political power of the families peaked after 1880. Though political activity can hardly be seen as part of the family's business, the third generation used politics to link their economic interests with the nation's and allowed no others to compete or interfere. (We will examine this aspect of their activities later).

The economic enterprises of members of the network—and as we shall see, their political and professional activities—displayed the cohesion and cooperation of its different families. The overseas kinship enterprise of the first-generation merchants is, of course, well known. Many examples of such family enterprises and of their advantages in a world devoid of international contracts can be found in the colonial period, and many authors have described this long-distance family enterprise and its cohesion.[12] But family cohesion in the guise of family network provided benefits for other types of economic enterprise as well. In the second and third generations, when the enterprise had changed from trade to the large landed estate or to mining or to the import-export business, family cohesion took other forms.

In the second generation of Buenos Aires families, the joint running of an estancia most frequently exemplified family cohesion in the network. The Pereyra and Iraola families, for example, were joined by a double marriage in their second generation. Together, they ran an estancia in which a Pereyra owned the land and an Iraola provided tools, equipment, and the cattle.[13] Innumerable combinations of these cooperative arrangements existed between family network members, enabling them to acquire estancias with very little capital. Four or five families who used land as common pasture might also form joint societies and then, as sons reached adulthood, partition it into individual estancias. Very frequently, these families intermarried, so some of the estancias contained pieces of land from the different partners.

In the third generation, cohesion mainly provided access to capital in the form of loans from each other or from banks where one or another family happened to be a director or on the board. At his death in 1883, Carlos Casares listed in his estate the outstanding debts on loans from at least four family network members and from the banks of which the Casares family were directors. Many of the debts were remnants of commercial accounts: to the Banco de la Provincia, to the Banco Nacional, to the Banco de Italia. Casares died while serving as president of the Banco de la Provincia. Clearly, he used bank loans for his own enterprises. He owed his brother Francisco $300,000. He also owed money to several others in the family network: Leonardo Pereyra, $300,000; Juan Lanús, $16,000; the firm Vicente Casares e Hijos, $120,000. The outstanding debts of his estancias came to $250,000. The debts totaled around eight million dollars in 1883 currency. (It was a period of enormous expansion in credit, the bubble that burst in 1890 with the Baring Crisis. To those who could get them, loans were very convenient, they purchased things to be paid on long terms with greatly devalued money.) Finally, credited to his account were 260,000 pesos owed to him by Juan Francisco Vivot, also a member of the family network.[14]

The transitions in family businesses over the three generations are well illustrated by two stories that show the range and specificity of the mercantile ventures of the first generation, the estancia-founding patterns of the second, and the development of the family businesses in the third. The two families started at different trade levels: one was an important merchant, the other a middle-sized trader.

Vicente Casares y Murrieta was one of the twelve merchants who reached the highest level of commerce and belonged to both the colonial group and the 154 network.[15] A Basque who arrived in the early 1800s, he soon became a member of the Consulado de Comercio. He had been preceded by his uncle, Vicente Murrieta, who had come as a commercial agent to Montevideo and to Buenos Aires, where he too was a member of the Consulado. Murrieta is not listed in Buenos Aires after 1800, so he presumably returned to Spain. The Murrietas, however, continued to be prominent in international commerce and, later, banking. Vicente Casares eventually headed the Buenos Aires branch of an international commercial firm.

Soon after his arrival, Vicente acquired his own barracas de cuero and, in the 1820s, a shipping company. In 1814, he married Gervasia Rodriguez Rojo, the daughter of a former official in the colonial bureaucracy of Buenos Aires, the treasurer of the viceroyalty of the Río de la Plata. She brought a sizable dowry to the marriage (14 million pesos in 1875 currency) and produced ten children.

Vicente started investing in land in the 1820s. This land was used for grazing until his sons reached the age to develop and build estancias. As each one of his sons reached midteens, he started his own estancia in partnership with his father. Vicente bought the land, registered it in his name and that of the son, who paid half the price of the land with his salary as administrator of the estancia. The eldest son returned to the city to run the shipping company in society with his father. The shipping company, estancia lands, and commercial firm were all gathered into one firm called "Vicente Casares e Hijos."

When another son, Francisco, returned to the city after settling an estancia, he started a lumber business with the lumber brought back from Entre Ríos by the family's shipping firm. At first, Vicente's ships had been used for international commerce. During the Brazilian blockade of 1828, the government gave Vicente a *patente de corso*, which enabled him to arm his ships against Brazil. Gradually, he shifted to smaller vessels that plied the Paraná River to bring, among other things, wood for construction to Buenos Aires. He held no governmental posts whatsoever, but he did become the first official representative of Spain to its former colony. His activities outside the business firm all revolved around his Spanish ties: he was decorated as a Caballero de la Orden de Carlos III; he held the money of other Spaniards for investment; and he founded the Sociedad Española de Socorros Mutuos, a mutual benefit society for Spaniards in Argentina.

Sheep and cattle estancias made up the basic economic holdings of the Casares family in the second generation. Vicente Casares had purchased land in a joint venture with a few other merchants, which they used as common grazing land and held under the name "Sociedad Pastoril."

Three other families from the 154—the Martínez de Hoz, the Agüeros, and the Torres—also belonged to this land society. Their jointly held land became a kind of family compound as all four families intermarried. Vicente E. Casares (second generation) married María Ignacia Martínez de Hoz y Agüero. He settled two estancias, one on the piece of land held in the Sociedad Pastoril. He ran the family's shipping firm, served on the Committee of Public Works for the Commercial Port of Buenos Aires and founded the Banco Nacional. His estancias, plus others from the Martínez de Hoz estate, passed onto his sons.

In the third generation, the Vicente Casares e Hijos firm continued exporting frutos del país. During that time, the Casares family combined livestock and agriculture on their estancias—a change made possible by the introduction of wire fencing—and became the first exporters of wheat. In this third generation, one Casares, Emilio, left Argentina for London to open a branch of the Casares commercial firm, thus reversing the movement of his grandfather.

But the Casares are not typical of the 154 families. Since in most cases we encounter a family after they have enjoyed a certain measure of success (when they appear in commercial guides), we cannot tell how many started as small retailers. By the time we find data on the first generation, it is after the 1820s or at the end of the first generation's life span. Altogether, 42 in the first generation reach the level of wholesalers. We can call only 23 of them retailers with any certainty and cannot determine the level of commerce at which the rest started. Since only 22 had been part of the Consulado de Comercio by the time it was dissolved in 1821, the trade level of the first generation was not the same as that of the mercantile community of the late eighteenth century. However, all of them were not small retailers.

Francisco Díaz Velez exemplifies the successful mercader, a role more typical of the group as a whole. He started neither at the top with capital and connections nor at the bottom as a small retailer. Velez was born in Andalusia, arrived in Buenos Aires in the 1780s, and began to trade between Buenos Aires and Tucumán, perhaps as an agent for a Buenos Aires merchant.[16] In Tucumán, he married María Petrona de Aráoz, daughter of Miguel de Aráoz, comandante de milicias. Soon after, he began his own trade in Buenos Aires. Most of his twelve children were born there. In 1803, he and his eldest son were accused of monopolizing the charcoal trade.[17] Later he was accused of trying to set up a monopoly in salt. His trade seems to have centered on transporting urban goods to rural areas and bringing back local products to sell in the city (charcoal, salt, hides). He had a warehouse close to the central market and became a wholesaler. His sons took on the oxen carts and small ships of this trade as soon as they came of age.

Although the economic base of the family was commercial in the first generation and they were important in trade in the second, the second generation became best known through the career of the seventh son. Eustaquio was one of the main military officers of the postindependence period and, as a result of his military career, became a major estanciero. He accumulated thousands of acres of estancias through land-lease grants from the government. These estancias were an important addition to the family trade, which then switched to selling estancia products.

Both the Casares and the Díaz Velez stories tell of businesses started by immigrants who came in the first wave of migration, predominantly from Spain. But in another wave in the 1820s and 1830s, other European immigrants dominated and became an important component of the 154 families—32 of the 154 families stem from the second wave of immigration. English, Americans, French, French Basques, Italians, and Germans were part of this group. They followed the generational business sequence, moving from trader to estanciero to public officer, but the evolution occurred in only two generations. The first generation moved into estancias sooner; they, rather than just their sons, became estancieros. Their sons became professionals more often and held public office sooner, though business on the estancia formed their economic base. These sons, in the latter part of their lives, resembled the third-generation of the pre-1810 immigrants more than they did the second.

The second immigrant wave included many commercial agents of foreign firms. Unlike the earlier group, this one contained more individuals who had specialized skills, and many of them were brought over by the Argentine government or private groups. This group also shows slightly different marriage patterns, which will be discussed below. But more important than these differences is the fact that all these new immigrants soon entered some form of trade and purchased estancia land. They too produced a second generation of estancieros. Though they were separated from the other immigrants by a generation, they replicated the earlier patterns. The stories of James Lawrie (a Scot) and Pedro Luro (a French Basque) illustrate the characteristics of this important subgroup of the 154 family network.

James Lawrie, blacksmith, came as part of the Santa Catalina agricultural colony.[18] Planned and organized by the Robertson brothers, who were English merchants, this colony settled on a piece of land that the Robertsons purchased in the province of Buenos Aires. The plan received a great deal of support from the government when Rivadavia was minister. When he left office, both governmental support and the colony itself collapsed. Lawrie moved to Buenos Aires and opened a smithy, making ornamental iron fences and gates for Buenos Aires quintas and houses. He also invented a system for branding animals and started a registry for the brands. He founded Saint Andrew's, a Protestant school, and served as an elder of Saint Andrew's Church. He bought estancia land for his sons.

His oldest, Santiago, became the owner of one of Buenos Aires's most famous estancias, Los Sajones, where other English-speaking immigrants had started breeding sheep. Santiago also became a well-known estanciero and horse breeder and one of the founders of the Jockey Club. He did not settle Los Sajones himself, however. He bought it—shepherds and all—when the original owner, an Irishman, died and his daughter needed the income. Most members of the European wave of the 1820s and 1830s follow this pattern, purchasing estancias already settled by others.

Pedro Luro was born in Gamarthe, a small town in the French Basque region. He came to Buenos Aires in 1837 when he was seventeen.[19] Starting out in a saladero of Barracas, he acquired a horse cart with which he transported passengers from Plaza Monserrat to Barracas. In 1853, he married Juana Pradère, a porteña and the daughter of French Basque immigrants.

With one of his brothers-in-law, Luro started a pulpería in Dolores, a small town in the estancia region south of Buenos Aires. The pulpería supplied local estancieros and gathered local products for resale in Buenos Aires. When one local estanciero fell into debt, Pedro Luro received his estancia in payment. This land became his estancia "Dos Talas." He then started a carting business between the rural areas around Dolores and the city of Buenos Aires. Around 1869, he opened a meat-salting plant in Tuyú and started some colonizing projects in the southern part of the province (in the valley of the Colorado River). The government leased him 375,000 hectares of land to raise cattle.

All of Luro's colonizing projects and lands were on the route his fleet of oxen carts traveled, and he took cattle with him to start cattle estancias further and further south. He continued to found small towns and start cattle estancias as he expanded his carting business. By the 1870s, at least eight important estancias were in his hands. He established one of the largest meat-salting plants in Ajó and became an active supporter of and partner in Mar del Plata, the famous sea resort in the province of

Buenos Aires that resembled Newport in the United States. He started another saladero in Mar del Plata with Patricio Peralta Ramos, another founder of the town and also a member of the 154 families. With the profits from it, he bought half of the town from Juan Barreiro, the other founding member of Mar del Plata. He built a dock and large warehouse for the hides and tallow from his saladero business and started a large general store, the well-known La Proveedora. He bought ships to transport goods between Buenos Aires and Mar del Plata and started to export hides and wool to Europe. He cultivated corn, wheat, barley, and linen in his surrounding estancias and set up a hydraulic mill to make flour from the local grains.

Luro's sons, true to earlier second-generational patterns, settled the estancia lands he had acquired. One firm, Sociedad Pedro Luro e Hijos, held all the estancias, mills, saladeros, carting, and shipping business. The oldest son, José, became the administrator of the family firm. In 1890, Pedro Luro died in France, where he had gone for medical treatment. His fourteen children received an inheritance that included about 400,000 hectares in estancia lands, 500,000 head of sheep, and 180,000 head of cattle.

Though José was a lawyer, he never left the family enterprises. After a brief stint in estancia administration, he became the administrator for the family's commercial operations and, like others of the late second generation, got involved in politics. He was governor of the area of La Pampa, where his father had extended his carting business and started cattle estancias. As president of the family firm in the 1880s, he made the initial proposals for the construction of the railroad to Mar del Plata and the building of the Bristol Hotel there. Santiago, the other son, also started by settling an estancia, "Ojo de Agua," on his father's lands. He became a lawyer, a legislator, and bank president. In addition, he became part of the Sansinena Meat Packing Company and shifted the family business from meat-salting to the handling of packed and refrigerated meat.

Profession, Public Office, and Politics

Professions

The main occupational pattern followed by the three generations was as follows: merchant or trader in the first, estanciero in the second, and public officer in the third (primarily, banks board member, and secondarily, railroad or corporation executive). Both the second and third generations moved into professional fields, but mainly in one area—law. Four members of the first generation, twelve of the second, and seventeen of the third were lawyers. Other professions remained numerically unimportant; in the course of three generations, only eighteen families enter other professions: four doctors, one pharmacist, five engineers, one notary, one archaeologist-historian, and (though not strictly professional in terms of degrees, but with university training) six journalists-writers. From our perspective, all the professionals have a nonprofessional look about them. They had professional degrees, but spent their lives following other pursuits. For example, the engineers Pellegrini and Pueyrredón are known to us for their paintings and their architecture.[20]

All the professions combined a good deal of political activity with their work. Eduardo Madero became the engineer of the Port of the City of Buenos Aires. The project became an important political event because two plans competed for approval. The so-called Madero Plan was proposed by Eduardo's brother Francisco B., legislator and Roca's vice-president in 1880. It placed the port by the center of the city of Buenos Aires rather than by the commercial port on the Riachuelo. It won the competition, and Pellegrini inaugurated the new port in 1889. Both the proposal and Eduardo's appointment, therefore, had important political support.

The writers and journalists of the group, in addition to founding newspapers and journals and writing on other subjects, were major political polemicists and, sometimes, activists. For example, when Juan Cruz Varelas's paper was closed for political reasons, the writer went to Montevideo to become chief leader of the opposition to Rosas. In charge of provisioning the army headed by Lavalle and of maintaining relations with the Uruguayan government and French agents, he went on a secret European mission to obtain support from the English and French governments to overturn Rosas. On return, he founded the newspaper *El Comercio del Plata*, dedicated to fighting Rosas's dictatorship.

Public Office and Politics

Some members of the first generation held public office, particularly civil or military posts in the colonial government (the latter will be considered separately). A few at the top of the mercantile scale became members of the cabildo, the most powerful local institution. During the first generation, these public offices seemed to provide income to those who had small commercial enterprises, for the largest merchants in the group did not hold them. In the second generation, the holding of public office became more common. Most frequently, the men of this group had finished settling estancias and returned to the city. A great number served in the legislature of Buenos Aires; others held related posts on government committees. By the third generation, office holding had become the main occupation, and the men held an impressive range of offices: president of the nation, governor of Buenos Aires Province, legislators of the nation and the provinces, directors of banks and railroads, members of the customs board or port committee. Without a doubt, the 154 held the most important offices in 'he country.

Family connections reinforced the office-holding patterns. A son might get a post in his father's department. The second-generation Pelligrini, for instance, started as secretary for the port committee, on which his father had long been prominent. But more important were the diversity and spread of office holding in one particular family and, particularly, the complementarity between political offices and family business.

The third generation of the Casares family illustrates these family and office-holding patterns. Carlos Casares, second generation, became governor of the province of Buenos Aires late in his life. His brother Vicente headed the Banco de la Nación. Vicente and Carlos joined two of the political parties, the Autonomista and the Nacional, and got both to join in support of one candidate. This new party, PAN, put General Julio Roca in the presidency. Cousin Alberto sat on the customs committee, and brother Emilio, as we have seen earlier, opened a branch of Vicente Casares e Hijos in London.

The First Generation

While I have stated that the predominant occupation of the first generation was that of merchant, seven members of the first generation held office in the royal government during colonial times or were brought by the government to perform some specific task after independence had been declared in the Rivadavian period. Four of them came as part of the Spanish Royal Army that was expanding its military establishment in the Río de la Plata region. One came as a member of the royal bureaucracy and was posted in Jujuy in the northern part of the viceroyalty. Rivadavia's government recruited the other two in Europe during the 1820s. Carlos E. Pellegrini, a French engineer, came at the invitation of Juan Larrea, Argentine chargé d'affaires in Paris in the 1920s. The government recruited Antonio Cambaceres to improve the meat-salting process. Instead, he started working with a private meat-salting concern, married the owner's daughter, and went into the meat-salting business himself.

Though a few came with a post already assigned, many merchants and large traders of the first generation acquired unpaid but powerful posts in the cabildo. Fourteen first generation and four second generation members held posts as alcalde de 1er, 2° voto, or regidor de cabildo. The cabildo posts were political in nature and lead us to the much more politicized posts of the next two generations.

The Second and Third Generations

By far the most important institution for the second generation was the Buenos Aires legislature. In the second generation, thirty-two members served as assemblymen (*diputados*) or senators (*senadores*) in the legislature (six first-generation members and twenty from the third). Ten members of the second generation also served in the National Congress, which makes the legislative participation of the second generation very high. The Buenos Aires legislature was very small but powerful; it had more concentrated power than the later national legislature.

The legislative function in the 1816–80 period is too checkered and complex to delineate here.[21] But members of the group held offices higher than that of legislator. At the top national executive level, they served as president or vice-president (or president of government junta or director supremo, titles for the highest office adopted immediately after independence) and as governor of Buenos Aires, the next most powerful office. One member of the first generation achieved the highest political position in the postrevolution period. Cornelio Saavedra headed the first junta of local government after the people decided not to accept the authority of the viceroy. Two members of the second generation, Alvear and Pueyrredón, also headed the Buenos Aires government. Alvear headed the Asamblea Constituyente in 1813; Pueyrredón became director supremo of the Provincias Unidas (chief of the United Provinces) from 1816–19.

Counting those who became president (or after independence, junta president, director supremo, etc.), vice-president of the nation, or governor of Buenos Aires, we find one (Saavedra) in the first generation, ten in the second, six in the third, and two in the fourth, for a total of nineteen in high public office. If we move one echelon lower and group together the offices of national minister, lieutenant governor, mayor, chief of police of Buenos Aires, or governor of one of the provinces other than

Buenos Aires, we find twenty-nine: two in the first generation, seventeen in the second, six in the third, and four in the fourth.

The second generation moved in significant numbers to politically important positions. However, the third generation achieved the highest offices on a national scale and in a much more comprehensive and stable way. A solid and powerful group ruled directly from the time of Roca's presidency to the end of Roque Saenz Peña's presidency (1914–16).[22]

Politics

Political actions in which these families participated over the three generations illustrate general trends.

On 22 May 1810, the Cabildo Abierto met and voted to remove the viceroy, taking the first step toward independence. This was also the first political event in which members of the 154 first aligned themselves politically; 16 families decided whether the viceroy should continue in power or be replaced by a local junta or council of government, (as did 29 of the 178 prominent merchant families studied by Socolow; 12 families belonged to both groups). Of the 16, 9 voted to depose the viceroy and transfer his authority to the cabildo. Two did not vote (Torres and his brother-in-law J. S. de Agüero). The vote of Ramos Mejía went unrecorded. Four of the 16 voted for the viceroy (Martínez de Hoz, Bosch, Molina, Quirno). A majority, therefore, favored his deposition.[23] Cornelio Saavedra was the proponent of the winning resolution and headed the local junta government.

The period in which Juan Manuel de Rosas governed the province of Buenos Aires (1830–52) was one of the most divisive in Argentine history. Groups within the society became bitter rivals, maintaining their enmity into the twentieth century. Most of the families became involved in their second major political alignment. Members of the first and second generations helped draft and lived under the legislation of this period. The third generation, identified with the liberal period that followed, consequently divided into allies and enemies of Rosas, which created bitter division among the families.

In the 1839 revolution of the "Hacendados del Sud," the owners of estancias south of the Salado River in the province of Buenos Aires, opposed Rosas. The armed revolt failed but deeply affected the Rosas regime, and it was mounted, led, and fought mainly by a group of second-generation members of the 154 families. Seventeen can be identified from the following families: Agüero, Acosta, Balcarce, Belgrano, Billinghurst, Cané, Campos, Del Carril, Castex, Madero, Martínez, Martínez de Hoz, Ramos Mejía, and Varela. Seven members of the 154 families, close allies of Rosas, held positions of political importance and benefited economically from his regime: Pereyra, a nephew of Rosas; Iraola, a family closely allied to Pereyra; Guerrico, Arana, Aguirre, Lastra, and Senillosa. Despite the violent opposition between the two sides, the families continued in their public posts after the fall of Rosas, acting as if nothing had happened.

The group in the Jockey Club and Sociedad Rural Club included those persecuted by Rosas and as well as some of his allies and relatives (the family of Rosas's son-in-law Terrero, for example, or the Pereyras). The closest and most powerful of Rosas's kin, the Anchorenas, were absent from both clubs' list of founding members from which the 154 were taken. However, the omission is short lived. The Anchorenas were not founding members but became members soon after, and an Anchorena was president of the Sociedad Rural in the 1920s. As after independence, the important families recovered their positions after the greatest of upheavals with more ease than any other social group.

With the third generation, the network of families became involved in politics at the national level. For example, Julio A. Roca and Carlos Pellegrini worked as a political team and dominated the era between 1880 and 1916.[24] Julio A. Roca was president twice, serving terms in 1880–86 and 1898–1904. Pellegrini was president from 1890 to 1892. Both Pellegrini and Roca alternated their presidencies with vice-presidencies and posts in the Ministries of War and Navy and of the Interior. The complex interweaving of their political offices, however, extended much further and included many other families of the network.

A brief sketch of such relationships shows Pellegrini linked to the Casares family. He served as minister to Carlos Casares, governor of Buenos Aires from 1875 to 1878. Then, after only a few months in this position, he became minister of war and navy under President Avellaneda; he replaced General Julio A. Roca, who had resigned in order to run for the presidency himself. As minister of war and navy, Pellegrini put down the Revolution of 1880, which had been led by Carlos Tejedor, the governor of Buenos Aires, against the federalization of the city of Buenos Aires. Earlier, Carlos Casares, as governor of Buenos Aires, had helped Roca equip his army for the Indian campaign—the Conquista del Desierto of 1878–79. The Casares family also forged the alliance of two political parties, the Partido Nacional, or PN, (supporters of former President Mitre) and the Partido Autonomista, or PA, (supporters of President Avellaneda). Pellegrini had been active secretary of the Autonomista.

The newly formed PAN party made Roca its candidate for president. In 1885, Roca named Pellegrini his minister of war and navy.

Another member of the family network, Cambaceres, served as president of the Committee of the Partido Autonomista Nacional in 1885 and proposed the winning presidential team of Pellegrini and Juarez Celman (Roca's cousin) for president and vice-president. When corruption and economic crisis sparked the Revolution of 1890 against Celman, Pellegrini as vice-president and Julio A. Roca as minister of war and navy put down the revolution and arranged for Celman's departure. Pellegrini succeeded him in office. In addition, two members of the Campos family, a military family in the 154, helped end the revolution. President Pellegrini then made Roca the minister of the interior.

The Revolution of 1890 also had serious financial implications. One of the elements that provoked the crisis was the Banco Nacional's default on the interest due on its loans from the London-based firm of Baring Brothers. The president of the bank was Vicente L. Casares, third-generation member of that ubiquitous family linked to Pellegrini and the PAN. Since Baring had overinvested in Argentina, the default threw the London market into a panic. An unofficial move by the Bank of England brought several banks to the rescue, and they reconstituted Baring as a limited company. It was at this point that Juarez Celman was removed from the presidency and Pellegrini replaced him. At Vicente L. Casares's bidding, he dissolved the Banco Nacional (as well as the Banco de la Provincia, also headed by the Casareses), founded the Banco de la Nación as a national bank, and appointed Casares as its first president.[25] Pellegrini passed the hat to pay the interest on the Banco Nacional's defaulted loan. British sources indicate that the Casares family financed the expansion of their concerns through loans that were questionable and financially irresponsible.[26] Bank loans and private concerns were never very clearly separated.

Another sidelight of the 1890 affair was the creation of the Unión Cívica, which later became the Unión Cívica Radical (UCR). This party, also involved in the revolt of 1890, started the political opposition to PAN and to the rule of the Roca-Pellegrini-Casares group and others. Yet the Unión Cívica was strongly tied to the family network. Vicente E. Casares, brother of the former governor of Buenos Aires, Carlos, acted as treasurer of the Unión Cívica. The powerful Pereyra Iraola family became involved in the second UCR revolution of 1893. After Pellegrini's term ended in 1892, Luis Saenz Peña, also a member of the 154 families, became president. José Uriburu, one of the army officers of the Unión Cívica revolt of 1890, was vice-president, and Campos, another member of the 154, was minister of war and navy.

A further look at the other top offices of the nation shows that other members of the 154, Luis Saenz Peña (1892–95) and his son Roque Saenz Peña (1910–14), succeeded Pellegrini to the presidency. After Luis Saenz Peña's term ended, Uriburu, his vice-president, presided until Julio Roca assumed office in 1898. When Saenz Peña resigned and Uriburu became president, Quirno Costa, another member of the 154, became minister of the interior and provisionally assumed the same post in the Ministry of War and Navy (1896–98). Quirno Costa served as vice-president between 1898 and 1904 and as minister of the interior during the presidency of Figueroa Alcorta (1906–10).

The political involvement of the network did not end with the third generation. Marcelo T. de Alvear, a fourth-generation member of the Alvear family—whose third-generation member had become first mayor of the newly federalized city of Buenos Aires in 1880—served as the UCR's president between 1922 and 1928 and as the representative of one of the two main branches of the UCR party (personalist of Irigoyen, antipersonalist of Marcelo T. de Alvear). The Alvears also appear as founders of the Jockey Club and Sociedad Rural. Peter Smith, in a study of the Unión Cívica's policies, has shown that government ministers serving under presidents who had been elected on the UCR ticket were frequently members of the Sociedad Rural. "In total Irigoyen and Alvear named in their presidential terms (1916–1930) twenty-nine men to their cabinet, and thirteen were members of the Sociedad Rural. This means that approximately forty-five percent of the UCR ministers were members of the Sociedad Rural. This percentage is higher than the total percentage for 1910–1943, and this suggests that the Radicals were as much in harmony with the Sociedad Rural as the Conservatives."[27] He has also shown that during these terms in office, the men made no major departure from the economic interests of the Sociedad Rural.

Between 1932 and 1938, General Agustín P. Justo, son of a fourth-generation member, and Julio A. Roca, Jr., son of President Roca, became the last family members to serve as president and vice-president. However, Justo's rise came more directly from his tie to the new base of political power, the army.

Other Posts
Banks and Railroads

Banking was also important to the network families. Over the three generations, 56 members held banking posts: 12 in the first generation, 28 in the second, 16 in the third. However, during the first and second generations, most members appeared as bank subscribers. For example, in 1828 when the first public bank was formed, 38 second-generation family members became subscribers (of a total of 264).[28] During the late second and the third generations, they occupied the top posts of president and vice-president in the main banks of Buenos Aires.

Two banks dominated the banking history of the second and third generations: the Banco de Provincia and the Banco de la Nación Argentina. Nineteen family names frequently appear on the list of board members of the Banco de la Nación between 1890 and 1940: Casares, Aguirre, Unzué, Lanús, Martínez de Hoz, Vela, Seré, Güiraldes, Hale, Pearson, Drysdale, Roca, Luro, Pereyra, Roca, Castro, Frías, Guerrico, and Leloir. As usual, more than one family member was involved, for example, Vicente L. Casares and his cousin Alberto Casares; third-generation Miguel Martínez de Hoz and fourth-generation Francisco, relatives of the Casares family; Mariano Unzué and Santos Unzué, of the fourth generation; Leonardo Pereyra and his son Leonardo Pereyra Iraola. The patterns in the board membership of the Banco de la Provincia are similar, though the domination by the Casares family is much greater.

The railroad boards have much less representation from our group, since they were owned and managed by English investors. But the first railroad was started with local capital, and four of its five founders were members of the 154 (Pereyra, Guerrico, Casares, Pellegrini). When the state bought out the private stock in 1863, Emilio Castro, another member of the network, became president of the board of directors. At one time or another, 24 of the 154, were on the railroad boards, and 23 of those 24 ended with the railroad running through or very close to their estancias.[29]

The Military

Posts in the military require separate treatment, because the period under study was one of transition for the army. The Spanish Royal Army and the urban militias of the colonial period made way for the militias, Guardias Nacionales, and, finally, a national professional army (1860s–1890s).

In the first generation, two groups were visible: those who came with positions in the Spanish Royal Army or Navy and those who rose through the urban militias. In the first and second generation, when military activity had not yet been professionalized, military service and family commercial enterprises intertwined and part-time military command was the norm. By the third generation, professionalization had occurred and military men gave up all other activities, except political ones.

Some of the first-generation immigrants arrived in Buenos Aires with appointments in the colonial army. They came to strengthen the Bourbon military establishment in Buenos Aires–Montevideo against the expansion of the Portuguese. First-generation members who held posts in the colonial army founded the most important military families (those who stayed in the military over the span of two or three generations). However, the nonprofessional, part-time nature of military activity is apparent even in these families. Sometimes, one individual filled several roles at once: trader, estanciero, military officer, legislator. The combined role of estanciero–military officer was particularly important because officers usually had the military command for the area in which their estancias were located. As leaders of the rural militias, they enjoyed certain advantages, not the least of which was recruiting for the militias. At times, they could use recruits to solve the perennial labor shortage on their Buenos Aires estancias. Military activity, therefore, enhanced local authority by enlarging legal powers. These, in turn, enhanced their economic base in the rural area.

In the second generation, a shift occurred from urban militias to rural ones because of the dominance of the military commander–estanciero. The third-generation military commanders increased their political activity to serve the national government in the city of Buenos Aires and began professionalization. Only at the end of the third generation did military officers spend their lives engaged only in military activity. Their political posts were usually limited to military intervention of provinces and positions as ministers of war and navy or of the interior.

Of the group of 154, 15 clearly can be called military families.[30] In these families, a young man entered his father's or brother's regiment or served under their command and eventually rose to the same command. More important, they tended to marry daughters of other military officers. As a group, the military were as endogamous as the merchants of the colonial period.

In the colonial period, 5 members of the 154 came with military posts: Alvear, Balcarce, Campos, Elía, and Quesada. They arrived in the 1760s and 1770s, part of the enlarged military establishment in the area of Buenos Aires–Montevideo countering the expansion of the Portuguese. They were important for their own military activities and for their roles as founders of military families. Their sons also rose to power in the military; three became noted political leaders.

Nine of the second generation chose military activity as their major occupation, serving as urban militia commanders during the English invasions of 1806–7 and the wars of independence. However, as Halperín-
Donghi has shown in the case of Pueyrredón, their military careers can
hardly be considered military when any of their biographies are fully
treated:

> Juan Manuel de Pueyrredón figures in Udaondo's *Biographical
> Dictionary* as a military leader, and he did in fact first attract
> public attention by leading a bold but unsuccessful attempt to
> counter the first British invasion. During that episode he had raised
> a regiment of hussars. But, sent by the Cabildo of Buenos Aires as
> its representative to the Court of Spain, his activity for three years
> was to be politics, accompanied by intrigues, imprisonment and
> successful escapes. This precursor of the Revolution was created an
> administrative official by it. He was Intendant first of Córdoba and
> later Charcas, and then returned for a few months to his military
> vocation, as commander-in-chief of the Army of the North. From
> then on, he was to experience abrupt falls and rises: he was a
> member of the Triumvirate, which exercised the supreme power,
> was dismissed and imprisoned in October 1812, and Supreme
> Director of the State from 1815 to 1819, but he never returned to a
> military command.[31]

One should also add about this "military" career that during the three
years Pueyrredón spent in Spain as representative of the Buenos Aires cabildo, he was active also in the commercial enterprise of his family,
which had a branch in Spain run by his uncles and cousins. Thus although the second generation saw military activity expand into all
realms of life and combine with estancia-based political activity, their
military was far from professional, for very few were only military officers. The second generation shows 26 members of the 154 families active
in the military.

In this period, the regular army could hardly be separated from the
militia, for the militia consisted of estancieros leading their peones. Even
the posts of commander general of militias and of justice of the peace
were often combined. Twenty-six of the 154 held the post of justice of the
peace in the area of their estancias: 5 in the first generation, 14 in the second, 8 in the third.

Military commanders also became estancieros. As we have seen, many
who led the milicias de campaña, particularly those posted to frontier
areas to the south of the province, received important land grants—
sometimes as payment for services from a cash-short government and

sometimes as incentives to settle land on frontier areas. Generals and colonels of the southern frontier areas got very large land grants. The 1826 enfiteusis law of Rivadavia started the large giveaway of public lands, but military campaigns, particularly the so-called Indian Expeditions, also became land-grant expeditions. The 1833 Indian expedition by Gral Juan Manuel de Rosas, the governor of Buenos Aires, had as its most lasting effect the creation of vast estates. The top officers and the urban families who helped finance and provision the expedition created them.[32] The 1839 revolution against Rosas also involved land distribution and epitomized the estanciero-military-politician connection. Sixteen families of the 154 participated in the uprising. When they lost, the government expropriated their estancia land and gave it to officers on the Rosas side and to members of his family and government.

Eustoquio Díaz Velez, one of the officers involved in the uprising and one of the 154 families, typifies the second-generation commander. Eustoquio was the son of the Andalusian merchant Francisco Díaz Velez, who had prospered in the colonial period. After independence, he pursued a military career. With each military campaign, he added estancia lands to the family business. He served as a general in the independence wars and exported the Buenos Aires revolution of May 1810 to the other provinces. As part of his military activity, he acted as lieutenant governor of different provinces (of Salta in 1813–14, of Santa Fe in 1814–15, of Buenos Aires in 1818–20). In 1827 alone, he received forty-six square leagues in the county of Monsalvo.[33] He also acquired large holdings in the county of Chascomús. As one of the military officers in the uprising of 1839 (with the Campos, Martínez de Hoz, Ramos Mejía, Castex, and Madero families), he took Tandil Fort to the south. When defeated, Rosas rescinded the leases on all his estancia lands and distributed them among his own military officers. Díaz Velez left for Montevideo where he remained until Rosas fell in 1852. On his return, he became part of the Buenos Aires legislature (1853–56) and worked to recover his estancia lands:

(September 19 of 1853) . . . my wife Doña Carmen Guerrero having died last year, I proceeded to make an inventory of furniture and domestic articles as well as urban properties. I could not do the same with my rural holdings because the disaster of the past times did not allow me to dispose of them nor to know what was on the estancia. Even today, affected by the disorder and the arbitrariness it is not possible to make a detailed inventory of these establishments, for the cattle has been roaming wild for years. But I wish to proceed with an inventory as soon as practicable and especially to pay the sacred debt which weighs over me, a debt I incurred for my family's support since 1840 when all properties and goods were embargoed and my house was sacked. All this time it has been necessary to take out loans at interest until the fall of Rosas could get our properties returned to us. The sad state they are in can be well seen from this description.[34]

While the second generation combined the roles of military officer and estanciero and politician, the third generation primarily combined military and political activity. After the 1860s, a few military commanders still headed rural militias from their estancia district, but most of the military became urban. The army/militia operated in the city of Buenos Aires or was sent by the government seated in the city to put down insurrections in the province of Buenos Aires or in other provinces. In other words, the military became a political arm of the national government and brought the rest of the territory under Buenos Aires's control. Members of the third generation were active in big conflagrations like the defeat of the Rosas government in 1852, the Mitre defeat of Urquiza in 1863, and the Paraguayan War. They also held positions of command in the revolts and revolutions that represented the struggle by the network of 154 to gain a commanding position in the city of Buenos Aires.

The group rose against Urquiza when he attempted to control Buenos Aires after the defeat of Rosas in 1852 (Revolución del 11 de Septiembre). They led the national government forces against the forces of the province of Buenos Aires, which opposed the federalization of the city into a national capital, and commanded the forces to defeat the uprising against President Juarez Celman in 1890.

Perhaps their contribution to the federalization of Buenos Aires in 1880 against the wishes of the province provides the best example of their political role. The top military leadership and government allied itself to the city, with its urban interests, even though they themselves were estancieros whose economic base remained in the rural sector. Although the top military leadership was not dominated by members of the family network, one of the 154's third generation became *interventor*, or military governor, of the defeated province, and the national government sent military commanders to operate as governors of all the provinces that opposed the policy of the Buenos Aires network then in power. The Campos family clearly illustrates the role of the military as defenders of the Buenos Aires network and depicts their intervention in the provinces. They epitomize the military family in all of its transformations over the centuries, and their story extends over four generations, since they arrived early in Argentina.[35]

Juan de Campos was born in Granada, Andalusia, arrived in Buenos Aires in the 1760s, and served as coronel de los Reales Ejércitos and as *maestro alarife* (master mason). For some time he was in the Banda Oriental, fighting the Portuguese by order of the governor of Buenos Aires, Pedro Cevallos. Later he served with the frontier forces who fought Indians south of Buenos Aires. Juan de Campos reinforced his ties with the southern frontier in 1764 when he married María Josefa Lopez Camelo, whose family had cattle in the Tuyú area.

In 1806, Campos's oldest son settled an estancia in this area. He requested a grant of land in that year, claiming prior settlement, but did not get it until 1818. In 1810, Gaspar José had fought against the English under the command of his brother-in-law Alejo Castex (a member of one of the military families in the 154). Castex led the Migueletes Voluntarios, a cavalry company.[36] Gaspar José served as captain during the second English invasion of 1807.

In the first invasion, Pueyrredón, another member of the 154, was attacked in the city by the English. Lopez Camelo, the alcalde of Las Conchas, recruited troops in the Banda Oriental and in the post of Las Conchas, including many of his kin: the Lopez Camelos, the Castexes, and the Camposes. They marched to the city and rescued Pueyrredón from the English siege. In 1818 when Pueyrredón became director supremo of the triumvirate chosen to govern the independent nation, he gave Gaspar José de Campos title to lands he had requested in the Tuyú, one of the first land grants given after independence and the start of the large Campos estancia holdings in The South. Gaspar José and his brother started not only the Tuyú estancia, but also one in Las Conchas. There Lopez Camelo had disembarked, perhaps also receiving a grant for services performed. Gaspar started the estancia with cattle and money given to him by Alejo Castex. (Campos paid him back by giving him a chacra of about fifteen acres that he had inherited from his father.)

The brothers ran the two estancias as one estate. The Tuyú estancia, with its 7,000 head of cattle and 900 horses had access to a small port at the mouth of the Salado River, and it shipped estancia products to the city. The estancia at Las Conchas served as a base for a train of ten oxcarts. The brothers collected and brought to the city grease, tallow, and hides, carrying back sugar, yerba mate, salt, paper, aguardiente (the local alcoholic drink), wine, and biscuits. Las Conchas had a pulpería in which city goods were sold and the cattle products collected and transported by oxcarts to Plaza Monserrat for resale. The estancia El Rincón in Las Conchas sold straw and wood, and José María Ferrari, the son of a Genoese whose daughter married into the Campos family, ran the pulpería.

Martín Teodoro Campos of the third generation was an estanciero and a military man. He and his brother both were military commanders during the 1839 revolution against Governor Rosas, and one of their nephews also served in the operation. They offered the port on the estancia Los Nogales in the south to French fleet admiral Leblanc if he would help them against Rosas. Leblanc refused. After the revolution's defeat, the two brothers spent many years in exile working as cattle drivers (*reseros*) in the Rio Grande do Sul area. After Rosas's defeat, Martín returned to his former posts as justice of the peace for Mar de Ajó (his estancia was in this town's jurisdiction) and commander in chief of the troops in the southern counties of Ajó and Tuyú.

In 1852, Martín and two of his sons joined the uprising led by the governor of Buenos Aires against Urquiza. He and his sons were jailed and then released but confined to their Las Conchas estancia. They were also prohibited from going south to the Tuyú. The government feared that Martín, in his role as commander of southern frontier forces, might raise troops again. Martín also became assemblyman and senator for the province of Buenos Aires. He had married, as had his grandfather, into the Lopez Camelo family; so throughout his military career, he added many thousands of acres to the original estancia grant in the south.

In the fourth generation, seven of Martín's thirteen surviving children became military men. During this period, the army began to professionalize, and the men worked very much as a team.

Martín, first lieutenant in the Guardias Nacionales, fought in Cepeda and Pavón (where, in 1859, President Mitre defeated Urquiza's Confederation forces). In 1880 he led the national government forces to overcome provincial opposition to the federalization of the city. He married his cousin, Concepción Escalada y Lopez Camelo, making the third marriage in four generations between Campos men and Lopez Camelo women. (The Escaladas, a military family into which General San Martín had married, had also married Lopez Camelos.)

Gaspar fought in the 1852 Buenos Aires uprising against the Confederation, and the government also restricted him to the family's northern estancia and prohibited him from their southern holdings. He was also in Cepeda and Pavón, served as lieutenant colonel under General Paunero in the Paraguayan War, and died in this war fighting under Colonel Miguel Martínez de Hoz, a member of the 154 families.

Julio was the other Campos in the 1852 uprising. He served in the Guardias Nacionales at Cepeda and then as military commander on the southern frontier at Azul. The national government later sent him to fight provincial caudillos in La Rioja and Catamarca. After fighting in the Paraguayan War, he became chief military commander for the southern frontier, a post which went to four generations of Campos. Elected to the National Congress in 1875, he later became president of the Banco Provincial. He fought in the 1890 revolution, which took Juarez Celman from power, but was killed during the fighting.

Manuel entered the military at age seventeen in 1864, fighting in the Paraguayan War under the command of his brother, Luis María. He also fought in the Conquista del Desierto with Roca. He became a general in 1885 and the military chief of the 1890 revolution. He served as chief of police of the city of Buenos Aires from 1894 to 1896. He was in the provincial legislature first, then in the National Congress. Finally, he became part of the Junta Superior de Guerra, the top professional military command, headed by Luis María.

Luis María is the most prominent member of the Campos family, militarily and politically. In 1859, he served in the Guardias Nacionales at Pavón with Mitre. With General Paunero and his own brother, he fought provincial caudillos in La Rioja and Catamarca. Later, he became military commander of Concepción del Uruguay in Entre Ríos, the base of Urquiza's government. There he married one of Urquiza's daughters. He was minister of war and navy in 1877 and 1879, chief of the army in 1893, again minister of war and navy from 1893 to 1896, and commander in chief of the Guardias Nacionales in 1896. As minister of war under Roca, he created the Escuela Superior de Guerra, the last act needed to professionalize the military.

The Belgranos provide another example of families in the second generation mixing and unifying estancia, commerce, and military activity.[37] The first Belgrano in Buenos Aires, Domingo Belgrano Peri, was born in 1730 in Genoa, Italy. He went to Cádiz on business, where he obtained Spanish citizenship, and emigrated to Buenos Aires in 1751. He became a very successful merchant in Buenos Aires and during the English invasions, as symbol of his success, donated the salary he received as alferez of the Regiment of Spaniards to the Real Hacienda. In addition to being made a captain by Viceroy Vertiz in 1772, he held several other posts: regidor de cabildo and síndico procurador (1781) and inspector and accountant of the customs house. (He was tried because of his friendship with the subsequent customs house administrator who bankrupted it, but he received no conviction.) In 1757 in Buenos Aires, he married María Josefa Gonzalez Casero, born in Santiago del Estero and a daughter of Juan Manuel Gonzalez Islas and María Inés Salazar. They had four-teen children.

Three of their sons became lawyers; two became military men. One of the lawyers was also a military man, the well-known Manuel Belgrano. Another of the lawyers was also a priest who reached a prominent church post as canónigo y presbítero of the cathedral. The two oldest sons were the lawyers, one the lawyer-priest, the other (Manuel) lawyer, military man, and politician. The third son, Joaquín, was like his father administrator of the customs house and was also finance minister before independence. In 1810, he was present at the open meeting of 22 May and voted to end the viceroy's government. After independence, he be-came alcade de primer voto and a member of the Tribunal del Consu-lado. In these positions, he looked after the family's commercial ven-tures. He also owned a lumber yard.

The Belgranos continued in commerce as a family. A nephew, son of one of the military officers, had an almacén of foodstuffs in the 1820s. The Mulhall Commercial Directory of Buenos Aires still lists Belgrano and Co. as importers in 1885. In politics, they became a formidable co-hort; four Belgranos appeared and voted in the Cabildo Abierto of 22 May. All voted for the removal of the viceroy and for putting decisions in the cabildo's hands (with ultimate responsibility in the hands of the sín-dico procurador general, a post their father had occupied in the past). Four of them held posts as alcaldes, regidores, government officers, and legislators after independence; one held high church office, two held military posts (sargento mayor de plaza, commandante of Las Conchas y San Fernando posts). Manuel, the most prominent member, held high political posts and was an important military commander. But a close look at his career reveals other activities as well.

He had been educated not only at the Colegio de San Carlos de Buenos Aires but also at the University of Salamanca, a sign of very high status. He was secretary of the Real Consulado during the viceroyalty. During the first English invasion, he acted as captain of the urban militias. After he voted with Saavedra for the viceroy's removal, he became part of the first government junta. He was made general of the Paraguayan Army, then given command of the Army of the Littoral for operations in the Banda Oriental. Later he was made chief of the Ejército del Norte to fight the Royalist forces in north. A period of diplomatic activity in Eu-ropean nations followed, then he returned to the command of the Ejér-cito del Norte. He died in 1820 while serving in this post.

The biographies do not state that the Belgranos also became estan-cieros in this second generation. One brother had estancias in the province of Buenos Aires, as did the nephew with an almacén (Olavarría). Belgrano the father, as an immigrant merchant, already appeared in 1791 in a lawsuit with a Juan Caldera Bernal over the profits of an estancia.[38]

Manuel Belgrano, in his role as secretary of the Real Consulado, was a vigorous promoter of agriculture and argued ardently for the creation of agricultural schools. He has also been identified by Tjarks as the most likely author of the "Representación de los Hacendados," a document written in behalf of the cattle interests for the opening of the Buenos Aires port to foreign trade. More important still, Tjarks shows that at some point in the last stage of the push for free trade, Belgrano spoke as the representative of the cattle interests of the Banda Oriental. Tjarks quotes a nineteenth-century contemporary, saying that Belgrano was anxious that the port open to trade with foreign powers and calling him one of the main movers in the matter.[39] The secretary of the Real Consulado, defender of agriculture, and chief of the army of the Littoral in the Banda Oriental was therefore also a Banda Oriental estanciero. Military command and the estanciero ownership in the same area became a frequent combination during the rest of the century.

Marriage

General Patterns

Marriage was the key institution binding the members of notable families together, from the second generation to the fourth. The patterns of marriage vary with each generation; the strategy differed with time, place, and position. Of great importance are the marriages that joined members of the 154 with the old colonial merchant group of 178 studied by Socolow: 19 in the first generation, 16 in the second, and 8 in the third married descendants of the colonial merchant families. If the whole cohorts were studied, the number would increase greatly. The very few complete cohorts available (for 18 families) show seventeen more marriages to members of this group. Since only twelve of the names from that group appear in the list of the two notable clubs, the marriages were with women of the colonial families.[40] The second pattern of importance is the intermarriages within the group of 154: forty-one marriages took place between main male members of the 154 families and women in the group (nine in the first generation, seventeen in the second, fifteen in the third).

In the first generation, European immigrants married local women, or porteñas. The second generation created alliances among the 154

through marriage. The third formed fewer alliances with members of
the same group. Kin marriage between uncle and niece took place more
frequently, and for the top echlon, there were marriages to Europeans,
some of them nobles. An important factor that altered the marriage patterns was the number of children.

Unfortunately, the information on children is much too scanty and
unreliable. In many cases where data exists, we do not know if the number of children is the number born or surviving. Only thirty-three cases
of the 154 in the first generation, twenty-three in the second, and fifteen
in the third are known with certainty. Given these small samples, we can
only point to a general trend, medians of nine children in the first generation (thirty-three families), five in the second (twenty-three), and
three (fifteen) in the third. What is most important in the trend is the
drop in numbers between the first and second generation. Further research may eventually throw more light on this subject.

Most obviously, the first generation's children had an extensive group
within which to form alliances. And they did—with the children of others who had come at the same time and with some of the children of the
established group of merchants of the colonial period. Examples of the
types of marriages in the three generations illustrate the patterns.

The First Generation

The first generation pattern shows immigrants marrying porteñas,
with a decided majority of the earliest immigrant group marrying
daughters of merchants or traders. Since these marriages created the
crucial tie between the newcomers and the local society, women played
the pivotal role in incorporating the new immigrants into society. They
provided access to urban capital and to the developing economy of the
estancia.

The second immigrant group of non-Hispanic Europeans followed exactly the same pattern of marrying local women, but these men sought
porteñas who were daughters of earlier settlers from their own places of
origin. Since few were available, they also married Hispanic women.
Only three married before emigrating. One married a woman who em-
migrated at the same time and was part of the same group of Scottish settlers brought to Buenos Aires to start an agricultural colony. But in the
second group of immigrants as in the first, the settlers also married into
families in the same businesses or professions. For example, Cambaceres
came to improve the saladero process. He married Rufina Alais, daughter of a saladero owner, and became a partner in the family business.
Pellegrini, who came from France to plan a port for Buenos Aires, mar-

ried the daughter of an English engineer who had been invited to Buenos Aires for the same purpose.

The Second Generation

The second generation forged alliances through multiple marriage (for example, two Casares brothers married two Martínez de Hoz sisters). Since the first generation had produced so many offspring, such alliances occurred frequently. Nineteen involved persons listed in the Sociedad Rural–Jockey Club membership and a brother. Many cousin marriages also took place in the second generation, the cousins generally being the children of two brothers. Marital alliances between families who had contiguous estancia land also commonly occurred in this generation, though we do not always know if the contiguous lands facilitated or resulted from the marriage.

In this generation, seventeen marriages took place between main male members and women of the 154 families (nine such marriages occurred in the first generation and fifteen in the third). If one considers the double marriages of the second generation and looks at the few whole cohorts available, one sees a multiplicity of connections between one family and others of the 154, a multiplicity the single-member approach cannot portray. The intermarriages of the main male members of the 154 and women from the same group are higher in number in the second than in the third generation, when the group coalesced into two clubs. This fact is surprising, since connections and alliances in the third generation seem to be more institutionalized and visible. Thus, the second-generation marriages served to hold together and strengthen the network. The institutional alliances in the third further reinforced it.

The Third Generation

Perhaps because of the smaller number of children produced by the second generation, new marriage patterns appear in the third generation. In the frequent kin marriages, uncle and niece marriages occur more often than those between cousins. In all such cases in this study, a man married the daughter of his sister, never of a brother. As Linda Lewin has observed for Brazil, testamentary laws made such marriages convenient since it consolidated the inheritances of two siblings in one family.[41]

The marriages of three generations of the Lanús family detail all the patterns described.[42] In 1785, Jean Lanús was born in Jerez de la Frontera of French parents. He came to Buenos Aires in 1806 (changing his name to Juan Lanús) and became a merchant. In Buenos Aires, he married Teresa Fernandez de Castro, a porteña, and settled for a time in Entre Ríos. He made several trips to the Malvinas with Luís Vernet, their colonizer and governor, and drowned on the last.

Lanús had six children. The fifth son, Juan, was a member of the Sociedad Rural, and Anacarsis Jr., his nephew (son of his brother Anacarsis), was a member of the Jockey Club. Two of Juan's brothers, Teófilo and Lucio, married two sisters in the Marmol y Reyna family. Juan married a niece, daughter of his older sister Clara; they had ten children. Juan's brother Anacarsis married and had five children, one of whom is the Anacarsis Jr. in the club lists. In the third generation, the Lanúses married several members of the group of 154 families. Luisa, the daughter of Anacarsis, married Galup Agüero, nephew of Julian Segundo de Agüero. Both the Agüeros and Galups belonged to the network. Juan's son, Florencio, married Celina Martínez de Hoz y Stegmann, daughter of Martínez de Hoz y Fernandez de Agüero. A son of Rosa Lanús de Alurralde, whose daughter had married Rosa's brother, married a Torres who was also related to the Agüeros. So three marriages in the third generation were into the Martínez de Hoz–Agüero–Torres clan.

Benigna Lanús, daughter of second-generation Leopoldo, married Roberto Cano, an important member of the 154. Anacarsis Lanús, Jr., third generation, moved to La Rioja (Chilecito) to pursue the mining interests of his family; there he married the daughter of Bustos, the governor. They had five children.

The second-generation marriages are by far the most interesting to observe and study because in them the complementarity of the family professions, the economic activities, and the landholding patterns develop. While the first-generation marriages tied the immigrant to the local society of Buenos Aires, the second-generation marriages of the most successful families created a variety of ties. The weakest families did not do the same; they become marginal to the group in the third generation and disappeared from sight.[43]

The Luros exemplify a family with very successful second-generation alliances.[44] Pedro Luro (1820–90) came to Buenos Aires in 1837, a late arrival. He was born in France's Basque country and, in 1844, married María Pradère, the daughter of another French Basque in Buenos Aires. She had been born in Gascogne and brought to Buenos Aires as a child. The couple had fourteen children, twelve of whom reached adulthood. Three of the sons were founding members of the Jockey Club.

The commercial story of the Luro family has been told elsewhere, but when viewed in light of the second generation's marriages, it becomes more significant. Pedro Luro, the immigrant who started a passenger carting service to Barracas and a pulpería in a small town south of Buenos Aires, later used his carting service to bring hides, wool, and meat to the city. Acquiring estancias with his business, he stretched his trade farther and farther south in the province. He opened a saladero in the Tuyú and traveled as far as the River Colorado, acquiring land then considered worthless because it was so far into Indian territory. His sons, when of age, started settling the lands as estancias. Luro opened more saladeros in Ajó and became a cofounder of Mar del Plata. He bought out half the lands from one of the three partners and started a general store and port in the town. His son José became director of the Society Pedro Luro e Hijos.

One of the sons of the business, Pedro O., married Arminda Roca, daughter of Colonel Ataliva Roca, Julio Roca's brother and one of the 154. The Luros's interests lay very much along the line of Roca's route in his southern campaign against the Indians, so their lands became both safe and valuable. Pedro was made director of the Banco de la Provincia, was legislator in the Buenos Aires legislature and then in the national legislature, 1898–1912, during the second presidency of his uncle-in-law. He was able to have a law passed for the creation of the new port of Mar del Plata, where the family had its large meat-salting plants and a large business exporting products from its estancias.

Another of Pedro's sons, Rufino Luro, married Susana Cambaceres. She was a daughter of the other large saladerista family, also of French origin and also a member of the 154. A daughter, Augustina Luro, married Francisco Sansinena Jacquemier, and one of the Luro sons became a founding member with Sansinena of a meat-packing firm to which the Luro family's meat production was redirected, away from its salting plants. Still another daughter married Prospero Rouaix, and Santiago Luro married María Gache. The spouses of both brother and sister were, once again, of French descent, and Rouaix was one of the 154. Santiago occupied legislative posts and headed the Conservative party. He was national legislator from 1886 to 1890, director of the Banco de la Provincia, and served on the board of the Banco Hipotecario under Pellegrini.

The Roca marriage put the Luro family in a position of political power in the financial sector, and it undoubtedly had strong implications for their southern estancias. The Cambaceres marriage allied them to the owners of the largest and most advanced meat-salting business in Buenos

Aires. The Sansinena marriage connected them with the new meat industry. An additional footnote to these interconnections: In 1882, Santiago was president of the legislature under Buenos Aires governor Dardo Rocha. At that time, brother José Luro placed a proposal before the governor and legislature to build a railroad between Buenos Aires and Mar del Plata. The legislature approved it.

The Peralta Ramos are another typical second-generation family started by Patricio Peralta Ramos (1814–87), who made his fortune by provisioning the government in Rosas's time.[45] He and his wife, Cecilia Robles, had six children. A brother had married the daughter of Carlos de Alvear, also in the family network and an important political figure after independence, and the family was tied to the Anchorenas through several marriages. Though the fall of Rosas supposedly ruined the Ramos, they soon regrouped, opening a saladero for the first Sociedad Rural near the future Mar del Plata. It was there the Martínez de Hoz family and others operated in society. In 1860, Peralta Ramos purchased thirty-two square leagues in the area from Coehlo de Meyrelles for the Sociedad Rural's meat-salting plant. He offered lands in the vicinity to Governor Mariano Acosta, a member of the 154, for the foundation of Mar del Plata in 1874. It was the biggest real estate deal of the century and made millionaires of the surrounding property owners. All were members of the 154: Luro, Peralta Ramos, and the members of the old Sociedad Rural, primarily the Martínez de Hoz clan. A son of Peralta Ramos married into the Irigoyen family, a prosperous merchant family in the colonial group of 178. The Peraltas participated in the Union Cívica revolution of 1890.

The Quirno family provides a classic example of first- and second-generation marriages.[46] Norberto Quirno—born in Navarra, Obispado de Pamplona, in 1777—arrived in Buenos Aires in 1797 and, two years later, married Manuela Josefa Gonzalez de Noriega, daughter of a capitán y regidor de cabildo. One of their daughters married Juan Bernabé Molina, one of the 154 and a cousin, since Norberto was related to the Molinas through his wife. In fact, with his cuñado Juan Fernandez de Molina (married to his wife's sister), Norberto Quirno opposed Viceroy Liniers in 1809 and was exiled for it. With Molina, he voted to keep the viceroy in the May 1810 cabildo.

Guillermo Quirno, the oldest son, had a saladero. He married Gonzalez de Noriega, a cousin from his mother's family. His brother Miguel married into the Pizarros, who, like the Quirnos, owned a saladero. With the Pizarros, Guillermo switched to breeding high-quality cattle. Norberto Quirno Pizarro, his son, had a great number of estancias (eleven) that he obtained by transfering capital from saladeros to develop his cattle and to supply the new meat market.

Gregorio, the next brother, was a colonel in Lavalle's army. His son Norberto Quirno Costa would become minister of foreign affairs (1886–89) then minister of the interior (1889–90) for President Juarez Celman. He also served Luís Saenz Peña (1892–94), Uriburu, and Alcorta (1896–97). From 1898 to 1904, he was vice-president under Roca. In other words, the Quirnos of the third generation, who strongly allied themselves to Molinas and Pizarros and very strong hacendados, dominated the post of ministro del interior, which controlled the police and army for internal security between 1880 and 1904.

The Ramos Mejía family belonged to the colonial group of 178 and our group of 154.[47] The marriages in the second and third generation follow the overall pattern. The first immigrant was a very early arrival: Gregorio Ramos Mejía, born in Seville in 1725, emigrated to Buenos Aires in 1761. He married twice. His first wife died in childbirth one year after the marriage. His second wife was the daughter of a local merchant. They had thirteen children. Gregorio became a powerful merchant in the colonial period, and his sons oversaw a vast network of international commerce.

Francisco, one of the sons dealing with commerce in La Paz, married María Antonia Segurola, daughter of one of the strong merchant families of the 178. Another brother, Idelfonso, married a Basavilbaso, also a commercial family of the 178. A pattern common in first- and second-generation lives appears in this generation of the Ramos Mejía family. When Francisco died, María married his widowed brother Idelfonso. (The pattern of the widow marrying a brother of the former husband appears mostly in first-generation marriages, and in the second generation of early arrivals.)

Francisco settled two estancias, one of them in Morón where he established a pulpería. This estancia, or chacra, measured 2,000 hectares. He bought it in 1808 with $32,000 from his father-in-law. The other estancia was south in the county of Maipú. There he became justice of the peace. His son Matías became military commander for the zone and was military leader of the Revolution of 1839 against Rosas, joining forces with General Lavalle. Matías married the daughter of Francisco B. Madero, a member of the 154, a military man in the 1839 revolution, and Julio Roca's vice-president in 1880. His brother Ezequiel, also in the revolution with General Lavalle, married Carmen Lavalle, the general's niece. Sister Magdalena married Isaías de Elía, a member of the 154 and a descendant of one of the merchants of the colonial group of the 178.

In sum, the second-generation men married daughters of important merchants of Buenos Aires. In the third generation brothers who were leaders of the Revolution of 1839 married daughters of military men in that uprising. The fourth generation married others in the group of 154.

The Bosch family illustrates marriages to daughters of important merchants, both old and new.[48] In 1775, as a young boy, Francisco Bosch came with his father to Buenos Aires from Catalonia and made his way in trade. He married the daughter of Cascallares, a merchant, who was part of the group of 154 and of the merchant colonial group. He was important enough to vote in the 1810 Cabildo Abierto, one of the few who voted to keep the viceroy. His brother Gerardo, who came to Argentina a little later, married the daughter of Aguirre, another prominent merchant of colonial times who also belonged to both the notable groups.

The second-generation Francisco alternated military and estancia activities in typical second-generation fashion. He married the daughter of Saenz Valiente, prominent merchant of the colonial period who overlapped both groups. Francisco's military grants made the Bosch family large landowners. He was chief of the Guardias Nacionales of four counties. In the Revolution of 1880, he fought on the government's side and was named chief of the garrison after the Buenos Aires provincial forces of Governor Tejedor were defeated. He was chief of police (1885–86) and in 1890 was sent to Méndoza to serve as interventor against a revolution there. Part of the Junta Superior de Guerra, he was named interventor of Buenos Aires Province in 1892 in order to put down the Unión Cívica's revolution. He then went to Tucumán to put down another uprising and followed this with a stint in Congress.

But the story is not complete without the activities of Bosch's kin. His cousin, the son of his uncle Gerardo was the main estanciero in the family and worked with his uncle Nicolas Anchorena. Nicolas, a merchant, set up an exporting firm with Saturnino Unzué, one of the group of 154. He imported pedigreed sheep from France for his brother-in-law, J. M. Cascallares.

The two Bosch brothers from Catalonia and their porteño brides, a Cascallares and an Aguirre, therefore produced a second generation that fulfilled the familial complementarity strategy and positioned the family for survival in uncertain times. They allied themselves to two powerful merchant colonial families from the very beginning. Francisco and Gerardo continued developing the alliances in the second generation through marriages between the colonial merchant and the 154 families. They also kept members of the family in different occupations: one operated as a merchant dealing in estancia products and running estancias with his uncle Anchorena, another as a wholesale merchant, and a third as a military man with large estancia holdings.

The Torres family gives us a concentrated picture of a recurring pattern, more detectable when we observe a cohort instead of one individual in each of three generations (starting with one individual who is a member of the Jockey Club or Sociedad Rural and moving back to his parents and to his grandparents).[49] Though only one individual in the Torres family is studied over three generations, an alliance with the same family repeats. At least twenty-five other cases of marriage alliances with the same family for two or three generations have been identified, but they have all been in the cohort of brothers and sisters (that is, identified not by the individual in the club lists or by his direct ancestors but by his brothers or sisters).

Sebastián Torres, born in the Spanish province of Álava, was in Salta in 1796 and then worked in Buenos Aires commerce. In 1797, he married Feliciana Andrea de Agüero. She was the daughter of the important colonial merchant Diego de Agüero, who was in the 178 and the 154 families. They had five children. Sebastián was at the Cabildo Abierto of 1810 but left with his brother-in-law, the priest Julián Segundo de Agüero, without voting.

Of the five children, three are known to have been married. Lorenzo Torres, the oldest son, married Clara Saenz Valiente y Pueyrredón, daughter of two important colonial merchant families in the 178 and in the 154. The second son, Eustaquio, who is our listed member of the Sociedad Rural and Jockey Club, married Juana Fernandez de Agüero y Agüero, another daughter of Diego. Daughter Juana also married an Agüero in this generation, the rarer case of a brother and sister rather than two brothers or two sisters marrying two members of another family. The third generation made alliances with the Aranas, the Martínez de Hozes, the Castexes, the Boschs, Duggans, and Camposes, all members of the 154.

Marriage and Complementarity

As we have seen individuals in many of the families combined occupations. In fact, the family often served as the major mechanism for making the combination—with its resulting complementarity—possible. By having members of the group engage in different occupational pursuits, the family could extend its influence in a number of directions. Complementarity through marriage, however, was the most important. Through it, the family gained what it did not already have: military office, a political base, estancia land. The family became more powerful and stable. A comparison of those family members who achieved the greatest success and most prominent positions and of those who became marginal in the third generation of the network confirms this. The most prominent factor in becoming marginal was failure to marry members of the 178 old colonial merchant families or of the group of 154 and failure to make varied marriages. Consolidation and the basic connections were made in the second-generation. The way to assure passage from the first-generation to the second-generation network seems to have been by varied marriages: with merchant families, with landholding families, with military families (the larger the number of children in the first generation, the better the possibilities). The more connections made through the marriages and the more varied the families, the greater the chances of forming part of the network and obtaining and retaining a dominant position. This factor is most noticeable in those of non-Hispanic origin who married those speaking their language.

The Lawries provide a good illustration.[50] Over three generations, they married English-speaking women. The first Lawrie married a fellow immigrant from Scotland, who was part of the same Scots 1825 agricultural colony. In the next two generations, the sons and daughters married other English-speaking immigrants, but none from the group of 154 or from the colonial merchant group.

Santiago Lawrie (second generation) had an important estancia, but he could not get bank credit in his later years and could not transform his estancia into a productive and varied great estate of the third generation. (The close connections of many of the 154 to banking made this possible for others.) Thus, even though Santiago Lawrie was a founder of the Jockey Club (a certificate given to first founders is in the family's possession), he was often omitted from the list of first founders. The family disappeared from view in the third generation.

The non-Hispanic families have been difficult to study, and only access to the family's carefully preserved personal documents have allowed me to put their story together. The bits and pieces from fifteen of the forty-four for whom too little or no data could be found point to the same marriage patterns as the Lawries. The Malcolms, for example, show three generations of marriages to descendants of others with English names who were not on the list of 154.[51]

The Founding Families of the Sociedad Rural and Jockey Club

Members of the second and third generation founded the Sociedad Rural and the Jockey Club in 1866 and 1882 respectively. The list of founders contains several members of the same family (second and third generation, usually father and son), and kinship links reveal that the clubs comprised a much smaller group of families than the 154 (for which information was found on the 122 studied and mentioned in this work). The membership lists have approximately forty families

First, of thirty families on the combined list from the two clubs, two or more individuals became members. The Casares and Martínez de Hoz families have five and four members respectively, but this figure only includes the immediate families. These two families intermarried (two second-generation Casares brothers married two Martínez de Hoz sisters) and functioned as a unit. In the first and second generation, multiple marriages connected the Martínez de Hoz family to the Agüeros, Fernandez de Agüeros, and the Torreses. All were partners in an early estancia land partnership called Sociedad Rural, a separate and earlier institution than the Sociedad Rural Club. It was founded in the 1820s and dissolved in 1868, two years after the Sociedad Rural Club was founded. The first president of the Sociedad Rural and of the 1866 club was a Martínez de Hoz. In sum, the club evolved out of an early land partnership that revolved around estancia interests. The Martínez de Hoz group and the Casareses headed this partnership of Casares, Martínez de Hoz, Agüero, Torres, and Fernandez de Agüero. Martínez de Hoz and Casares had the largest number of family members in the clubs. In fact, the total group can be seen as their kin and political and economic allies.

The clubs gathered this intermarried group, allowing them to make connections. It also weakened the network by establishing other means for individuals to form connections.

The Spatial Coordinates of the Family Network

The residential and land ownership patterns of the family networks may provide the best way to study the complex relationship between the city and the hinterland in Latin America. Only some general comments will be made here about common patterns in the family network. The minutiae of the interplay between city and rural environments needs its own examination and cannot be treated in this synthesis.

House and City

The first generation was thoroughly urban. It resided in Buenos Aires, the small city to which the majority migrated during the two decades before independence. The most important merchants and traders lived in

Mutilated remains of the Elía house, first generation, Buenos Aires. In spite of its ruined state, the house's plain massing and mirador are still visible. Photograph by Diana Balmori, 1972.

two areas, the Catedral Sud parish to the south of the central plaza and the commercial center to the northwest of the plaza. The second generation still concentrated its residences in the Catedral Sud but extended itself to the Catedral Norte parish and spread itself over a much more extensive commercial center. The third generation made a dramatic residential move. It built large mansions in the Barrio Norte, a new sector of the city that became its own. In this much more restricted sector, the network acquired residential buildings of a different type, style, and size (see map 3).

Quinta and City Outskirts

The first generation resided in the city. Its residential extension in the rural environment involved only the addition of a quinta, a country house or villa on the outskirts of the city (in most cases, a trek of ten to fifteen city blocks). A few went out to the San Isidro area on the embankments of the river. Families moved to these country houses in the summer, carrying servants, pet parakeets, and pianos with them. This move

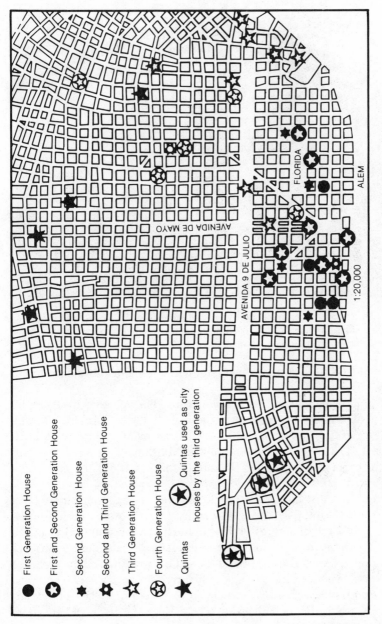

First Generation House

First and Second Generation House

Second Generation House

Second and Third Generation House

Third Generation House

Fourth Generation House

Quintas

Quintas used as city houses by the third generation

AVENIDA DE MAYO

AVENIDA 9 DE JULIO

FLORIDA

ALEM

1:20,000

Locations of some houses and quintas of eighteen Buenos Aires families over three generations.

Cané-Andrade house, second generation, corner of Moreno and Balcarce, Buenos Aires. In spite of several facade changes, the basic form of this house has survived, a two-story house around two patios. Photograph by Diana Balmori, 1972.

of a few blocks for a summer was considered a major movement out of the city.

The quintas were usually operative farms. They produced vegetables and fruits, bringing an income to the family. Ortiz Basualdo's family quinta, for example, was in San José de Flores, west of the city. It had a good deal of land and was a complex establishment. In one month of 1848, the expenses for running the quinta totalled $25,000, and its products earned $30,000.[52]

This quinta must have been an old chacra (or chácara, a large farm without a substantial house); its wealthy owners built a house on it, turning it into a weekend resort. The house had a mirador, or lookout, a feature common to both quintas and estancias. It also had a carriage house, a shed, a stable, three ranchos, a small almacén, a chapel, a house with a large oven in it for baking on the premises, and a corral and pasture (potrero) with a shelter in which animals were kept. Two of the ranchos belonged to Doña Fulgencia, Doña Eugenia de Selva, and one, called the gate house, to Don Feliciano.

The style of the buildings was similar to that of the city houses: brick walls, tile roofs (earlier, adobe and palm or straw thatch), and distinc-

Diaz Velez quinta, Montes de Oca 98–222 Buenos Aires. New City mansion, third-generation site of old family quinta. Photograph by Diana Balmori, 1972.

tive open galerías, covered porches surrounding one or more sides of the building. Like the urban houses, they were quite plain and unadorned, built without any virtuosity in craft or in materials. But they could be refined in their plainness and became a genre of the vernacular architecture.

The quintas flourished during the times of the first and second generation and became a mark of urban prosperity. The second generation built the largest numbers of quintas. The third built very few, since the estancia absorbed their social and productive functions. The few quintas built by the third generation were located on old quinta grounds, now so well situated inside the city limits that they were appropriate sites for building new city mansions instead of typical quinta dwellings. When third-generation members lived outside the network compound of Barrio Norte, this also happened.

The first generation members traveled a few blocks outside the city: in some cases just north, in others west along the road to San José de Flores, and in others south along the road to Barracas (the commercial port). The second generation extended its reach slightly further along the same routes. The city stretched and grew along these routes.

Cano quinta (third generation) about 1900. Negative from glass slide found for sale in antique shop in Buenos Aires.

Estancias and Hinterland

The real movement of the families to the hinterland came when the second generation settled the estancias. This took them further west toward the county of Rojas, south to the Salado River, and gradually, further and further south.

Except for the few years that young, second-generation males lived there, the estancia did not provide a permanent residence for anyone but the capataz and a few cowhands. The families of the second-generation settlers still resided in the city. The estancia usually consisted only of a rancho of adobe walls and straw roof and, in many cases, another rancho that served as a store, the famous countryside pulpería. The estancia was tied to city: first, through the presence of the young men who settled, managed, and exchanged goods with it; second, because it depended on urban development capital. Though distant from the city and unconnected except by slow trains of oxcarts, the estancias gradually became a more active place where rural products and city supplies were exchanged and the working population grew.

Lawrie quinta, second generation, Brandsen, province of Buenos Aires. Photograph taken in 1890s, courtesy of Nelly Lawrie Pearson.

During the late second generation, a wave of building activity started on the estancias. Family members built permanent residences of solid material; these would serve as their summer residences and social gathering places. Until the 1870s, they were built in the style of the old quinta houses. They incorporated such quinta features as miradores, which were justified as Indian lookouts (though this may or may not have been their original purpose). Architecturally, the move was from city to country, and the architecture of quintas preceded that of the estancias.

The colossal wave of building on the estancias peaked in the third generation. Started by the family network of the Barrio Norte and made possible by the development of the railroads, it quickly spread from the urban mansions to the estancias, with an abrupt change in style, form, and scale. The new estancia structures displayed family wealth and made the social group visible; they had little to do with rural life or urban productivity. The buildings incorporated urban amenities. Foreign materials and foreign craftsmen, particularly new Italian immigrants, built them. Some became salons, places for receiving foreign dignitaries. Others simply were possessions that established the social position of country gentlemen. But unlike the English aristocracy that had its build-

Guerrico house, second generation. Photograph by Diana Balmori, 1972.

Lawrie estancia, "Los Sajones," built mid-nineteenth century. Photograph courtesy of Nelly Lawrie Pearson.

ing spree in the seventeenth century, the families never became ensconced in their country estates. They were urban, and their estancias remained vacation palaces for summers or weekends. A description of Carlos Casares's estancia mansion conveys a sense of their nature.

When Carlos Casares died in 1883, his estancia could be called a country estate. The pastures had been newly fenced with wire, the trees had just been planted, and a house, which seems to have been a smaller residence and may have been for a mayordomo, was just being built. The estate had all the refined items needed by a city gentleman: a greenhouse with potted plants and a heater, a room nearby for a gardener, a building housing gymnastic equipment, and ponies with saddles and a pony cart. Ladies' saddles indicated the new presence of urban women. The artificial lake, shaped in elliptical form, had a water fountain. The nearby pavillion, a ten-sided polygon, was made of cast iron. It had a wooden floor, zinc roof, and an aljibe with thirty pipes, a marble opening, and a lacy metal arch that held the chain and bucket. The inventory listed the dining room first, since dining had become a preeminent pastime. Paintings, two bas reliefs of horses, a marble fireplace, and an icebox provided its interior decoration.

Only a few details can suggest the flavor of the rest of the house. Paintings of horses predominated, though the living room also had a stuffed lion, a statue of a horse, and a bronze cannon. The great innovation was running water, though only the main house had it. Another large house

Hannah estancia, "Negrete," built 1860. Photograph courtesy of Noel Sbarra.

was being built for Carlos Ford, the mayordomo, whose name suggests he was probably a gringo and thus highly prized for this kind of job.[53]

Construction is a mark of the third generation in both city and country. This generation (and the fourth) were responsible for still another construction boom and another set of mansions in resort towns like Mar del Plata, the Argentine Newport.[54] In nineteenth-century Latin America, the establishment of the family networks in city after city brought about a boom in construction of family palaces in the city and on rural estates. The building of private residences and estates (as distinguished from Church or public building) indicates economic expansion and the rise of a particular socioeconomic group. Both the scale and quantity of the private construction projects probably exceeded any earlier ones. Social crystallization and the building boom here are clearly linked.

The Aftermath of the Family Network

Research on the network families ends with the fourth generation and does not go further in time than the first decade of the twentieth century.

Speculation about what followed after the family network's power waned, however, is appropriate here.

Network power ebbed gradually. First, the military challenged all other groups in the 1930 coup and replaced Irigoyen and his vice-president, Enrique Martínez (a fourth-generation member of the family network). Only with the rise of Perón in the 1940s, however, was the network's power checked completely.

In Argentina, the first challenge posed by the military occurred in the nineteenth century, though it was not perceived as such then. Juarez Celman (Roca's relative) and Carlos Pellegrini (the other most direct representative of the interests of the family network) were overthrown. The son of a French engineer who immigrated, Pellegrini was a professional who served the family network, primarily the Casares family. The Casareses governed for the family network when it had enough control that it did not need to place members of its central core of families directly into power. The military coup that overthrew Juarez Celman was not seen as an act of military intervention but as the act of a faction of the family network in the military wrestling for power. The Campos family played a crucial and central role in the coup and made it seem even more like a family affair. These military officers played a crucial role in being the instrument of the family network in the capital city to bring the other areas ruled by groups of families in the interior under the Buenos Aires network's control. But once the army started recruiting on a more professional basis, the officers who reached the highest echelons were not only from the network. Eventually, the military became the only other group organized well enough to wrest control from the network. Thus, the 1892 coup illustrates the rise of a power group that eventually would function as an entity separate and distinct from the network.

While in power, the network supported a weak executive who had more power to veto than to initiate and who was at the beck and call of one group. Any executive who wished to do more needed a very powerful personal following. Since no structural form gave the executive any power, he needed to gain the support of whatever groups were available: first, the family network; then, the armed forces. When Perón gained power, he undermined the military's power by constructing a political base in the trade unions. With them and a buoyant postwar economy, Perón could govern better than previous executives. In all these instances, however, because of the incomplete and hazy separation of powers and of the public and private realm, the executive branch was controlled by private interests of a group.

The network's power waned, but the power of individual families did not. They could even continue to place certain family members in high office. Today individuals from network families still have preferential access to important posts, though they gain office because of their expertise, economic power, or skills rather than their names alone. Such is the recent case of the minister of economy, José Martínez de Hoz, who served in the military regime of General Jorge Videla (1976–81).

Though the family networks could not compete with public institutions, individual families did survive when and if they institutionalized their holdings, turning them into twentieth-century business and legal structures. In this, they resembled the "dynastic" families who dominated American business, the Rockefellers, DuPonts, Kempners, and Moodys. They used the legal devices of corporations to help them, serving as board members or executive officers in different companies. They also had sizeable overseas investments that protected them from national instability and changing governments. Many of the Argentine network families survived by using the techniques of the dynastic families that anthropologist George E. Marcus has studied in Galveston:

> A legally devised plan to transfer and conserve patrimonial capital in one generation becomes in the next generation an organizational framework for extended family relations—actually a formal model or surrogate of the family, with law rather than the founding entrepreneurial patriarch as its source of authority. This legal surrogate comes to figure importantly in relations among descendants, who are tied to it by their hereditary entitlements, especially as some of them attempt to alter their given positions in the formal organization of family interests. During the past century, American business dynasties—termed here family/business formations—have achieved durability as descent groups in a bureaucratized society by assimilating, rather than resisting, characteristics of formal organization which are usually assumed to be antithetical to kin-based groups. . . . These formations have endured as both extended family and business organizations well into the twentieth century under political, economic, and cultural conditions manifestly unfavorable to their survival.[55]

Today, then, family network remnants can be found in such family-business formations in different Latin American countries. Their most important legacy lies in the semiprivate nature of public office—above all in the top executive posts of the presidency and ministries—which the armed forces rather than family networks now control.

5

The Family Network
IN THE
Historical Literature

We have seen archetypal examples of notable family networks in Guatemala, Northwest Mexico, and Buenos Aires. The first is an old, "backwater" area, a society already 250 years old in 1770, shaken by commercial revolution and earthquake. The second is a vast new region, colonized by settlers who established mining operations, haciendas, and commercial trades and who, relatively few in number, formed networks to advance their position. The third is a new city, a port that was opened, expanded, and created by the eighteenth-century commercial revolution and by new merchants.

To what extent does the network develop as a strategy in other areas of Ibero-America? Where did commercial and political forces compel variations in the family network? What remains to be studied; where is the research insufficient to apply the model? This is the subject of this chapter.

The material on old families usually comes from a body of literature that develops a number of well-established themes. They include works on families and enterprises or great estates. Charles Harris's *A Mexican Family Empire* (1975) and Edith Couturier's *Hacienda de Hueyapán* (1976) belong to this group. The strength of these studies lies in the span of time they cover. Next in importance are the mercantile studies that shed light on the family network. Traditionally, mercantile endeavors were family enterprises, sometimes with an international scope. These studies do not generally cover the same span as the hacienda studies (usually two generations). Most of them concentrate on the late eighteenth century, the heyday of merchant power, and do not treat the family in the nineteenth century.[1] Equally important are the studies of elites.

Each author usually defines the term to include or exclude a particular section or profession, but all concentrate on the prominent. Though we also concentrate on prominent families, we try to avoid using the word "elite"; it emphasizes a social sector but does not consider its most important characteristic, its family organization.

By focusing on notable family networks, we examine an organization based on kinship and family ties and an organization that uses its basic structure to obtain notable status. Many studies indicate that only the prominent, the elite, the wealthy, the notable have extended families. We reverse the argument by asserting that the extended family is the sine qua non of notability. For this reason, family notability and the extended family appear together. The ambitious seek family connections to further their social positions and to give them stability and lasting power. Studies of elites, particularly in late-eighteenth-century and nineteenth-century Latin America, inevitably consider family and kinship relations.

Rather than listing every relevant work, we will mention the authors who have made specific contributions to specific themes. We try to identify the works that shed new light on a family-related subject or area.

The First Generation

The Iberian Heritage

Family alliances have been critically important to Iberian civilization since at least the medieval period. The dominant family, the marriage, and the testament are essential for the maintainance of authority and tradition in the Spain of the reconquista as well as in colonial Ibero-America. The eighteenth century transformed the strategies employed by families, providing notable families with the ability to preserve themselves despite economic and political failings. As society became more complex, as change came more rapidly, and with commercial and political fluctuations, networking developed as a far more complex strategy than before.

The eighteenth-century commercial revolution brought a flood of new peoples, new territorial expansion, new valuable commodities, and new Bourbon rules. Buenos Aires is certainly the epitome of this grand transformation. But so too were older areas such as Caracas, Bogotá, Santiago, and Guadalajara. If we take the growth of Guadalajara alone, we see a city that expanded 400 percent throughout the eighteenth century both because of migration and because of natural growth. The old traditional families had either to accept these changes, adapt and join with new groups through marriage or alliance, or perish.[2] International commercial networks, more complicated internal economic relationships, more sophisticated and better developed bureaucracies all became linked to traditional social positions. And with the liberal age, national ideological factions were joined to the network.

Networking rose in importance as traditional privilege declined. The old sources of privilege—Church funds and cabildo domination, among others—dried up as capital invaded and as Bourbon reforms altered laws. This did not mean the old traditions ended. New families sought titles and privileges as had the old. Status in itself was critically important. But the strategy of privilege was no longer relevant. There was, for example, the paradox of the great increase in titled nobility in both eighteenth-century New Spain and in Chile at a time when such titles scarcely provided economic protection, as most unhappy heirs discovered. Still, titles were coveted and continued to have economic as well as social significance, albeit less than before. The same can be said for front church pews, housing near the centers of power, and cabildo seats.

We are concerned with what constitutes notability. Evenmore, we are concerned with the preservation of notability, the continuation of authority through networking of leading families, be they merchant, titled, or landed. We are interested in how leading families overcame Lesley Byrd Simpson's and others' dictum that "all creole family history consists in the passing from shirt sleeves to shirt sleeves in three generations."[3] We do not dispute the phenomena. It was rare that families did not lose their economic preponderance after three generations. Susan Socolow talks about it in Buenos Aires. So does David Brading in Mexico. We are interested in how families preserved their social predominance after they returned to economic or political "shirt sleeves."

In our view, the eighteenth century provided a tool not only for economic and social advancement, the creation of titles and new family lineages, but also for preserving status beyond the classic third-generation fall. Families that lost their mines or their political position with the independence wars still were able to continue on in the hierarchy of the postindependence period. From time-to-time, they reemerged in the nineteenth century, in politics or in business, in league with foreign capital.

The Colonial Tradition

Although the network represents a change from past patterns, we insist that the eighteenth-century transformation maintained older values and practices. This was a period of continuity, of gradual change rather than a radical break in social structure. The family tradition was, after all, ancient and well-grounded; not even the commercial revolution or the ideological challenge of the early nineteenth century were sufficient to destroy it. The eighteenth-century family maintained its coat of arms, which called back the Spain and Portugal of the reconquista when nobility used family linkages to maintain and expand its titles (the union of Ferdinand of Castille and Isabella of Aragon is the most obvious example). The eighteenth-century merchant family continued to maintain its limpieza de sangre, its lineage to the conquistadores or to the most noble families of the peninsula. The use of family networks to link enterprises in colonial towns and in the peninsula recalls the conquistadores, who also turned their trust to their families. Who best to cite but Christopher Columbus, who relied upon his brothers to safeguard the world he discovered? Or, perhaps the five Pizarro brothers who used their alliance to defeat Spanish usurpers, Incan rebels, and, for a time, the crown itself.

In sixteenth- as well as eighteenth-century Ibero-America, the family was the most obvious defense of privileges and wealth. The ties of marriage, blood, regions, and trade cemented commercial and other relationships between the distant mother country and the New World throughout the colonial period. The rapid expansion of trade in the heady, early days of the empire also required family linkages and regional loyalties to avoid the betrayals of rival conquistadores and merchants. The pattern of the familial mercantile company pervades the period. The company headed by Francisco de Churraca in the 1520s is a case in point. All members of the company were Basque. While Churraca stayed in Cádiz, his older brother Martín de Zubizarretta traded in the Caribbean. Other members stayed in Biscay. Similarly, three families made up a 1520 company headed by Alonso de Nebreda, with agents in Seville, Santo Domingo, Cuba, Seville, and (even this early) in Mexico. A generation later, Francisco de Escobar of Seville secured his fortune by trading through his nephew in Panama, his sisters and brothers-in-law in Lima and his brother in Chile.[4]

Land and Cabildo

After the conquest period, as society settled, Iberian institutions developed to protect the dominant groups' position. Authority was based, above all, upon privilege, privilege either in the colony or in Spain. Privilege was derived from the control of land; neither commerce nor mining was sufficient. Without privilege, social position, economic power, and political authority could not long endure. Of course, government positions, commerce, and property were also significant, but these were all temporary. Bureaucratic positions in the audiencia or in the Church could not be passed on; without privileges derived from tradition or from the crown, they were singular opportunities that could not be made permanent. Merchants might maintain their power through one generation, but this too was a passing privilege, vulnerable to the ups and downs of commerce. If we use the seventeenth-century cabildo of Mexico City as an example, merchants were outsiders, rarely gaining entrance to the forum. From 1620 until 1650 only three merchants were regidores. Merchants did hold significant if short-lived political power through the consulado and through their authority over credit and tax collection, but never did it approach that of merchants a century later.

Power came from the land, and even if the vicissitudes of agriculture did destroy familial fortunes from time to time, families aspired to be property owners. As Louisa Hoberman points out, merchants sought entrance into the ranks of the landed elite either by the establishment of mercedes, by marriage, or by purchase. They became proprietors of wheat farms, cattle ranches, and grazing land for sheep and goats as well as sugar plantations. However, over one or two generations, land was not sufficient to maintain economic power, although it brought political power in the cabildo and social status. The landed oligarchy thus had to seek allies among the merchants. There was indeed a "circulation of elite."[5]

Throughout Ibero-America, the pattern is roughly similar: notable families were defined by the land and their political control through the cabildo and associated institutions (such as ecclesiastic cabildos, sodalities, etc.). Outsiders bought or married into this landed authority, either taking over from or bolstering declining fortunes.

In Lima, the Mediterranean family structure was strong and descendants of sixteenth-century founders were dominant. Travelers reported a "nobility" of two hundred families controlling local society in the early eighteenth century. One observer called Liman society a true "feudal aristocracy." In 1776, it comprised a duke who was a grandee in Spain, 58 marquises, 45 counts, a viscount, and 135 knights of the Order of Santiago. "Numerous ties of patronage, marriage, godparentage, property ownership, and friendship bound the creole bureaucrats to the creole nobility of Lima, of which they were indeed members from birth."[6] In Quito and Santiago de Chile, patrimonial society was dominated by small groups of interconnected families. The wealthy Brazilian sugar planters controlled their captaincies, linked "through kinship and common interest." In São Paulo, as Elizabeth Anne Kuznesof has shown, towns, expeditions, feuds, and political participation were organized around the family from the sixteenth through the eighteenth century.[7] "Political power in the cities," Germán Colmenares reports about seventeenth-century Nueva Granada, "was perpetuated by means of lines and clans knowingly reinforced with matrimonial alliances. . . . Business, landholding, mines, nothing remained outside the familial control."[8] Although the leading families saw their encomiendas drying up at the beginning of the seventeenth century as the population of Indians declined, the old families were able to maintain their authority through the cabildo and to control the land, mines, remaining labor supply, and even the monopoly of navigation rights on the rivers. The 306 creoles who were alcaldes in Cali between 1566 and 1799 had only forty-two last names.[9]

The Mediterranean heritage of familial control extended to the hinterland. The "true owners" of François Chevalier's *grande domaine* were "families and lineages rather than individuals." Although distant from political institutions, huge Mexican and Central American estates were owned jointly by a number of relatives. Many others were entailed. Here, on the vast cattle ranches of southern Mexico, some 90,000 square miles of cattle and sheep estancias were "huge family circles made up of relatives and intimates, tugged by blood ties and ancestries, and the feuds or rivalries between families."[10]

The Pattern of Continuity

The continuity between the new and old periods, the eighteenth and earlier centuries, is most obvious in the frailty of rural families in agricultural regions close to commercial and mining centers, the domination by urban groups, and the drive by some members of the urban population to acquire land, to become hidalgos for social rather than economic reasons. Consider David Brading's conclusion for the late-eighteenth-century Bajio of Mexico. Without denying the persistence of a class of dominant families, he suggests that there was considerable flux or circulation within the class. Families lost their capital in unprofitable haciendas, which passed to the Church. They became dependent upon peninsular relations to manage family enterprises successfully. Brading suggests this phenomenon is a consequence of the unsettling influence of the commercial revolution during the late colonial period.[11]

The weakness of the rural class and the invasion of new, more power-ful merchant and bureaucractic groups, although intensified by the in-dustrial and commercial revolutions, was not new. Throughout the colo-nial period and throughout Latin America, most privileged families preserved themselves through marriage to the recent arrivals. Compare, for example, Brading's conclusions with Louisa Hoberman's observa-tions on early seventeenth-century Mexico. As we have discussed, mer-chants sought out landed estates for social stability despite a lack of prof-itability. Late-eighteenth-century Bajio and early and mid-seventeenth-century Cali appear similar in this circulation among the dominant group, in the coming of new peninsular groups, and in the economic de-cline of landed classes.

Rather than a break with earlier values, Jacques Barbier's examina-tion of eighteenth-century Santiago reveals a more closely knit society than the older and smaller traditional oligarchy, even with a greater willingness to enter into marriage alliances with outsiders. "Far from be-ing a time of new politics," he concludes, "the late eighteenth century may well have been a golden age for the practice of the old."[12] The new eighteenth-century family sought not only to intermarry but also to gain honors, emulating its colonial heritage. Two-thirds of the entailed es-tates awarded by the crown from 1684 until independence were award-ed after 1748. "The year 1755 is important in the social history of Chile" because it marks the start of a period of inflation of honors—honors re-ceived "by relatively new men, connected to official circles, and often characterized by an interest in trade."[13]

The Eighteenth-Century Family: Merchants, Miners, Bureaucrats, Farmers

The new eighteenth-century family merged with older oligarches; it did not suppress them. This was social reform, not revolution. From New Granada to New Spain, Bourbon bureaucrats, merchants, and miners came, joined with, and frequently overcame the economic posi-tion of old landed groups to form a notable class. Sixteenth-century lati-fundias in Cali were divided up among eighteenth-century miners and merchants as the old families married with the new class. "None of the 18th Century 'nobles' bore the same name as 16th century," Colmenares deduced "but their privileges still existed, married into by immi-grants."[14] Similarly, the late-eighteenth-century stereotype in New Spain of "the opportunistic immigrant who inveigled his way into the confidence of a rich relative, married his Creole daughter, and displaced his son from the patrimony" has been confirmed as accurate. "The experiences of the most successful Spanish merchants at the turn of the century precisely fit the stereotype."[15]

Brading's conclusions of the circulation of elite and the frailty of the agricultural sector are supported by other studies. Without denying fundamental changes wrought by the commercial and intellectual revolutions, these works confirm for us the continuity of earlier economic and social patterns. Eric Van Young's study of Guadalajara reveals that migration from Spain was virtually constant throughout the eighteenth century.[16] As did Brading, Van Young sees the mineral boom in the second half of the eighteenth century as altering the colonial economy. Landholding became more linked to the colonial economy, more in need of credit, and less profitable. With land falling in value, the eighteenth-century notable family had to maintain commerce to maintain the landed ideal.

The term "hacendado" came to be meaningless in late-eighteenth-century Guadalajara, Van Young suggests. Landowners in Guadalajara were not endogamous but recruited members from other economic groups. Hacendados, merchants, and bureaucrats all intermarried. "The categories are so blurred, and intermarriage among elite individuals and families was so general, that any attempt to sift out the social characteristics of the land-owning group is hazardous." There was so much intermarriage that "the upper-class of late-colonial Guadalajara was in some ways simply a huge extended family."[17] The statement, we might add, is as applicable to seventeenth-century New Granada or Guatemala as it is eighteenth-century Guadalajara. As elsewhere, the patriarchs of prominent eighteenth-century landowning families in Guadalajara were usually Spanish, but the Spanish founders might have come at the beginning as well as the end of the century.

Van Young believes that the significant change affecting Guadalajara landholders was political and came after 1750, with the end of the hegemony of landowners in the cabildo. In the last half of the century, city merchants shared power with the landowners, thereby linking commercial money with political authority for the first time.

Preliminary conclusions by Margaret Chowning and Frederick P. Bowser in their study of Michoacán coincide with Van Young's observations. Spaniards and Mexicans worked hand in hand in similar economic pursuits. Neither the division between land and commerce nor that between gachupine and creole seems to have much validity for most of the late eighteenth century. Indeed, as the Chowning and Bowser study illustrates, we see current historiography challenging nineteenth-century liberal historiography, which posits the hostility between native and peninsular-born, between merchant and farmer. Listen to the words of these modern historians and compare them to a criollo commentary of 1811:

> Though cultural cousins slowly drifting apart, the [*gachupines* and *criollos*] intermarried, were business partners, the guarantors of each other's loans, shared powers of attorney, acted as executors of mutual estates and (perhaps) even cried at the grave. . . . Money and social connections far out-stripped rivalries between *gachupines* and *criollos* when the qualities of a future in-law were being weighed. Through the part of the colonial period which we have studied, wealthy Spanish merchants were considered by Mexicans to be desirable business associates and, were there a stray daughter around, welcome additions to the family.[18]

> The Europeans were our relatives, they were married to our daughters or sisters, they were our good friends and we did business with them. Our interests and wealth were mixed with theirs and indeed depended upon them absolutely.[19]

Differences did arise very late in the colonial period between one element of peninsular society and one of creole society. But the linkage between the groups ran deep—after all, who were the most dominant creoles but the sons or grandsons of peninsulares?

We do not deny the rise in merchant power throughout the Americas, a rise that is closely linked to the transformation from subsistence economies to one based on international commerce. We are suggesting that commerce and agriculture were and had been before interconnected and interdependent, both socially as well as economically. In the eighteenth century, with more complex economic and political tools for notables to employ, this connection was developed into networking. This was as true in Guadalajara, the Bajio, or Michoacán as it was in Guatemala or in Brazil. In Bahía, merchants rose in power in the late eighteenth century, being absorbed into a dominant class that had previously been monopolized by landowners. During the same period, businessmen in São Paulo emerged in municipal government—67 percent of council members were engaged in trade while only 19 percent were agriculturalists—with the collaboration of traditional families with whom they were tied through marriage.[20]

This description of eighteenth-century Michoacán might apply to most towns of Latin America one hundred years earlier. It describes the foundation upon which the notable family network was built:

We conclude from the archival evidence that Michoacán in the
eighteenth century was dominated by an inbred, smugly
prosperous elite, formed generations earlier. They successfully
competed with Spain in the ranks of the bureaucracy and the
clergy, and even in commerce. In keeping with a long tradition,
they married their daughters to *gachupines* on the rise; there was a
sentimental loyalty to the Crown. . . . The preservation of these
[families] involved more than the wedding of offspring to the
proper people. It also meant reliance on a complicated network of
brothers, cousins, uncles and in-laws to provide business contacts,
press law suits, make discreet loans, raise orphaned children and—
since it was always comforting to have a priest in the family—
intervene with the Almighty.[21]

The typical first-generation pattern in this new family network linked
nouveaux arrivés, who arrived anytime from 1715 to 1808, with older
families. Some of the newcomers were merchants, but others were government officials or in the military. The history of the house of Regla
provides the most typical example of this pattern in New Spain.

Pedro Romero de Terreros came to New Spain in 1733 from a "moder-
ately wealthy family" in Seville and with familial connections in Mexico
through his uncle, a merchant in Queretaro. Very much like the Guatemalan Aycinena later on, Romero established a business with mule
trains between the Gulf of Mexico and the central valley. As did Aycinena, he married into a powerful criollo family, the house of Miravalle,
which had been in the New World since the sixteenth century and had titles from the late seventeenth century.

Local power and earnings from commerce combined with luck to produce Romero a small fortune. He used his profits from the mule trade to
invest in mines in Pachuca and, in 1759, hit a bonanza. From there he
expanded his operations over the entire province. Through connections
in his wife's family, he was able to secure his political position with the
viceroy. Romero bought up a portion of seized Jesuit property as well as
the water rights to many of his neighbors' haciendas. By the time he died
in 1780, Romero, now count of Regla, owned silver mines, refining
mills, transport facilities, credit institutions, as well as many large
farms. "He was, indeed, the richest man in Mexico since Cortes."[22]

The rags-to-rags generalization applies well to the Romero clan. The
second generation expanded the power of the family more than its income, and the third sold off the original mines. Warfare and floods eroded the family's economic position. But the immense wealth and social
prestige of the house of Regla preserved it long after it lost its property.

While administrators rented the Romero lands and mines, the children married into Mexico's elite. The second count of Regla married the eldest daughter of the count of San Bartolomé de Jala, who through his pulque estates was one of the most powerful and wealthy men in New Spain. The count's sister, María Dolores Romero de Terreros, married a regent of New Spain, a future member of the Council of the Indies. By the turn of the century, the Romero house had close connections at the royal court in New Spain as well as with the viceroy in Mexico, who was compadre of one of the count's children. In the nineteenth century, the Regla fortune was dissipated, but nonetheless, most Mexican aristocratic families intermarried with the Romeros. The third countess of Regla was a close confidant of Guadalupe Victoria and became involved in the political machinations of the period. [23]

The persistence of noble, as opposed to notable, families, is of course critical to this study. The modern, eighteenth-century Mexican nobility rose and dominated the old society much in the same manner that eighteenth-century merchants overcame traditional families. As in Chile, new titles proliferated in this period: in the first half of the eighteenth century, the Bourbon monarch distributed twice as many noble titles as had the Hapsburgs in the whole seventeenth century. But the nobility had to guard its position as much as other groups. Titled families were as vulnerable to mining, agricultural, and commercial failures or to dispersion of wealth among heirs as other groups and therefore employed the same strategy: first-generation nobles sought to preserve their position in the second generation, marrying creole women and then marrying their daughters to peninsular men.

Most of Mexico's nobility derived from the new bureaucracy. Others rose on the profits of the new mineral boom, purchased titles, land, and entails. Of fifty-five noblemen studied by Doris Ladd, forty-four had interests in rural property. These nobles had no common political philosophy. They were both liberal and conservative, both for and against independence, and they followed the political doctrine that best favored their interests. Regardless of whether their ideology prevailed, many remained in independent Mexico, able to overcome the disasterous effects of the independence struggles—be they the sacking of mines and farms and the withdrawal of capital to Europe or the abolition of titles and entails—and to maintain their positions through well-extended networks through the mid nineteenth century. [24]

In Havana, a different process created the first generation of the nineteenth-century network. The late-eighteenth-century military government of Havana worked in close cooperation with the thirty traditional families of the port to stimulate commerce in the heady days of Bourbon reform. Old families merged with new, farmers with merchants and with bureaucrats, establishing an oligarchy. Their authority grew with the nineteenth-century sugar boom. They networked through marriage and commercial relationships. In the second half of the nineteenth century, when new Spanish merchants arrived with additional capital and modern technology, in essence attacking the old group, the older sugar families were able to maintain social prominence. Many continue to endure well into the twentieth century.[25]

In Buenos Aires, almost all of the notable families in 1778 traced their origins to recent immigrants. The average merchant in 1778 had been born in Spain; those that were Argentine-born were sons of traders who had emigrated that century. Merchants turned mostly to sons-in-law to preserve their fortunes, and thus, consanguineous and affinal ties produced merchant networks.[26] As in Guatemala, the political ideology of the merchants depended much upon their economic position. The Spanish party was dependent upon monopolistic trade practices. The independence party was composed of sons of merchants who were in the bureaucracy or the military and who had seen their power eroded by Spanish-born brothers-in-law. But both sides were connected by blood; even though they lost, the position of some members of the Spanish party was, in part, protected by their in-laws in the independence party.

From the Yucatán to Chile we see a similar pattern: powerful colonial families using networks to adjust to independence and increase their wealth, landholdings, and political power through the early twentieth century. In the Yucatán, the Peón family is representative. Don Alonso Manuel de Peón Valdéz came to the Yucatán in 1759 in the military service of the crown. He married an encomendera, Leonor de Cárdenas y Díaz, "setting a pattern," the Peón biographer Allen Wells tells us, "which future male heirs would follow: serve in the military and marry with landed family."[27] After independence, the Peóns were fierce partisans of the conservatives. Despite their political losses, they were able to survive using their links with other families to create major henequén holdings that became the basis of the family's huge wealth during the henequén boom in the late nineteenth century.

In Chile, the historian Alberto Edwards argues that a fundamental change took place in the eighteenth century, with new families entering and merging with old. They formed, as Jacques Barbier concluded, closely knit noble-merchant families. They bought titles. With independence, some of the families left and returned to Spain. Others remained. Mary Lowenthal Felstiner has explored how branches of the Larraín

family not only participated in the independence struggle b
tral to it. Out of it they networked into the other leading ,.
coming an integral part of postindependence society.[28]

The Second Generation

Recent works—most of them Ph.D. dissertations or articles—shed light on two major subjects: the family's complementarity in business, marriage, and politics and the connections between family networks and the regions whose ultimate political and economic fates they decided or brokered.

The Family's Complementarity in Business, Marriage, and Politics

While the first-generation merchant can be found quickly and identified easily in the historical literature of the Americas—he is a common figure, particularly in the late eighteenth century—the second-generation member is more difficult to recognize. Not only does he not come labeled as such, but the patterns of his businesses, social activities, and marriages are more complex. Some telltale signs, however, lead us to second-generation members, and these appear throughout the historical literature of different parts of Hispanic America. The most visible mark of a second-generation member is that he is a "mixed-occupation" type: a merchant-miner in one part of the Americas, a merchant-estanciero in another, and a merchant-planter in still another.

This type emerged when the second generation added additional activity to that which it "inherited" from the first. In nineteenth-century Bahía, Flory and Smith tell us, it is "an intermediate social type which might best be termed the landed merchant or merchant-planter . . . its existence calls into question the traditional view of Bahía society which stresses the division between the rural aristocracy and the urban merchant class."[29] He appeared as a merchant-miner in Mexico or Chile, a merchant-estanciero in Buenos Aires, a merchant-hacendado in Peru. In Panama society prior to 1850, Ignacio Mendez finds the merchant-businessman and the merchant-hacendado.

Whatever the combination, however, the mercantile enterprise always continued. As Flory and Smith have said of Bahía: "It should be emphasized that as the businessman developed rural properties, he continued to function as a merchant." The Bahía merchant-planter, like other "mixed-occupation" types, emerged partly from his merchant father's planning: "While providing business opportunities for young immigrants the successful established merchants directed their own sons away from commerce as a principal occupation. . . . Precisely those men capable of founding merchant dynasties chose instead to establish their sons in the Recôncavo as planters as soon as possible. Alternatively they placed their sons in the professions as *letrados* or priests."[30]

This type, however, simply embodies a more important underlying characteristic of this generation's occupations: complementarity in all activities.

> Joaõ Lopes Fuiza (Bahían merchant), left extensive agricultural holdings to his three children. His eldest son and namesake became a senhor de engenho, his only daughter wed a millowner and inherited one of the Fiuza sugar mills, and the remaining son became a Jesuit priest. When there was continuity in commerce over two or more generations, it was usually through the female lines as businessmen married off their daughters to ambitious newcomers—another way of facilitating the rapid establishment of immigrant merchants.[31]

The sons' professions and the daughters' marriages are part of this complementarity.

The case of the Yermos in Mexico in the second half of the eighteenth century, described by María Teresa Huerta, clearly illustrates the commercial start in the import-export area and the move into another commercial sector (sugar and meat markets) that developed on newly acquired haciendas. Of Basque origin, the Yermos arrived in Guanajuato in the 1780s and soon intermarried with those in the town of San Miguel el Grande. They served as the storers of the Consulado de Mexico, dealt in the import-export market, and through a nephew, became connected with Nuevo León commerce. Eventually, in the nineteenth century, they controlled meat supplies for Mexico City, acquired land and cattle, and expanded and controlled the meat market. One nephew who was brought in to handle this commerce married his cousin, a daughter of the first immigrant. He established the family in the sugar and meat businesses, using products supplied by their haciendas, but he always continued the import-export trade.[32]

As we have seen, Brading observed that in late colonial Mexico, fortunes made in commerce, mining, or political office were invested in the purchase of landed estates. He sees the peninsular immigrants who dominated commerce as "ascending the social scale and the creole landowners descending it."[33] He is right in observing that the immigrant *almaceneros* (wholesalers) emerged as the dominant figures in the colonial economy, but in the next generation, the sons had to make a major transition if the family was to survive in the new economy.[34] By far the most important transition was into land, which made the second generation merchant-hacendados.

In Medellín, Colombia, a prominent group of entrepreneurs emerged in the late eighteenth century. Coming from commerce and mining in the nineteenth century, this group became, according to Ann Twinam, "the colonizers, bankers, tobacco growers, railroad builders, coffee producers, and industrialists of Colombia."[35] But more important, if a Medellíner had a peninsular two or three generations earlier, he had the greatest possibility of belonging to the group of notable families.

Charles Harris tells the story of the Sanchez Navarros family. It takes place in Northern Mexico in the nineteenth century and reveals many of these aspects of family complementarity. It also shows that a merchant's son could have a career in the priesthood without repudiating the family's commercial interests. The founder of the latifundio was a priest who as a young man was assigned to the parish of Monclova. There he built up a profitable business by supplying trade goods to haciendas, military outposts, and missions. The Monclova store and sheep trade provided the cash to acquire land. The priest took his brothers and, later, his nephew as partners. Other family members, living in places such as Saltillo and Mexico City, acted as agents and sources of the political and financial information needed to manage the latifundio. The cooperation of family members made it possible to avoid splitting up the latifundio through inheritance.[36]

The notable families of nineteenth-century Yucatán, which Alan Wells has described, were composed of growers and planters of henequén: multifaceted individuals "who played the combined roles of planter, merchant, and speculator juggling investments continually in an effort to solve the demanding rhythms of the henequén economy."[37] Second-generation activity created the family network and the family fortune through complementarity. Wells identifies two types of families who became notable: "traditional landholding families whose prestige and influence dated back to the colonial era and a group of families whose principal source of wealth was fashioned from the growing import-export trade."[38] The assets of both seemed necessary for economic success in this period. What Wells calls his "elite" is "a network of closely knit families, . . . thirty families which dominated . . . land, marketing and capital."[39] Complementarity provided the means for the alliances: in marriages, professions, businesses, government posts, and, at times, in adjoining land.

The most common arrangement was the marriage of an immigrant trader to the daughter of traditional landed family. Their sons then combined the two activites. A certain time span was needed to solidify these combinations: in very general terms, the period between 1820 and 1860. During this period, the import and raw material markets in the world economy and improved transportation (ships with larger holds) began to favor exports of bulk materials, such as foodstuffs and hides, that were not as valuable per weight unit.

The series of monographs about family businesses in Mexico during the period 1830–60, *Formación y Desarrollo de la Burguesía en Mexico, siglo XIX*, deals with second-generation family businesses: the Escandón family business was run by sons of an Asturian merchant immigrant; the Beistegui were sons of a Basque merchant; and the Somera were sons of a Santander wine merchant.[40] This work provides the best detail about the second generation's enterprises and its complementarity. The Somera family is almost a "classic" second generation. The first-generation capital made possible the multitude of other activities in the second. The sons of the Santander wine merchant invested in a line of diligencias for the Mexico-Veracruz run, and then they purchased empty lands that they developed and sold off in small lots in a colonia. Public posts helped them to develop the substructure of services (water, paving, etc.) for the colonia. The Martínez del Río activities started with a Panamanian merchant who conducted business with Quito and Lima in wax, iron, and mules. The second generation transformed them into a Mexican firm that had vast land holdings as well as the mercantile business. The Beisteguis began with a Basque merchant enterprise. The two stores in Guanajuato and in Mexico City were transformed into a vast business that included mines, landed estates, loan credit, and investments in utility companies, banks, railroads, and credit companies. The Mier de Terán family business started in commerce and shifted to commercial agriculture—sugar and wheat—in the second generation.[41]

Missing from these studies of family businesses are the interconnections between them, a crucial ingredient in their individual successes. Valentín Rivero, for example, had business ties with the Martínez del Ríos and the Beisteguis.[42] The credit links, carefully detailed in some of these studies, reveal that each had access to capital from the other, and this sets them apart from other members of society. In the interesting case of Rivero, there are even connections with Murrieta and Co., a banking firm in London comprising relatives of one of the most powerful families in the Buenos Aires network.

In addition, some of the works contain good examples of the later im-migration of non-Hispanic Europeans during the second generation's time. The successful ones followed the steps of the first-generation Span-ish immigrant, and they emerged as part of the network in the 1860–79 period. They came most frequently as agents of foreign houses (English, American, French, German). English-speaking immigrants predomi-nated (English, Irish, Scots, Americans). The crucial steps included marriage to a local woman and access to land through kinship ties, po-litical ties, power, or trade. Following the shift from trade to land, they also kept the trade connection. Their businesses show the same charac-teristics of complementarity though all the steps occur in one generation. First and second patterns mixed, as if the newcomers had to fall into step with a mainstream generation if they were to succeed. Patricio Milmo in Mexico and Henry Swayne in Peru are good examples of these later im-migrants and their careful mix of business activities and marriages.[43]

But as we have said earlier, nothing was new in what these families did over a three-generation span. Both the second-generation and the period between 1830–60, however, were marked by diversity and com-plementarity. All we can do here is to point out that this second genera-tion sought complementarity and that in the context of the nineteenth century, given the changes taking place in the world economy and in the political and economic status of the colonies, this activity assumed new dimensions.

Contiguity and Credit Links
Two themes are hinted at in the literature but are never stated as ma-jor components of the family alliances or the major socioeconomic pat-terns, and they may turn out to be crucial ingredients of the family net-work. Here, we will treat them as footnotes to the discussion of business complementarity. The first theme is spatial contiguity. Linda Lewin says, in her survey of the Nóbrega family of Paraíba, Northeast Brazil (1790–1920): "The four generations surveyed were numerous, lived to maturity . . . and shared geographical proximity. . . . The residence patterns of Paraíba elite families during the Old Republic reflected a pattern of contiguous estates for the same family members; their land ti-tles revealed that property was often held in joint ownership usually overlapping a given number of family owners on different estates."[44] Kuznesof shows kin capable of being organized on a bairro basis in São Paulo: "Most important to the marshalling of local kinship structures for community benefit were the bairro militia companies, the officers of

which were committed to both the economic ends of the merchant elite and the kin and ritual kin group which constituted the social network of the bairro."[45]

We do not have enough studies of the residency patterns of the notable families in Latin American cities to draw any conclusions, and the traditional assumption that they placed their residences around the central plaza has been challenged by the new studies of historical geographers.[46] In Santiago, Buenos Aires, and Caracas the family network, once it reached its peak, created a new borough or neighborhood on empty land in the outskirts of the city. In these cities, the families' earlier residences had clustered in a small area near to the central plaza. The residences of some network families frequently adjoined or, in many cases, were on the same block. As the Brazilian case studied by Lewin indicates, rural estates were also often contiguous. In some cases, this occurred when a group of merchants bought the land jointly. Then in the next generation, several marriages took place among the families. In these cases, marriage connections allowed families to consolidate lands into larger estates.

Credit is another frequent theme in the historical literature on families in a colonial society that has been described as cash poor and credit ridden. Credit networks among families have surfaced recently. In the credit networks of the second-generation families studied in Mexico, many of the same names appear in the different studies.[47]

Several authors have referred to the importance of private credit linkages in Latin American cities during the late eighteenth and early nineteenth centuries until the 1860s, when banking structures developed. Hyland, for example, sees that a series of public and private credit linkages, developed in the period from 1851 to 1904, transmuted the impact of foreign commerce on the domestic economies of a country like Colombia.[48] Huerta argues that the transfer of Mexican lands to merchant-financiers in the first decades of the nineteenth century was a result of a shift in systems of credit from a Church financing system to a commercial, capital one.[49] Both Hyland and Huerta say that the elimination of the Church as a credit institution created a vacuum after independence. Commercial and mortgage banks did not yet exist nor was foreign capital or credit widely available. Hyland sees "the families of the elite (in the 1860s) falling back upon their long-established internal credit and capital networks" and uses the Barona family to illustrate this process:

> Manuel María Barona, scion of a distinguished landowning and
> merchant family with strong ties and investments on the east bank

of the Cauca River, was among those Cali Conservatives supporting the losing cause during the War of 1860. He managed to raise 51,575 pesos for the Conservative cause, largely by tapping the capital resources of his and allied families. As security, he mortgaged all the family properties: one hacienda, four large pastures, three urban dwellings, and a two-story warehouse-store in Cali. Upon his death in 1863, and the defeat of the Conservatives in the same year, his widow was obliged to surrender the properties to her husband's creditors. The pain of this sacrifice was short-lived: often within days of the debt payments, her merchant son, Joaquín Policarpo, systematically repurchased each of the properties. This task was greatly eased by a variety of intrafamily arrangements, discounts, and tacit understandings that appear between the lines of the formal legal verbiage of the notarial documents. Thus, although the Hacienda Guabito, together with an urban property, was turned over to creditors on May 11, 1864, in settlement of 17,413 pesos in debts, we find the same properties repurchased five days later at 14,080 pesos.

By the terms of the repurchase, the creditors, who happened to be don Joaquín's aunt and her husband, waived 4,333 pesos in accumulated interest and provided a generous five-year repayment period at no interest. By December 1867, Barona was even able to put up 6,400 pesos to underwrite a new pharmaceutical firm in Cali. Five years later, the family had recouped its losses and once again was one of the most powerful in the city.[50]

By the third generation, these families had transformed the credit networks into banks:

With the founding of the Banco del Cauca on November 29, 1873, the diverse patterns of economic change set in motion after 1851 came together in the same institution. . . . each of the major family-clans of Cali had invested generous sums in the bank, an investment paralleled closely by their already substantial investments in urban property.

In structure and financial backing, the bank was manifestly an enterprise of the landowning and commercial elite of the Valley.[51]

Richard B. Lyndley's study of the credit links among the Guadalajara notable families (1800–30) is the best-documented example for the first generation, and it shows the formation of the credit network. With the second generation society moved from its mercantile and colonial orientation to a commercial and capital one. Only by the third generation did a fully formed banking system emerge with new systems of credits. Lyndley sees credit as the "key to the structure of the Guadalajara oligarchy."[52]

With no system of banks in Mexico until the middle of the nineteenth century, with a government only beginning to experiment with public banking by establishing the mining tribunal and more likely to borrow from the private sector than to lend, and finally with the disappearance of the Church as a money-lending institution, the economic value of credit links increased among the prominent. Lyndley, however, sees British capital (which arrived after independence) as harbinger of a new economy that allowed the development of new enterprises without help from the notable household. However, more work on the subject may show that the kinship credit network in the period 1830–60 became, if anything, more crucial. Only the players were new: those who rose as market conditions changed were freed from the old colonial merchant loans. But they married into the credit network and added to it. For example, Hyland does say that after the 1830s, the integration of economic activities would start through public institutions like banks, markets regulated by prices that limited liability, business and corporations, and a land market open to anyone who had money, but it would not be fully realized until the 1860s. The second-generation families' credit network reveals itself not only in financial loans, but in all kinds of sharing arrangements: joint purchase of lands, joint running of haciendas, and exchanges of properties. As Hyland has remarked, land consistently and regularly functioned as credit within the kin network, and Lyndley maintains that

> in various ways the process of independence encouraged the
> development of something that had not existed before—a land
> market. . . . Land moved in the direction of becoming a
> marketable item whose value was predicated as much on its
> exchangeability as its utility, a commodity that one could acquire
> for money, rather than through a complicated social strategy
> involving numerous, interrelated kinship and credit
> commitments.[53]

In most places, at the end of the first generation and clearly by the second generation, the merchant-hacendado and merchant-miner appeared. Lyndley argues that the need for credit produced them.

> This is precisely where the data from the present study led us—to
> the conclusion that the need for mobilizing credit was the central
> motive for the agricultural-commercial family enterprise. The
> family business evolved into a structure that encompassed
> metropolis and province, city and countryside, government and the
> governed, agriculture and commerce. This combination of

resources permitted the elite household to create credit for investment and secure it with a stable asset and source of income. At the same time, the matrimonial alliance and its complementary kinship relations created a system for distributing credit and allocating scarce resources. Instead of impersonal lending institutions that dispensed credit according to the chances for gain or loss in an equally impersonal structure of loans and investments a merchant invested his liquid assets in his father-in-law's or other relative's hacienda, while the hacendado sold his products through his merchant kinsman in a city market regulated by his relatives and rivals.[54]

Cases from the historical literature that illustrate the second generation's complementarity in its economic ventures are easier to come by than those illustrating the marriage complementarity. Yet in this generation, brothers and brothers-in-law became powerful cohorts.

Marriage

In the literature on families, marriage is treated frequently, but very rarely beyond the discussion of the marriage of a particular individual. However, immigrant marriage—that is, those of the first generation in our scheme—has been dealt with more often. Many authors have described the prevailing pattern of the peninsular trader marrying a local woman in different parts of Iberian America. As Kuznesof shows in São Paulo:

Marriage provided immediate and complete incorporation of the immigrant into the family network of his bride and into the political and economic associations of his father-in-law. Traditional *paulista* families were attracted to the idea of merchant immigrant sons-in-law because of the small number of local wealthy families, the constant diminution of estates through property division, and the poor returns in agriculture. . . . Marriage to an immigrant without family had the additional benefit that the estate of the immigrant stood a good chance of being willed to his wife's family. In effect, the way in which immigrant merchants were able to gain access to resources controlled by the traditional elite was through being incorporated into their families as sons-in-law and thereby maintaining the control of the traditional elite over community resources. Marriage was the most important mechanism by which merchant immigrants gained access to the resources of *paulista* society.[55]

But the marriage patterns of the children of that first immigrant have not been observed in detail, particularly those of the whole cohort in the second generation. The second generation seems to have been the most successful in bonding the greatest number of families through marriage, but they also sought to join lands into large estates, to pool capital, to acquire brothers-in-law with political power, military command, mercantile outlets, and means of transportation.

The mechanisms and combinations of marriage arrangements are not clear for the second generation, except in their broadest outlines. That sibling exchanges were part of it, that they were important and frequent, seems clear. But in order to understand the whole, cohorts rather than individuals in the different generations need to be analyzed. The broad outline of the second generation reveals an exogamous generation, though one in which marriages were carefully planned. The survival and success of the family depended on it. The sibling exchange made the connection to one family preeminent; those two families usually adopted a double name to mark their double union. But some preferential unions took place vertically, too. Some families reinforced connections with another family by establishing more marriages with that family in the next generation, sometimes in two or more generations. Other than that, complementarity seems the rule. Reinforcement and the multiple marriages between two families also can be seen in the remarriage of a widowed partner to the brother or sister of the spouse.

None of these patterns are new; they were widespread during the colonial period. Blank has traced the preferred ties of some families in seventeenth-century Caracas. "Three of the elite kindred are distinguished by their solidarity within themselves and with each other, whereas the connections of the other families are scattered. The strength of these families is in part a result of their demographic vitality. Stemming from sibling groups, all of whose members produced surviving offspring, they had rich demographic resources for making both internal and external alliances."[56]

The social benefits gained by the husband from his wife's social position, which we have seen in our nineteenth-century case studies, can be seen already in Blank's description of seventeenth-century Caracas marriage. "More important than property was the status women conferred upon marriage. . . . In Caracas the foreign spouses of the daughters of the elite were adopted into the structure at the position of their wives. They served in the same places in the municipal government as their local born brothers-in-law."[57] Lavrin and Couturier have also illustrated how men acquired status through the women they married in their study of women's socioeconomic role in colonial Guadalajara.[58] What seems missing in the nineteenth century, however, is the dowry. Though dowries are only beginning to be studied, the information we have shows that they seem to have diminished. The status or connections that the bride's family could confer, however, did not.

In the nineteenth century, certain parts of these old patterns were adapted to new circumstances. The second generation mainly married into families that were allied by economic interests in a particular region, sometimes families to whom they were already linked by land contiguity or financial credit. Women in the second generation preferentially married men from the new group of non-Hispanic immigrants who had come to America as representatives of foreign houses. A vertical extension also reinforced marriage alliances, but the lateral extension in which brothers-in-law created cohorts seemed to prevail.

Lewin's study of the three dozen extended families in Brazil's northeastern state of Paraíba is particularly important as a complete examination of a network's marriage connections.[59] From 1889 to 1930, this group had complete control. Lewin pursued these families further back through the nineteenth century but did not separate them generationally. Though she has stressed the male sibling bond in the late nineteenth and early twentieth centuries (the time of the third and fourth generations) it is also present a generation earlier:

> Data extracted from a published genealogy of Paraíba's prestigious Nóbrega family offer a useful sample from which to generalize about the frequency of parallel or cross-cousin patterns of marriage. As a ruling family dominant in the backlands *municipios* of Santa Lusia and Patos, the Nóbregas possessed kinship links with half-a-dozen other principle parentelas who collectively controlled Paraíba's interior. They produced senators, congressmen, vice-governors and state assemblymen during the Old Republic and in the preceding Empire and therefore present an excellent choice from which to sample marriage patterns. The four generations surveyed were numerous, lived to maturity to a remarkable degree, and shared geographical proximity. . . . The very high frequency of marriages between parallel cousins demonstrated the importance of strong sibling bonds, especially between brothers, for maintaining the family's core over generations. Nearly two-thirds of all cousin marriages occurred between patrilateral or matrilateral parallel cousins (92 of the total 145 identifiable cases), but it was marriage between the offspring of brothers which emerged as the nearly dominant pattern. . . . The leadership stratum of the state oligarchy illustrated this advantageous manipulation of links with female kin. With one minor exception, five of the six men who led the oligarchy between 1890 and 1930

became successful politically by virtue of ties with either their wives or their mothers' kin.[60]

For the non-Hispanic late arrivals, as for the first generation, the father-in-law connection would be more crucial. Patrick Milmo's case, described by Cardoso, provides a good example.[61] Born in Ireland in 1826, Patrick arrived in Monterrey in 1849. In 1857 he married the daughter of a regional political leader named Vidaurri. He started in commerce but soon branched into a hacienda, which he owned jointly with his father-in-law. He also was his father-in-law's partner in many business transactions. He loaned money to his father- and brothers-in-law and, through Vidaurri, also lent money at interest to the government of Nuevo León. He eventually expanded into mining and industry, his entry aided, of course, by the political power of his father-in-law.

Other ritual forms reinforced connections between specific families. Godparenthood remained important through the second generation. As the network gathered strength, the custom of using the brothers and sisters of the spouse as godparents reinforced family connections and, in some cases, led to more sibling marriages. Felstiner says of the Larraín family in Chile, "In each Larraín branch, godparents were chosen from the immediate kin, rarely from outside the family or from the other branch."[62] Games and social gatherings, which joined all the godparents of one family's children, also seemed designed to foster close ties in the second generation.

Public Posts

The business complementarity of the second generation can be found in the historical studies of individual family businesses or family estates. More difficult to find are the connections between businesses and posts, particularly public posts. One of the few examples has already been mentioned—the Rivero family's use of their municipality posts to develop the services of a colonia.[63] Many references to the control of public posts by families exist, and even the literature of early colonial times shows this pattern. For example, Peter Marzahl in his study of the cabildo of Popayán, Colombia, says:

> Corporate forms of organization remained underdeveloped, among them the cabildo. Sets of families, rather than institutions and corporations, served as the integrating clamp of this society, with such family combinations possessing vertical and lateral dimensions. The former are visible only occasionally, in their effects, as when the Hurtados and Velascos managed to mobilize

their respective adherents in the struggle about the governorship in 1701. . . . Co-optation of newcomers, in fact, added a third dimension extending over time designed to preempt the future. The continuing contour of this society in its upper echelons was represented by changeable congeries of families, around which everything else was arranged, at times in symmetrical fashion. The cabildo, in this context, played only a minor role.[64]

Louisa Hoberman describes family power in Mexico:

By the late 1620s, the cabildo constituted a tightly knit group of families. A Monroy, Figueroa, Trejo, Barrera, Cervantes, or Carbajal may not have held office for a long period of time, but when he sold or bequeathed the position, it was to a relative or prospective relative. Merchants might be found among these. Between 1621 and 1645 at least four regidores were sons or relations of merchants who had been in business in the 1590s. But there was another reason for a lack of congruence between consulado and cabildo. Both second generation merchants and the few merchants who bought the office of regidor for themselves shed their official merchant status once they became aldermen.[65]

In the same vein, Kuznesof has portrayed the commissioned militia offi-cers in early nineteenth-century São Paulo as a "territorial and kinship-based elite power group of critical importance to the management of the community."[66]

Whatever local control some families possessed in colonial times, by independence and the removal of the crown's authority, the relations be-tween families and public posts became all the more important and deci-sive. The best study of political posts and families in the period with which we are concerned is Mary Lowenthal Felstiner's excellent article "Kinship Politics in the Chilean Independence Movement." It describes what happened when Spanish rule was removed:

As members of families, the patriots envisioned a society in which the family system could thrive, in which political relations had the intimacy and security of family relations. If their new society looks like the old society in many ways, it is because they turned to what they had. For organization they turned to kinship alliances. For political and social positions they drew on kinship qualifications. For ideology they called up the image of the family, which justified both rebellion and family interest in the state. So a pivotal revolutionary institution, by ensuring connections, patrimony, and continuity from past to future, also fostered generational ties between old and new regimes. . . . From the early junta movement, patriots envisioned the natural state of society as family sovereignty—which was not to be confused with popular sovereignty: "misfortune has interrupted our relations with the sovereign and we should for the time being consider ourselves in the primitive state. In this state each head of the family is its natural governor; from every district or *federation of families* the magistrate or town councillor is elected. . . . Images of the polity as family or a federation of families pervaded revolutionary ideology."[67]

By the end of the nineteenth century, this "federation of families" appeared in country after country in Latin America and in what we have described as the family networks.

Just as in colonial times, families achieved control of the cabildos, so in the national period did they gain control of provincial legislatures. What the historical literature of the nineteenth century shows is that the importance of political office increased for a family as an additional and necessary complement to its business interests. The studies of different families and their businesses point to a certain group of posts that families sought and, if they could not capture them directly, tried to obtain through marriage. For the second generation, these posts included provincial legislator, customs official, militia officer (preferably rural militia), justice of the peace (this was often combined with a militia post), port commissioner, municipal officer, or officer of a political party. The most prominent and important was that of provincial governor.

Alan Wells, in his study of the Molinas in Yucatán, shows the basis of the provincial governor's power and how it extended into the first years of the twentieth century. The network's business versatility coupled with its far-reaching political connections originally placed one member in the governorship of Yucatán: Olegario attached himself to a liberal cause as secretary to General Cepeda Peraza, and several brothers received positions in the new administration after the Liberal victory. One of the brothers, partner in Olegario Molina and Co., was state customs administrator in Progreso. Olegario became state deputy, then judge, then governor of Yucatán, and finally emerged in national politics (the hope of every regional leader) as secretario de fomento of Porfirio Díaz. But apart from his individual success, the study shows the political posts of the whole family cohort. These brought continuous prosperity to the family business.[68]

Mary Lowenthal Felstiner has made clear the degree to which prominent patriots clustered according to kinship. "In October 1811, Joaquín Larraín told José Miguel Carrera: 'We have all the presidencies in the family. I am President of Congress, my brother-in-law of the Executive, and my nephew of the Audiencia.'" In 1813, the Chilean junta removed several members of the Carreras family from military command so that all the armies "would not be located in one family."[69]

Doris Ladd, looking at the transition made by the Mexican nobility during the period of independence, sees the family as their vehicle for crossing from the colonial to the national period and for their nimble maneuvering through politics and professions to keep themselves safe from political storms and economic changes.

> Neither the wars of independence nor the new Republic destroyed the Mexican nobility . . . the dynamic relationships of elite society in Mexico worked to blur the stereotyped polarities of Spaniard and Creole, rural and urban, financier and producer, colonialist and imperialist, provincial and cosmopolitan, loyalist and patriot, liberal and conservative . . . whatever happened patriarchs without question remained patriarchs.[70]

Linda Lewin has used the term *política de familia* to define the actions of a family network of nineteenth-century Paraíba.[71] She has best illustrated the way different family members complemented their activities to ensure local control: they monopolized elective office and appointive bureaucratic posts in Paraíba; they mobilized sizable public or private armed forces; they appropriated local tax revenues while at the peak of their power in the third generation. Lewin particularly examines a second-generation feature: "the fundamental bonding at the level of male siblings." This bonding among brothers-in-law is particularly important in politics; for there, the families relied on brothers-in-law to coordinate local power.[72] Men bonded as political allies by marrying sisters. If the sisters they exchanged were also their cousins, the family core became more tightly woven.

Between the 1830s and 1860s (the timetable is not exactly the same for each place but falls within these parameters), a similar phenomenon occurred in other Latin American regions where brothers-in-law coordinated local power in provincial assemblies. Though few examine provincial assemblies of this period or the family connections of their members (there are not near the number of studies of cabildo members), analyses of nineteenth-century notable families indicate that a seat in the local legislature was a common family post and that families strove to make alliances to control electoral districts.

Lewin has pointed out that Peter Dobkin Hall has discussed similar cousin marriages and strong political bonding of male siblings among

Boston Brahmins.[73] Thomas Purvis has shown that just as Boston Brahmins developed political bonds through marriage during the 1780–1850
period, notable interconnected families dominated the New Jersey legislature during the 1703–76 period.

> New Jersey's political life was already oligarchic in 1703 and grew
> progressively so during the next seven decades. Wealth and family
> consolidation became conspicuous elements in the backgrounds of
> both assembly leaders and backbenchers. . . . Especially during
> the years after 1737 when native-born assemblymen predominated
> in the house, kinship connections in most counties came to center in
> one or two prominent families. . . . Family ties among
> assemblymen invariably connected legislators residing within the
> same county . . . kinship connections among representatives
> demonstrated a high degree of interrelatedness beginning with the
> first election in 1703 and increasing throughout the century.[74]

But Purvis, unlike Hall, refers to an earlier period than the one with
which we are concerned, and he identifies other studies that indicate
that in this period, all middle colonies were similarly controlled by notable families and their kin in the assemblies and courts.

At one level, the findings in Purvis's study compare with those concerning the prominent families who dominated the cabildo posts in colonial Latin America. But one wonders if such activity also occurred in the
national period after independence as it did in Latin America. Not in
New Jersey, according to Purvis: "The American Revolution reversed
this drift toward oligarchic consolidation. The imperial crisis after 1763
led to a noticeable democratization of politics, especially evident in the
appearance by the 1780s of less affluent representatives unrelated to
members of the pre-war elite."[75]

But at independence and shortly thereafter, new people also appeared
in the Latin American legislatures. Had the families simply reassembled
from a new base after independence? Is that not the case of Boston? Neither the Latin American nor the North American studies satisfactorily
answer this question. Though the resemblances are striking, particularly
in the case of the Boston family network and the Latin American cases,
the relation of the Boston Brahmins to the political structure needs to be
compared to the Latin American cases in more detail. The relation in Peter Hall's study seems less strong and less close. Perhaps, as Purvis has
pointed out in his New Jersey study, it did end with the American Revolution. Perhaps, however, as in Latin American cities, the independence
movement put an end to the rule of a particular group of notable families
and a new, more powerful group arose by the second half of the century.

The political power of family members resided not only in the posts they occupied directly. An example from Juan Englesen's study of nine-teenth-century coastal Peru, that of hacendado Domingo Elías, illus-trates this well: "Elías backed a person he liked for an official position such as Port Customs official or Regional Tax Collector. He worked for the nomination of a particular person, and when he was appointed he provided the finances and bond or securities necessary for his confirma-tion."[76] Elías was an hacendado and the merchant son of a Spanish bu-reaucrat and a Peruvian woman from a provincial hacendado family. He played the role of regional caudillo, though officially he held only one post: that of tax collector for education and charity for the South Central region to which he had been appointed in 1837 by his business partner Andrés de la Cruz, president of Peru. By the 1840s, Elías entered the national political scene and remained there until his death in 1867. As a result, he had the opportunity to use the extensive state apparatus to further his own and his family's interests.

> As a member of the Council of State—a policy-making body in Castilla's Presidency. . . . Elías did not oppose any of Castilla's policies and he obtained with the latter's approval, the financially rewarding guano contract. . . . In 1855 he was Minister of Finance. Between 1849 and 1862, he held the guano contract, one of the most lucrative activities in Peru. With the expansion of the guano trade Elías expanded his already extensive land venture.[77]

Though involved in other political activities, Elías ran for the presi-dency, was defeated, led insurrections from the provinces against one of the regimes, and was defeated again. His political activity typified that of the second generation, and he is the prototypical head of a regionally prominent family who strove to obtain a national footing. But most im-portant are his direct use of political office for benefits or gains in his business ventures and the close ties between his state posts and his busi-ness. He not only got the guano contract but used government money to build a small railroad line in the guano islands. The railroad not only di-rectly benefited his business, but he himself had been paid by the gov-ernment for building the railroad that carried his cargo.[78]

Domingo Elías ran his businesses mainly through four people: his brother; his brother-in-law, Quintana; his wife, Isabel Quintana; and an old friend, also a merchant. Of his twelve children, the five sons be-came administrators of fundos, the eldest representing his father in the most important transactions and running the mine operations. In addi-tion, a cousin and two uncles of Elías's wife became part of the family's

business complex. The two uncles, who were brothers and important hacendados and merchants, provided shipping for Elías's goods and supported him with money and troops in his bid for the presidency. Still other relatives lived in the South Central Valley. Englesen quotes Pedro F.
Vicuña, a Chilean exile, who said that wherever Elías stopped during his
journey to the south he was greeted by a relative.

In some works, another aspect of the political activities of the second-
generation families appears: the mobilization of the network's finances
to support political parties, though this did not become clearly institutionalized and visible until the third generation. Elías, for example, got
the backing of what was considered the first organized political party—
the Progressive Club—for his presidential campaign. The Civilista party
would not emerge until the 1870s, but it institutionalized the political interests of the coastal hacendados who were connected to each other by
kinship ties.[79] This can be seen even more clearly when families in the
Cauca Valley mobilized to the Conservative cause. In Richard Hyland's
study of these families, he shows that Manuel Barona, scion of a distinguished landowning and merchant family that had strong ties and investments on the east bank of the Cauca River, tapped his resources and
those of allied families. He raised 51,575 pesos for the Conservatives.[80]

Through these means and the same kin patterns, a powerful group of
families controlled cities or regions of the new nations by the third generation.

Regions and Families

The second theme in the historical literature on families is that of regionalism. In the histories and activities of a few families, we see the full
implications and importance of the formation of the regional family network. Specifically, in the events of the 1820s to the 1860s, we see a group
of families who banded together in a particular region to gain control
and to serve as brokers to obtain privilege in a newly formed nation. We
witness the dissolution of Spanish units in the Americas and the realign-
ment of whole areas after independence. Michael Hamerly in his study
of the area of Guayaquíl does not refer to the dominant group in the city
but does show the period after independence as one in which the main issue to be resolved by those who dominate the city is whether they will be
subjects of Quito or Lima. Independence starts with their break with
Gran Colombia.[81] David Cubitt takes the study of this area a step further and shows the emergence of postindependence Guayaquíl through
the political maneuverings and actions of a group of merchants and hacendados with cacao plantations.[82]

Different regions tried to obtain favorable positions for themselves in the emerging nation by vying to become the capital city or by forming coalitions to resist moves made by other regions to become the capital. They entered into alliances with the capital to gain privileged positions for themselves: national office for members of the families and for the economy of the region. In each place, a coalition of a few notable families decided the ultimate fate and particular configuration of the final national unit. Several works deal with this major subject, though not all give families the importance they deserve.

Wibel's study of nineteenth-century Arequipa shows the connections between a region and a group of families.[83] The leaders of eighteenth-century Arequipa were landowners, merchants, and officials of state. Their roles overlapped so that the labels were used interchangeably. In the period after independence, kinship ties among prominent local families appeared in their familiar guises, for example, land contiguity:

Networks of common land ownership tied together many of Arequipa's most prosperous agricultural areas. They were produced and strengthened by the repeated intermarriage of Arequipa's landed elite. Lands divided by inheritance in one valley were joined with similarly fragmented estates in the same valley or other valleys through marital alliances. A majority of the chacareros of Arequipa, the viñateros of Vitor and the landowners of neighboring districts were related to each other by both blood and marriage. . . . These patterns of common property ownership and family ties were the basic elements of the cohesion of the landed elite whose nucleus was in the city.[84]

Family ties also structured Arequipa's commerce. In one local marriage, Raimundo Gutierrez de Otero, an immigrant merchant from Santander in northern Spain, married the daughter of montañés Mateo Cossío, colonel of militia and landowner. Raimundo was in commerce in the north with his brother Simón. He had another brother in Cádiz, who was also a merchant and who served as his contact with Spain. He had a nephew who was a merchant in Guayaquíl. Another brother Luís, a deputy in the Consulado de Tarapacá, married into the wealthiest mining family in the intendancy.[85] The cohesion of the region was sustained by contacts between the "elites." "Elite relationships made up the region. . . . When independence came they supported or rejected the sovereignty of Spain according to their ability to perpetuate local domination and to benefit from ties to sovereign authorities."[86]

According to Wibel, a distinct occupational shift took place in the 1780 to 1845 period because agricultural expansion was limited. As a result, many more family members became professionals after independence, particularly army officers. But one asks if this shift was not just the addition of one more activity to what remained a family enterprise in agriculture, since the shift to political and army positions in the second and third generation became a necessary complementarity activity for protecting family holdings and businesses. "The elites monopolized the opportunities in church, government, and military," Wibel says, and in the process, they left both agriculture and commerce. The close ties between the families gave them a monopoly of posts. The landowners were also professionals, so they still kept control of the land. The merchants, however, did lose out to British and other North European merchants.

The economic ties between the Arequipa region and Bolivia broke down when Bolivia became a separate nation and the Arequipa region became dependent upon it, until its final political subjection to Lima. In this interplay with Lima, the families moved into national politics and, from there, represented the region and served as brokers for it and as mediators for its position in the nation. This interrelated group from Arequipa, therefore, became "a political elite in its own region, and its most notable families reached the national level and Lima; . . . most Latin American nations continue to be mediated by such political elites in the national capital."[87]

Englesen's study shows us the same picture in coastal Peru. The dominant group of families battled in the region and outside, trying to decide if an alliance with Bolivia or with Lima was more convenient. This can be seen in their support for different parties. Various families are illustrated, but their final moves are identical: they propelled themselves and their regions' interests into national politics and Lima.[88]

Roger Haigh, in his pioneering work on the province of Salta's (Northwest Argentina) "kinship elite," has described with great accuracy the provincial family network and its brokerage of the region's fortunes vis-à vis Buenos Aires. His description can serve as the basic model of such relations:

> The break with Spain in 1810, by eliminating Spanish officials, greatly augmented the power of the families. From 1810 to 1821 this family structure provided the basic source of strength that enabled Salta to repulse seven invasions and to earn the title "Bulwark of the North." . . .
> Further research into the nature of these families revealed that they controlled most of the wealth of the province and were directly related to those who controlled the remainder. These relationships were the result of a multiplicity of kinship

connections, a network of families that made up the socio-
economic elite of the province. . . .

In summing up the relationship of [the caudillo] Güemes to the
kinship elite, the continued domination of the family structure is
apparent. He was selected by it and was successful only when he
enjoyed its support. On points of discord between Güemes and his
supporting group he was either defeated or forced to compromise
his position. Güemes was dead within a week after the final break
ensued, and the family structure immediately reassumed complete
control of the province. It appears that Güemes was more an
instrument of the kinship elite than the tyrant of Salta.[89]

Fred Hollander in his study of Salta and oil contracts in the twentieth
century takes Haigh's work as his departure point and elaborates on the
kinship elite's relations with Buenos Aires:

Following the victory of Buenos Aires over the interior provinces
in 1862, the Buenos Aires oligarchy consolidated national control
by supporting cooperative family coteries within each provincial
oligarchy. These family coteries in turn were integrated into the
national governments that followed; hence the succession of
provincial presidents in the latter half of the nineteenth century.
After 1880, intermarriages between the dominant families of the
northwestern oligarchies and the oligarchies of Buenos Aires and
the littoral provinces forged a true national oligarchy from the
tentative political alliance of the two regions. The role of the
northwestern oligarchies in the national government, which won
the selective protection of the sugar industry, continued until the
national oligarchy was fragmented and politically expropriated by
the electoral victory of the middle class Radicals in 1916.[90]

The ties of the provincial network of families with the capital did propel several of its members into national office, including the greatest
prize of all, the presidency. Moreover, the notable family network of
Buenos Aires granted protection to the northern provinces' sugar industry. But the Buenos Aires families also established their own cattle and
grain economy as that of the nation. The resolutions of the conflicts between the regions headed by groups of families and their pacts with the
capital city are, however, a third-generation topic. What is important to
stress here is that the nucleus of the family network was always in the
city (the capital city for the dominant region), though the families' economic base may have been in the city's rural hinterland. The families'
second generation fought the battles and made alignments; the third
generation assumed regional control. Works dealing with the third gen-

eration, therefore, can illustrate this topic more extensively, since the family networks can be seen in command of different regions.

This political and social resolution of the relations between regions through a city-based group of families has had important implications for the resulting political system in Latin America and for the present difficulties in governing, so much so that some present-day political analysts still call for a system of oligarchies to serve as brokers for the different sectors and interests in order to produce governable nations.[91]

The Third Generation

Case studies on notable families are sparse for the third generation, which coincides roughly with the last third of the nineteenth century. This neglect is paradoxical given the prominence of the period in Latin American historiography in general. But perhaps the very prevalence of research on the late nineteenth century helps explain the relative paucity of family studies. Other themes have taken precedence: dependency, economic development, modernization, nation building.

It has been largely from such themes that case studies on notable families (often only brief, irregular glimpses) have come. Many studies have focused on influential or ruling groups: oligarchies, elites, incipient classes, or economic interests such as entrepreneurs. Historians of the period have begun to perceive the family as important, even central, in such groups. For some, such as Nils Jacobsen in his study of hacendados in southern Peru, the family remains peripheral. For others, like Frederick Hollander in his study of the Salta oligarchy in Northwest Argentina, the family network is an integral part of the analysis, but it is only rarely detailed in action. Still others provide vivid descriptions of the workings of the notable families, but fail to analyze them at more than a surface level, for example, Richard P. Hyland, in his study of the elite in the Cauca Valley in Colombia. By contrast, the evidence and analysis of Mark Wasserman and Allen Wells in their regional studies of Chihuahua and the Yucatán have increasingly focused on the role of the notable family.[92]

At the opposite end of the historiographical spectrum are several studies of individual families, usually covering several generations, with the late nineteenth century occupying the temporal center of the monograph. They provide, in fascinating detail, a glimpse of notable family life during the period. In varying degrees and levels of sophistication, they reach out to make connections with the general circumstances in which regional society functions and the families must operate. Darrell

Levi's monograph on the Prados of São Paulo is the most comprehensive in this regard, suggesting that the Prados are an archetype for the "modernizing elite family" in nineteenth-century Brazil.[93]

Only two studies (other than this work)—those by Linda Lewin on Northeast Brazil and Robert Oppenheimer on Santiago, Chile—explore a network of families as a historical pattern in its own right. In these studies, the emphasis is on describing and explaining the evolution of the network and the patterns by which it functioned. But the interaction of the network with larger historical circumstances, both in cause and effect, is also considered.[94]

These group and individual studies, with their differing perspectives on the notable family network, reveal more patterns in the third generation than in the second. The notables' responses to the historical circumstances are less marked, more complex. There are prominent themes to which they move, but also numerous variations. By contrast, the situations in which the notables found themselves appear to have a greater degree of commonality across regions than in the preceding two generations: the growth in power and resources of state and national government; the rapid acceleration of a foreign presence; the technological transformations (especially in transportation, communications, modes of production, and public services); and a marked acceleration in the rate of economic and social change. The monographs that touch on the family network do demonstrate important exceptions to one or more of these fundamental historical conditions. In the Cauca Valley, economic expansion was delayed until 1890, while in southern Peru and in at least two areas in Brazil, there was little foreign presence or social change and economic alterations were limited. In Salta, economic conditions were generally adverse throughout the whole period.[95]

In part, the varying responses of the notable families—the more complex patterns among the networks—were the result of such exceptions to the general rule in the larger context of historical circumstances.[96] But they were due more, it appears, to the cumulative decisions of earlier generations. In some regions, a set of circumstances prevalent in the third generation began in the latter half of the second generation. The networks there had devised patterns that would become more generalized in a succeeding generation elsewhere, themselves moving on to more complex variations of the same pattern or on to new ones during their third generation. Brazil and Chile were countries where political stability, economic expansion based on exports, and technological change arrived by mid century. In the littorals of Argentina and Peru, only economic expansion was prevalent by that time. Cumulative effects of more specific circumstances (such as civil disorders, natural calamities, degree of foreign contact), as well as family idiosyncracies (number of children, individual personalities and inclinations), also contributed to the varied patterns and choice of strategies among the networks of the third generation. These variations, multiple and complex as they were, do not, however, obscure the significant number of common patterns among family networks revealed in the monographic studies to date.

Continued Economic Diversification

Most prevalent among these common patterns was the sophistication and complexity of the family business enterprise. The diversification of economic activities that became general in the second generation reached its greatest intensity and extension in the third. Exceptions, of course, should be noted. In southern Peru, sierra hacendados found little inducement for diversification given the substantial short-run profits from expanding existing sheep-ranching operations. In Salta, circumstances would not permit it (though in the fourth generation, Hollander details the rise of the Patrón Costas family through diversification). Nevertheless, extensive diversification was the general rule, and Wasserman provides the most thorough documentation of its scope in his study of the notables in Chihuahua. Julia Alfaro Vallejos and Susana Chueca Posadas, in their study of a new Italian immigrant family in the Lima-Callao area, demonstrate the powerful inducements to diversify.[97]

Most of the regional and individual studies stress the creation of institutionalized credit resources as the important core of diversification and of the marked expansion of family interests in the third generation. In the prior two generations, credit arrangements were based on personal loans and network credit alliances with real estate as the customary collateral. But beginning in the 1850s in some areas, as in Chile, and encompassing most regions by the 1880s, the family credit alliances were centralized and institutionalized in financial companies, particularly banks. Oppenhemier details how in Santiago "families made sure they had some control of the process by controlling the various corporations." Usually they took the initiative in founding banks, and even if they did not own or operate them outright, "in most cases where the family held large quantities of stock, family members were on the boards of directors or managed the banks."[98]

Notable families also made sure their members were on the decision-making bodies of railroad ventures. If banks were crucial to gaining access to capital for diversification in the third generation, the network's members also understood that improved transportation and communications were the key to creating and controlling production and markets. Levi and Joseph Sweigart show the close relation between coffee expansion and railroad ventures in central Brazil, and Wells describes the decisive control over rail lines achieved by such families as the Peóns and Molinas in the spread of henequén cultivation in the Yucatán.[99]

Other economic strategies are less consistent. Though industry (in the processing of primary products and the manufacture of consumer goods for the expanding population centers) was pointing toward the future—becoming the central activity for the expansion of wealth in the twentieth century—only a few of the studies detail such ventures. Levi and Wasserman demonstrate its emergence as an important component in the Prado and Terrazas family enterprises. Alfaro and Chueca elucidate with minute detail the pivotal role that industrial ventures came to play in the Piaggio family's rising fortunes from the late nineteenth century to the present.[100] Similarly, public services were an outlet for diversification, responding to technological innovations, urbanization, and the integrative possibilities with industry.[101] Large capital requirements and foreign domination generally restricted notable families to speculation in extractive enterprises (in particular, mining). The Piaggios, however, did play a pioneering role in the development of the oil industry in coastal Peru.[102]

Investment in real estate was pervasive, as the acceleration of economic activity led to steadily rising land values. Yet network family strategies varied considerably. In Chihuahua and the Yucatán, where insecurities (and often poor transportation) had rendered huge tracts of land unprofitable, the most successful families cashed in on speculative acquisitions made during hard times and added to their prodigious holdings. In São Paulo, coffee expansion was based on the obtainment of undeveloped land. By contrast, most notables in the Cauca Valley completed the shift in emphasis begun during the tumultuous conditions of the second generation from agricultural holdings to urban property. In southern Peru, as in many other regions, the rising profitability of export markets induced altiplano hacendados to convert subsistence plots and community pastures into lands for wool export.[103]

Patterns Complementary to Diversification

There were also corollary, or complementary, patterns that facilitated diversification of the family enterprise. Indeed, employment or neglect of these strategies in great part determined the success or failure of the process. Incorporation was increasingly widespread among network families. Most authors describe family-owned stock companies or family memberships on boards of directors. Beato, Oppenheimer, Englesen, and Alfaro and Chueca make the utilization of incorporation an integral part of their interpretative analysis.

> There was a shift of family wealth from individuals and partnerships to formal corporations that controlled family wealth and business activities. . . . Soon, corporations became an integral part of family investment patterns. . . . The corporation and corporate law separated capital from the immediate family and limited the families' legal liabilities.
>   The families not only held stock in groups or alliances, but tended to buy and sell blocks of stock as a unit. . . . Seldom did one member of the family buy or sell stock without the same action being taken by the rest of the family investors. When this did occur, the other family members or the family commercial house bought the stock.[104]

In most regions, frequent business relationships with foreigners also proved important for the diversification of the family enterprise. At the heart of Wasserman's thesis is the interweaving of the interests of the various levels of notables with those of foreigners. He provides abundant examples of these connections: in particular, notables were clients of foreign entrepreneurs, and in the case of the Terrazas clan, were partners in ventures and employers of trained and skilled immigrants, incorporating some as in-laws. Wells shows that an essential ingredient in the Molinas' rise to preeminence in the henequén trade was their close ties with North Americans, which culminated in their role as intermediaries for International Harvester. In Salta, their few economic supports in marked decline, the notable families in the early twentieth century were steadily driven to a strategy of clientage to Standard Oil.[105]

An emphasis on the professions in the third generation is a corollary pattern to diversification often described by scholars, but explored systematically far less. In business negotiations and management, in administration of government, in the introduction and maintenance of public services, and in the delineation of cultural refinement in an era of "progress," a wide range of professions were pursued and employed by the family networks: law, medicine, engineering, business administration, accounting, education, agronomy, literature. In the studies of Marc Hoffnagel, Chandler, and Lewin on Northeast Brazil, legal training is seen as becoming almost a prerequisite for political office. Roberto C. Hernández Elizondo notes the use made in the Rivero family business in Nuevo León (Mexico) of the commercial training of three sons in London and Paris. Levi not only points out the Prado family's stress on legal training, but also the role of their educational experiences in Europe in establishing them as innovators and trendsetters in São Paulo.[106]

There was also a spatial context to diversification, and the most successful notable families understood the need to be flexible. Rio merchant-planter entrepreneurs with sufficient capital migrated to São Paulo. Pernambuco planters secured an urban base in Recife to preserve their dominance. The Terrazas network's enormous interests rested not only on their extension into almost every nook and cranny of Chihuahua, but as well in the expansion of their enterprises into other Mexican states and the national capital. In stark contrast, the Feitosas failed even to maintain their century-long domination of the Inhamuns district in Ceará (Northeast Brazil), in large part because of their spatial inflexibility. Paradoxically, as the geographical context of the interests of successful families expanded, that of their living patterns—residence, social gatherings, personal relations—generally narrowed. Oppenheimer, Levi, and Lomnitz and Pérez devote special attention to this trend.[107]

More systematic and most important as a pattern complementing the diversification of network interests was the full integration of politics into the family enterprise. Successful families turned the growing power of state and national governments to their advantage rather than succumbing to them. Numerous family members assumed political careers, while many more held public office for limited periods. In policy positions (especially legislative bodies and executive offices), they promoted and protected network interests. In bureaucratic posts, they found secure and often profitable incomes as well as grubstakes for the pursuit of private interests. Occupation of political offices also fostered connections with politicos at higher levels. As participants on officially instituted juntas, family members implemented government policies and carried on governmental functions that were closely related to the networks' interests in education, public services and improvements, and property assessments.

In the wake of a crucial provincial election, the head of the Sousa Leão family in Pernambuco described to a relative in the frankest of terms the interrelation of politics and family interests: "This struggle is not a mere conflict of personalities, but a struggle for our family's political survival. The price of our laxity would be the elimination of our family as a political force in the province."[108]

Unlike the Sousa Leãos, the Prados in São Paulo in the latter part of the third generation were "eliminated as a political force." Building

upon the pattern of the second generation, the family had increased its
political influence by the 1880s to the point where, as agricultural minister, Antonio Prado was able to use imperial government policy to assist
paulista enterpreneurs in shifting to immigrant labor—this, in addition
to the family's prominent role in provincial politics. With the institution
of the Republic, at the very time that São Paulo gained considerable influence in the national political sphere, the Prados withdrew from politics, retiring to the sidelines except at the municipal level, where they
served a number of years as mayors. Levi attributes their political decline to cultural, intellectual, and psychological factors: they could not
stomach the petty machinations and groveling compromises of the new
republican political structure of coalitions of state machines. Thus there
was little political assistance as their economic interests began to slip in
the early twentieth century.[109]

Fewer Santiago network members were directly involved in political
office in the third generation. Oppenheimer contends they withdrew in
part because it no longer seemed necessary to hold these posts. Family
alliances were firmly solidified, they already controlled the principal
corporations, and there was a government generally sympathetic to
their interests. But Oppenheimer's case is the exception. Elsewhere networks moved to control government wherever they could, through their
own personnel or clients, and through such control, to promote their familial enterprises. No one has demonstrated this more clearly and more
fully than Wasserman in his research on the Terrazas network in Chihuahua. Luis Terrazas (second generation) mastered the lessons of economics in politics and tutored the succeeding generation of children, in-
laws, and network members.[110] The network's political and economic
power became virtually synonymous:

> Terrazas' control of the state government, particularly after 1902,
> meant that every economic venture of any consequence had to have
> the family's approval; one way or another, the Terrazas had to
> receive their "payoff.". . . Everyone paid.[111]

Varied Marriage Strategy

Of the various patterns among the third generation, marriage strategy
appears to be the most varied. Here the accumulative generational effect
had perhaps its greatest impact (that is, on family size and composition,
degree of prior network interlinkage). If there is a trend apparent in the
studies to date, it points toward exogamy, in the minimum sense of outside the extended family and in the larger sense of outside the network.

In Northeast Brazil, where fundamental change had been largely absent for several generations, family strategy was centered on vertical cohesion of generations, minimizing contests for limited resources and the dispersal of family interests. But with circumstances beginning to alter considerably in the second half of the nineteenth century and in the face of powerful challenges beyond kin bounds, the emphasis on family solidarity declined: "A diversifying economy as well as an encroaching state subjected the elite parentela to more severe pressures to draw its collective expertise from the wider society."[112] Both Lewin and Levi quantitatively measure this shift to exogamous marriages in the third and fourth generations.[113]

The basis of family organization became weighted horizontally. "The rising frequency of exogamous marriage," Lewin explains, "reflected the need to recruit talented 'strangers' as resourceful brothers-in-law who could be incorporated for the greater political utility and security of the group."[114] For Pernambuco planters, that meant the incorporation of successful Recife professionals and politicos; for Salta notables, the strengthening of prior kinship bonds to networks in Tucumán and Córdoba for linkage to the national Argentine network based in Buenos Aires. The Piaggio family in Lima reached out to professionally trained fellow immigrants, who became key figures in the family enterprise. In Chihuahua, the happenstance of a large family (twelve surviving children in the third generation) was employed by Luis Terrazas to cement his leadership in the existing state capital network and to incorporate important business partners and other families whose political influence was rising.[115]

In Santiago, where the five elements who came to form the national capital network had all established themselves and begun intermarrying by the mid nineteenth century, the third generation protected the network through supportive alliances. The result was a mixed strategy, with more kin marriages and some marital ties to foreigners. The fact that economic expansion and political stability had come earlier to Chile reinforced this pattern.[116] Similar marriage strategies have been observed in Northwest Mexico and Buenos Aires, though as we have seen, historical conditions in the former were different.

Levels of Notability

A final pattern traced in monographs arises from the interrelations of the networks themselves. After two generations of progressive extension of notable family interests beyond the localities—which had been their

solid though restricted base in the colonial period—distinct levels of notability had begun to emerge. Only a few of the studies focus on networks that attained a national level of prominence and power (Oppenheimer's, Balmori's, and Wortman's). A large number concentrate on
networks or individual families at the state-provincial level, correlating
the rise of such networks and their client status vis-à-vis national regimes. Wells's and Hollander's work on the Yucatán and Salta provinces
detail this pattern clearly. Wasserman's study of Chihuahua shows considerable prerogative exercised by the Terrazas network. A number of
other studies limit themselves to local networks and families, whose notability expanded (or in the case of the Feitosa of Inhamuns, declined)
within their locality but not outside it.

Lewin proposes such a three-tiered pattern of notability in her article
on family-based kinship politics in the Brazilian northeast. A closer look
at the evidence contained in the monographs as a whole suggests a more
complex pattern. In between the three layers, one finds families (often
groups of them) whose economic interests and political connections extend beyond the level that serves as their base of operation. These extended ties give them more leeway, more prerogative, vis-à-vis the networks above them. More opportunities are open to them, and not a few
are able to move to the next level of notability. Hollander's study details
examples of just such "in-between" notable families at the provincial level in Northwest Argentina, some of whom (such as the Avellaneda and
Roca-Paz families) joined the national network in Buenos Aires. These
in-between notables also were frequently the instruments through
which higher network levels tried to expand their control downward,
eroding the autonomy of the notable networks below them. Wasserman
details this process in Chihuahua, especially after the Terrazas network
achieved full control at the state level at the turn of the century, citing in
particular the Samaniego-Ochoa family, based in the border town of
Ciudad Juárez.[117]

Though relations between state and national networks vary—from
subservience, through varying degrees of prerogative, to a few cases of
alienation—in those between the state and the localities, a common pattern through the third generation appears in the studies. Local networks, long accustomed to a considerable degree of autonomy, felt the
steadily increasing pressure of those at the state level. Lewin, Chandler,
Hoffnagel, and Wright in their studies on Northeast Brazil record the reactions of local notable families to the intensifying efforts of those at the
state level to centralize political power at their expense, stripping them
of most of their accustomed prerogatives and often restricting their eco-

nomic opportunities in the process. To counter this threat, local networks usually sided with the "outs" or new challengers at the state level, or played competing groups against one another. However, in many countries, especially by the turn of the century, state networks had firmly implanted themselves in power. In response, some local families bided their time or broke ranks to cut special deals, becoming the agents of state encroachment. Others sought alliances with other social groups or political movements to challenge what they considered undue encroachment on their prerogatives. In Chihuahua and many other states of Mexico, local notables supported (often participated in) the Revolution of 1910–20. In Salta and other Argentine provinces, they affiliated with the middle-class reform movement of the Radical party.[118]

This growing tension between the levels of notable networks was symptomatic of a general challenge after the turn of the century to the hegemony obtained by third-generation families at all levels. It became the primary public context in which the fourth generation lived and in which most struggled to maintain their position.

The Fourth Generation

Though our study focuses on three generations, there is always an epilogue to any temporally drawn boundaries. If our purpose has been to demonstrate the rise of notable family networks to preeminence in Latin American society through the course of the nineteenth century, then we must also note the decline of that hegemony, which began during the fourth generation in the early twentieth century and culminated in the profound political, economic, and social alterations resulting from the Depression of the 1930s.

The period from 1870 to 1930 is commonly seen as a whole in Latin American historiography. The export-based economies, dependent upon the world market, became widespread and reached their zenith during these six decades, and their demise came suddenly with the Great Depression. The national regimes that in most countries consolidated power in the late nineteenth century were not dislodged or significantly altered until the 1930s. The Mexican Revolution and the triumph of middle-class reform movements in Uruguay and Argentina are noteworthy exceptions to the general trend.

From another perspective, however, if the first half of the period saw the consolidation of power, wealth, and authority, then the second half (the early twentieth century) marked the initial unraveling of that export-oriented, oligarchic, imitative system. Available monographs point to the fact that notable family networks, which were at the center of that system, experienced a similar fate. If the third generation found themselves at the summit, the fourth generation felt the gathering momentum of decline.

Levi concludes that the Prados of São Paulo were representative of what he labels the "elite modernizing family," the foremost symbol and focal point of the modernizing paradox in Latin America of a postcolonial society seeking independence and development but finding, in the end, a new dependence and skewed development. The very modernizing trends that in the short run brought them preeminence and that they themselves promoted, in the long run tended to undermine the families' solidarity and their power and authority.[119]

It was during the fourth generation that the corner was turned. The very scale of economic organization, embodied in the corporation, that they had adopted to expand their interests to unprecedented scope began to outgrow the level at which family operation (in personnel and decision making) was most profitable and productive in the marketplace. Politically, the very governmental and party structures whose growth in size and organization notables had profited from through the occupation of political posts by family personnel and submissive clients began to exceed the level at which families could control them. Interest-based political organizations and increasingly impersonal bureaucratic structures presented challenges that the families found more and more difficult to dominate.[120]

This concept of promoting something that becomes too large to handle appears often in the monographs that include the fourth and fifth generations. Lewin, for example, notes that the scope of the network by the fourth generation (especially where exogamous marriage strategies had been pursued) in time began to weaken the corporate character, the solidarity of individual families and of the network as a whole. The Prado and Gómez families employed stratification to promote links with a larger network, while maintaining a level of cohesion with the family. But the class orientations becoming prevalent in society, which they adopted, increasingly separated elements of the family from one another and reciprocal obligations disintegrated. Levi infers that the Prados found that the economic scale of enterprise was becoming too large for family management and that personalistic methods in politics were no longer bringing the family more than token results. The contrasting success of the immigrant Piaggio family does not negate his argument. Their late start (a two-generation delay) meant that the scale of their family enterprises remained corporately manageable through much of the twentieth century.[121]

Because of this generation lag, Alfaro and Chueca emphasize the beneficial side of the modernizing process in economic matters for notable families. The family allowed business dealings to be kept secret, provided a pool of human resources for the firm, lessened tensions and problems in business relations, and provided a powerful mechanism for supporting and extending its enterprises. Nevertheless the Gómez family, by contrast, found themselves increasingly on the "down side" of the corporate business process. Resources (capital, technological, human) were increasingly removed from the personal circles in which the family moved. The top-heavy, centralized administration, embodied in trusted relatives, was less and less efficient and more and more out of touch with administrative and technological innovation.[122]

Wasserman points out that as politically powerful as the Terrazas network became in Chihuahua after the turn of the century, when the family enterprise began to be entrusted to the fourth generation, they were out of touch with the multiplying social and economic forces in the state. The same sense of circumstances beyond the family's firm grasp pervades Levi's analysis of the fourth generation of the Prados.[123]

A decline, however, is not a fall. Nor does a corner turned mean the end of the road. The family networks' hegemony may have disintegrated through the course of the fourth generation, but their economic interests, political influence, and social prestige persisted and were in no small part due to the strength of the familial ties that remained and the families' continued adaptability to the circumstances around them. The Terrazas network and their clients, who became such symbols and targets for Mexican revolutionaries, nevertheless retained substantial economic power and rebuilt a considerable portion of their political influence. They intermarried with important revolutionary figures, renewed business contacts with important personages in Mexico City and abroad, and penetrated some of the many political interest groups that arose during and after the Revolution, in particular, the cattleraisers' association. The Prados, who failed to transfer the base of their interests from coffee to industry before the Depression descended upon them, married into immigrant families who had concentrated in industry. Salta notables who had been seriously hurt by the series of economic misfortunes that beset the province between 1918 and 1933, and who were resentful at the strengthened position of those who had not, crossed the class boundaries of the Radical movement and gained control of the party's leadership. However, they were also quick to join forces with other notables to preserve their interests during those stormy years and even recovered much of their national influence until 1943.[124]

Notable family networks in the twentieth century no longer dominate Latin American society. They have had to scramble and manuever along with the other economic and political interest groups. But to do so they have had a long tradition of family influence from the colonial period to build upon, and the more recent memory and example of family authority and power in Latin American society at its zenith. That era, it should be remembered, is at most only two generations away. In Nicaragua, it is still measured in years.

APPENDIX

FOUNDING MEMBERS,
SOCIEDAD RURAL AND JOCKEY CLUB

Acebal, Enrique
Acebal, Juan
Acebal, Pedro
Acosta, Eliseo
Acosta, Mariano
Agüero, Lorenzo
Aguirre, M. A.
Alegre, Martín
Alegre, Pedro
Alfonzo, Mariano
Alvear, Torcuato de
Amadeo, Daniel
Amadeo, Luis
Anasagasti, Irineo
Anderson, Guillermo
Arana, Daniel
Areco, José A.
Armstrong, Thomas
Artayeta Castex, Bernabé
Balcarce, German G.
Balsa, Eudoro J.
Belgrano, Manuel
Bell, Diego
Bell, Tomas
Bemberg, Otto S.
Benítez, Apolinario
Benítez, Mariano
Biaus, Enrique

Bibolian, Agustín
Billinghurst, Mariano
Bosch, Francisco B.
Bret, Santiago
Briddger, Federico
Brown, J.
Cabral, Mariano
Cambaceres, Antonio
Campos, Luis María
Campos, Manuel J.
Cané, Miguel
Cano, Juan
Cano, Mariano
Cano, Roberto
Cárdenas, Ezequiel
Carril, Salvador María del
Carthy, Diego
Casares, Alberto
Casares, Emilio
Casares, Mariano
Casares, Sebastián
Casares, Vicente L.
Cascallares, J. Antonio
Casey, Eduardo
Casey, Lorenzo
Casey, Santiago
Castaing, Esteban
Castaño, José N.

231

Castex, Mariano
Castro, Emilio
Chapar, Pedro
Chivit, Diego
Cobo, Rafael de
Coffin, B. C.
Coffin, J. B.
Corrales, Guillermo J.
Crisol, Miguel
Davis, Carlos A.
Diaz de Bedoya, J.
Diaz Velez, Eustaquio
Diehl, Carlos
Dowling, J.
Drysdale, Thomas
Duggan, Thomas
Duhamel, Dipertal Emilio
Eastman, R.
Elía, Ezequiel
Elías, Isaias de
Elizalde, German de
Elizalde, Pedro de
Fernandez, Francisco
Fernandez, Juan M.
Fernandez, Juan N.
Frías, Estanislao
Gahan, Eugenio G.
Gahan, Santiago B.
Gahan, Tomás A.
Galindez, Lauro
Galup, Diego
Galup, Sebastián
García y Gonzalez
Garraghan, Lorenzo
Glew, Juan
Gonzalez Moreno, Remigio
Gorostiaga, José B.
Goya, Luis
Guerrico, Manuel
Güiraldes, Manuel J.
Halbach, C. I.
Hale, Samuel
Ham, Patricio
Hannah, Juan

Harrat, Enrique
Hughes, Juan
Iraola, Martin
Jurado, José M.
Justo, Agustin P.
Kemmis, Guillermo
Lanús, Anacarsis
Lanús, Juan
Lastra, Nicolás
Latham, Wilfrid
Lawrie, Santiago
Leloir, Alejandro
Leloir, Federico
Leslie, Guillermo
Lezama, Gregorio J.
Lowe, Nicolás
Luro, Pedro O.
Luro, Rufino F.
Luro, Santiago
Madero, Ernesto
Madero, Francisco B.
Malcolm, Juan
Marenco, Mariano F.
Martín, Bartolomé
Martínez, Julián
Martínez, Miguel F.
Martínez de Hoz, Federico
Martínez de Hoz, José
Martínez de Hoz, Narciso
Mattos, Manuel J.
Mendez, Tulio
Molina, Angel
Molina, Juan C.
Mouján, Calixto
Murphy, Eduardo
Nash, J. W.
Newton, Ricardo
Newton, Ricardo B.
Niera, Federico
Nougier, Emilio
Oldendorff, Ernesto
Olivera, Eduardo
Ortiz Basualdo, Alberto
Pacheco, José

Pellegrini, Carlos
Peralta, Patricio
Pereira, Leonardo
Perez Millán, Blas
Perez Millán, Patricio
Piñeiro, Ramón
Pueyrredón, Prilidiano
Quesada, Héctor G.
Quirno (Pizarro), Norberto
Ramírez, Eliseo
Ramos Mejía, Ezequiel
Ramos Mejía, Matías
Ramos Mejía, Matías
Roca, Ataliva
Roca, Jerónimo
Rodríguez, Carlos P.
Rodríguez, Esteban
Rodríguez, Marcelino
Rodríguez, Victoriano
Rouaix, Próspero
Rufino, José Felipe
Saavedra, Hilario
Saenz Valiente
Saenz Peña, Luis
Sallerno, Juan
Sanchez, Ignacio
Schang, Augusto

Senillosa, Felipe
Senillosa, Pastor
Seré, Pedro
Shaw, Alejandro
Shaw, Juan
Stegmann, Claudio
Stegmann, Jorge
Taylor, Guillermo H.
Temperley, Jorge
Terrero, Federico
Torres, Eustaquio
Trelles, Pío
Unzué, Saturnino
Urioste, Carlos
Valle, Aristóbulo del
Varela, Rufino
Vela, Agustín
Videla Dorna
Villagra, Juan M.
Villar, Nicandro
Villate, Carlos
Villarico, Manuel
Vitón, Ramón
Vivot, Bartolo
Vivot, Narciso
Zemborain, Augustín
Zoilo Miguens, José

NOTES

Introduction

1. Alan Wells, "Family Elites in a Boom-and-Bust Economy: The Molinas and Peóns of Profirian Yucatán," *Hispanic American Historical Review* (HAHR) 62 (1982):224.

2. Linda Lewin, "Some Historical Implications of Kinship Organization for Family-Based Politics in the Brazilian Northeast," *Comparative Studies in Society and History* (CSSH) 2 (1979):262–92.

3. Diana Balmori and Robert Oppenheimer, "Family Clusters: The Generational Nucleation of Families in Nineteenth-Century Argentina and Chile," *CSSH* 2 (1979):231–61.

4. In the eighteenth century, the *Diccionario de Autoridades* (Madrid, 1732) defined notable as *digno de nota, reparo, atención,* or *cuidado,* the term in current use.

5. For a succinct overview of this period's generational theories, see Julian Marías, *A Historical Method* (University, Ala.: University of Alabama Press, 1970).

6. The second generation of the family networks can also be seen as a cohort. Looking at the two general explanations for change in human behavior over time, we come up against period and cohort. Using Andrew Cherlin's work, we define the period explanations as those that refer to the consequences of events that occur during the period studied. Cohort explanations refer to the consequences in later life of the early experiences or shared characteristics of particular birth cohorts. The second generation is one that shares the early experiences of a society; later in their lives, a set of changes produced by their actions is set in motion. See Andrew Cherlin, *Marriage, Divorce, Remarriage* (Cambridge: Harvard University Press, 1978), pp. 33–44.

7. The best examination of this kind of move to gain economic and political control is Roger M. Haigh's study of the families in control of the northern Ar-

gentinian region of Salta. Their control did not differ at all from that of colonial families, except in its range, which extended to finances and the top political offices. The downfall of the Güemes clan, who through local political power attempted to direct their own financial and political matters, clearly illustrates the ultimate conflict the family network created in the emerging political structures: unclear definition of the public and private spheres. See Roger M. Haigh, *Martin Güemes: Tyrant or Tool* (Fort Worth: Texas Christian University Press, 1968).

8. In some instances alliances occurred that joined families' contiguous rural lands to create a colossal estate and joined resources for running such a place. But this was the case particularly for land and not, for example, for mercantile ventures. Some examples of the successful and unsuccessful will be cited in the case studies (chapters 2–4). Success is here narrowly interpreted to mean socioeconomic preeminence over time.

9. The dividing line between notables and non-notables had nothing to do with elites and nonelites. Such modern distinctions imply fairly sharp differentiations between those who control whatever yields wealth and the avenues of political power that assure access to it and those who do not. The notables possessed status as families woven into networks, and the families often overlapped the finer lines of "elite" criteria. Some members, branches, and even whole families did not possess the requisite "elite" control in the political and economic system, but others did. The former held high status because they possessed not only direct access to those with such control, but also the potential, through family network membership, to acquire that control themselves.

10. See, for example, the rise of the Boston Brahmin group in Peter Hall, "Marital Selection and Business in Massachusetts Merchant Families, 1700–1900," in *The Family: Its Structure and Functions*, edited by Rose Lamb Coser (New York: St. Martins Press, 1974); and the colonial merchant group in Bernard Bailyn, *The New England Merchants in the Seventeenth Century* (Cambridge: Harvard University Press, 1955).

11. See Lawrence Stone, *The Crisis of the Aristocracy* (Oxford: Oxford University Press, 1965).

12. See Elizabeth Anne Kuznesof, "Household Composition and Headship as Related to Changes in Mode of Production: São Paulo, 1765 to 1836," *CSSH* 22 (1980):79–109, "The Role of the Female-Headed Household in Brazilian Modernization: São Paulo, 1765 to 1836," *Journal of Social History* 13 (1980):589–613; Donald Ramos, "City and Country: The Family in Minas Gerais, 1804–1838," *Journal of Family History* 3 (1978):361–75, "Marriage and the Family in Colonial Vila Rica," *HAHR* 55 (1975):200–225.

13. Examples of these regional studies of prominent colonial families include Louisa Schell Hoberman, "Merchants in Seventeenth-Century Mexico City: A Preliminary Portrait," *HAHR* 57 (1977):479–503; Stephanie Blank, "Patrons, Clients, and Kin in Seventeenth-Century Caracas: A Methodological Essay in Colonial Spanish American Social History," *HAHR* 54 (1974):260–83; Peter Marzahl, "Creoles and Government: The Cabildo of Popayán," *HAHR* 54

(1974):636–56; Ann Twinam, "Enterprise and Elites in Eighteenth-Century Medellín," *HAHR* 59 (1979):444–75.

14. Linda Lewin's study of Northeast Brazil cited above is the only other family study to date that has such breadth of coverage and scope.

Chapter One

1. Darrell E. Levi, "The Prados of São Paulo: An Elite Brazilian Family in a Changing Society, 1840–1920" (Ph.D. diss., Yale University, 1974). The particular examples of the Serna-González and Iñigo families can be found in chapter 3.

2. The problem in drawing conclusions about the nature and chronological dating of these network alliances is that most available studies do not comprehensively deal with marriage patterns. Those that do rarely extend over three generations. First-generation marriage alliances were of great importance in the formation of the network that became centered around the Aycinenas in Guatemala, as those in the third generation were in the consolidation of the state network in Chihuahua under the Terrazas. See Mark Wasserman, "Capitalists and Caciques: Elite and Foreign Enterprise in Chihuahua, Mexico, 1821–1911" (Manuscript).

3. Albert Stagg, *The Almadas and Álamos, 1783–1867*. (Tucson: University of Arizona Press, 1978), pp. 8–9; Wasserman, "Capitalists and Caciques," pp. 36–45.

4. See Balmori and Oppenheimer, "Family Clusters," p. 241.

5. See the numerous regional studies on Brazil discussed in chapter 5.

6. André Bourgiére, Introduction to *Family and Society*, edited by Robert Forster and Orest Ranum (Baltimore: Johns Hopkins University Press), p. vii.

7. See, for example, Blank, "Patrons, Clients, and Kin."

8. Mary Lowenthal Felstiner, "Kinship Politics in the Chilean Independence Movement," *HAHR* 56 (1976):58–80; Jacques Barbier, "Elites and Cadres in Bourbon Chile," *HAHR* 52 (1972):416–35.

9. Leon Campbell discusses how the Visitador Gálvez and other officials accepted the complicity of creoles in the Tupac Amaru affair ("A Colonial Establishment: Creole Domination of the Audiencia of Lima during the Late Eighteenth Century," *HAHR* 52 [1972]:17).

10. See ibid., pp. 9–10, for a discussion of the amounts candidates for audiencia positions donated to the crown. These sums were as high as 30,000 pesos.

11. The discarding of traditional obligations by the notables is detailed in Edith B. Couturier's "Hacienda of Hueyapán: The History of a Mexican Social and Economic Institution, 1550–1940" (Ph.D. diss., Columbia University, 1965), pp. 188–231; and is vividly illustrated in the novels of Mariano Azuela, *Los Caciques* (Mexico City, 1917), and Jorge Icaza, *Huasipungo* (Quito, 1934).

Chapter Two

1. Miles L. Wortman, *Government and Society in Central America, 1680–1840* (New York: Columbia University Press, 1982). For a discussion of the "rags-

to-rags" generalization see Lesley Byrd Simpson, *Many Mexicos* 3d ed. (Berkeley: University of California Press, 1957), p. 232.

2. See Wortman, *Government and Society in Central America.*

3. Antonio Vázquez de Espinosa, *Compendium and Description of the West Indies* (Washington, D.C.: Smithsonian Institution, 1942), pp. 573, 607, 655, 692, 702, 713, 740, 755; Murdo J. MacLeod, *Spanish Central America: A Socioeconomic History* (Berkeley: University of California Press, 1973), p. 218; A.G.I. Guatemala 156, Bishop Fr. Juan de Zapata, 6/5/1623; Christopher Lutz, "Santiago de Guatemala, 1541–1773: The Socio-Demographic History of a Spanish American Colonial City" (Ph.D. diss., University of Wisconsin, 1976), pp. 516–20.

4. William L. Sherman, *Forced Native Labor in Sixteenth-Century America* (Lincoln: University of Nebraska Press, 1979); MacLeod, *Spanish Central America;* Lutz, "Santiago de Guatemala."

5. Testaments of Josepha Inez de Asperilla and of Juana de Osegueza, A.G.G. Al.20 Leg. 486, pp. 202–7ff.

6. Wortman, *Government and Society,* pp. 111–84.

7. Ibid.

8. Arthur M. Wilson, "The Logwood Trade in the Seventeenth and Eighteenth Centuries," in *Essays in the History of Modern Europe,* ed. Donald C. McKay, (Freeport, N.Y.: Books for Libraries Press, 1968), pp. 1–15; Susan Fairlie, "Dyestuffs in the Eighteenth Century," *Economic History Review,* 2d ser., 17 (1965):488–510; Wortman, *Government and Society,* pp. 89–90, 304; Troy Floyd, *The Anglo-Spanish Struggle for Mosquitia* (Albuquerque: University of New Mexico Press, 1967), pp. 55–61.

9. Testimonio de los autos formados sobre que en el puerto de San Fernando de Omoa . . . se cobre el Impuesto de 4 pesos por cada Zurrón de Anil, A.G.I. Guatemala 235; Petitions to build and run a vessel between Guatemala and Cádiz, A.G.I. Guatemala 540, 12/5/1758 and 1763.

10. Wortman, *Government and Society,* pp. 111–129.

11. Ibid, pp. 129–56.

12. Extracto autorisado en competente forma de las justificaciones de calidad y descendencia de los Vidaurres, Minas y Carriones, A.G.I. Guatemala 923.

13. Ibid.

14. Records of the Cabildo of Guatemala 9/30/1739 in Archivo General de Guatemala and A.G.I. Contaduría 976, Cuenta of 1725, Guatemala 342; Estado de los empleos provistos en individuos pertenecientes a ramificaciones de una familia, A.G.I. Guatemala 530.

15. Troy Floyd, "The Guatemalan Merchants, the Government, and the Provincianos, 1750–1800," *HAHR* 41 (1965):90–110, and "The Indigo Merchant: Promoter of Central American Economic Development, 1750–1808," *Business History Review* (1965):348. For Gaspar Juarros, see A.G.I. Contratación 2605.

16. Contratación 1595, A.G.I. 1595; A.G.I. Guatemala 745; Troy Floyd, "The Guatemalan Merchants"; Ramón Salazar, *Mariano de Aycinena* (Guatemala: Biblioteca de Cultural Popular, 1952); Edgar Juan Aparicio y Aparicio,

Conquistadores de Guatemala y fundadores de familias Guatemaltecas, 2d ed. (Mexico, 1961), p. 51.

17. The published material on the Aycinenas is mired in political rhetoric because of the close connection between the family and the Guatemalan Conservative party. Ramón Salazar's work, *Mariano de Aycinena*, is a liberal attack to which Edwin Enrique del Cid Fernández responded in his four-volume *Origen histórico de la casa y marquesado de Aycinena* (Guatemala: privately published, 1969). Also see Floyd, "The Guatemalan Merchants," pp. 97–98, and "The Indigo Merchant," pp. 90–110; Letters from Mariano Aycinena, in *La anexión de Centro América a México*, comp. Rafael Heliodoro Valle (Mexico: Secretariá de Relaciones Exteriores, 1924–49), 3:235, 4:131–33; Aparicio y Aparicio, *Conquistadores*, p. 20.

18. The literature on Romero de Terreros is voluminous. Most recently, see the research accomplished by Couturier in "Hacienda of Hueyapán." Also see Doris Ladd, *The Mexican Nobility at Independence, 1780–1826* (Austin: University of Texas, 1976), and David Brading, *Miners and Merchants in Bourbon Mexico, 1763–1810* (Cambridge: Cambridge University Press, 1971). For Chile see Alberto Edwards, *La fronda aristocrática* (Santiago, 1928).

19. Germán Colmenares, *Cali: Terratenientes, mineros y comerciantes, siglo xviii* (Cali: La Universidad Aurónoma de Cali 1975), and *Historia económica y social de Colombia* (Cali, 1971). For São Paulo, see the works of Elizabeth Anne Kuznesof, in particular, "Clans, the Militia, and Territorial Government: The Articulation of Kinship with Polity in Eighteenth-Century São Paulo," in *Social Fabric and Spatial Structure in Colonial Latin America*, ed. David Robinson, (Syracuse: University Microfilms International, 1979). For New Spain, see Ladd, *The Mexican Nobility*, and for Buenos Aires, Susan Migden Socolow, *The Merchants of Buenos Aires, 1778–1810: Family and Commerce* (Cambridge: Cambridge University Press, 1978).

20. Edgar Juan Aparicio y Aparicio, "Datos genealógicos de los trece próceres que firmaron el Acta de la Independencia de Centroamérica en 1821," *Revista de la Academia Guatemalteca de Estudios Genealógicos Heráldicos y Históricos* 12 (1973):12–13.

21. Salazar, *Mariano de Aycinena*, Cid Fernandez, *Origen histórico;* Wortman, *Government and Society.*

22. For a partial summation of Aycinena wealth, see "Consulta de la cámara de las Indias 10 de febrero de 1783," in *Colección de documentos para la historia de la formación social de Hispanoamerica*, ed. Richard Konetzke (Madrid: Consejo Superior de Investigaciones Científicas, 1962), 3:502–06. Also see slave contracts in A.G.I. Guatemala 745.

23. Wortman, *Government and Society*, pp. 158–62; The implications of the controversy are carefully outlined by an eighty-five-year-old prelate: See Pedro Martínez de Molina 9/17/1773, A.G.I. Guatemala 661.

24. Ralph Lee Woodward, Jr., "Economic and Social Origins of the Guatemalan Political Parties, 1773–1823," *HAHR* 45 (November 1965):544–66; Proyecto . . . para la traslación de la capital, A.G.I. Indiferente General 1747. See in

Guatemala 561, año de 1778: Sobre . . . averiguar el producto de los Reales No-
venos; Real Cédula, 7/18/1778; President of Guatemala, 8/25/1778; El Fiscal del
Consejo de Indias, 11/21/1778.

25. Governor of Comayagua, 10/16/1774, A.G.I. Guatemala 450; Intendant
of Comayagua, 4/20/1795, Guatemala 919; President of Guatemala, 7/8/1776,
Guatemala 450.

26. For the plans of the Aycinena house see Mapas y Planos, A.G.I. Guatemala 243; "Consulta de la cámara de las Indias 10 de febrero de 1783," in Konetzke,
Colección 3:502–6.

27. Testimonio de los autos, sobre si devera pagar alcavala de las haciendas
nombradas la Concepción y Sn Juan de Vista que Dn Juan de Taranco ha cedido
al Sr. Marquesa de Aycinena, A.G.I. Guatemala 573, año de 1785, fols. 1–6,
53–57.

28. Estado de los empleos provistos en individuos pertenecientes a ramificaciones de una familia (3 Octubre de 1820), A.G.I. Guatemala 530. This document was reprinted soon after in the loyalist, conservative newspaper *El Amigo
de la Patria* and was reprinted again in the liberal diatribe of Ramón Salazar,
Mariano de Aycinena.

29. For the judicial proceedings against the Aycinenas see Testimonio . . . a
representación del Sr. Marques de Aycinena sobre no pagar mas derechos . . . ,
A.G.I. Guatemala 673, año de 1814; A.G.G. A1.5.5 Leg. 51, Exp. 1273, fol. 18;
Salazar, *Mariano de Aycinena*, pp. 57–62.

30. See the petitions of Juan Fermín de Aycinena, 1/12/1819, and Gregorio
Castriones and the "Sociedad Urruela y Barreda," 1/16/1818, A.G.I. Guatemala
679.

31. See the diverse correspondence between Mariano Aycinena and Agustín
Iturbide in Valle, *La anexión de Centro América a Mexico*, 2:45–47, 142–44,
212; 3:112, 197. Also see Vicente Filisola, *La cooperación de México en la independencia de Centro América* (Mexico: Librería de la Vda. de Ch. Bouret,
1911), 2:31.

32. Wortman, *Government and Society*, pp. 240–46.

33. George Thompson, *Narrative of an Official Visit to Guatemala* (London:
John Murray, 1829), p. 191.

34. Wortman, *Government and Society*, p. 250. The liberal view of the period
is detailed in a contemporary account, Alejandro Marure, *Bosquejo histórico de
las revoluciones de Centro-América* (Guatemala: Tipografía de "El Progreso,"
1877–78); the conservative response came in Manuel Montúfar *Memorias para la
historia de la revolución de Centro América* (Jalapa: Aburto y Blanco, 1832).

35. Ralph Lee Woodward, Jr., "Social Revolution in Guatemala: The Carrera
Revolt." *Applied Enlightenment: Nineteenth-Century Liberalism*, Middle
American Research Institute Publication no. 23 (New Orleans: Tulane University, 1972), pp. 45–70. See *Guía de forasteros de Guatemala para el año 1853*, pp.
21, 80; Lorenzo Montúfar, *Reseña historia de Centro-América*, (Guatemala:
Tip. de "El Progreso," 1878–79), vols. 4, 5; *Libro azul de Guatemala* (Guatemala, 1915), p. 219.

36. The alcalde ordinario of San Salvador, representing the entrenched families, was Joseph Arce, the ancestor of Manuel Arce, one of the primary figures in the independence and federation period. Testimonio de las Diligencias practicadas sobre el nombramiento echo de Thenientes de la Provincia de Sn Salvador, San Miguel y Villa de Sn Vicente de Austria, A.G.I. Guatemala 242, año de 1758; Joseph de Pinedo, 7/22/1752, A.G.I. Guatemala 246.

37. See William V. Wells description of the Zelaya family in *Explorations and Adventures in Honduras* (London: Sampson, Low, 1857), pp. 271–89.

38. Edgar Juan Aparicio y Aparicio, *Conquistadores*, p. 20; Testimonio de los autos sobre la erección de la compañía que se quiere establecer en esta ciudad para el beneficio de Minas y Saca de frutos del reino, A.G.I. Guatemala 232, año de 1744; *Breve Muestra de las Muchas Utilidades que puede producir . . . una compañía que se podrá establecer* (Guatemala ?, 1741).

39. Relación de contribuyentes y contribuciones, que nosotros los dos comisionados por la Junta de Comercio . . . , A.G.G. A3.6 Leg. 1012, Exp. 18613; A.G.G. A1.2 Leg. 2189, Exp. 15,737, fol. 152.

40. Aparicio y Aparicio, *Familias Guatemaltecas*, pp. 49–50.

41. *Revista de la Academia Guatemalteca de Estudios Genealógicos Heráldicos y Históricos* 1 (1967):18–25.

42. Aparicio y Aparicio, *Conquistadores*, pp. 26, 33–34.

43. Relación de contribuyentes . . . , A.G.G. A3.6 Leg. 1012, Exp. 18613.

44. A.G.I. Contratación 1595, 2498, 2598, 2599, 2605, 2607, 2612; Guatemala 880; Aparicio y Aparicio, *Familias Guatemaltecas*, pp. 55–56.

45. Estado de los empleos provistos en individuos pertenecientes a ramificaciones de una familia, A.G.I. Guatemala 530, fol. 3.

Chapter Three

1. "Northwest" is used not in a purely geographical sense. It is an attempt to define a historical space, a given geographical area that has had a common, distinctive experience over a significant period of time. The area comprising the present-day states of Sonora and Sinaloa forms the core of this historical region.

2. For a similar conception of the central role of such families in society, see Felstiner, "Kinship Politics in the Chilean Independence Movement," pp. 58–80. It was a vision of "progress," for want of a better word: progress without "positivistic" capitalization, a sense of steady improvement and growing refinement.

3. Linda Lewin discusses a shift in marriage strategy among notables of Northeast Brazil in the late nineteenth century in response to changing conditions in "Historical Implications of Kinship Organization," pp. 262–92.

4. Stuart F. Voss, *On the Periphery of Nineteenth-Century Mexico: Sonora and Sinaloa, 1810–1877* (Tucson: University of Arizona Press, 1982), pp. 1–17.

5. Ibid., pp. 19–24, 27–29.

6. This struggle for power between newcomers and an existing colonial establishment at the end of the colonial period has been well-illustrated in Felstiner's "Kinship Politics."

7. Donald Ramos, in two studies of Minas Gerais (Central Brazil), has quantitatively demonstrated the limited extent of the patriarchal extended family,
commonly thought to be the dominant form of family organization: see "Marriage and the Family," pp. 200–225, and "City and Country," pp. 361–75.

8. Leonard Kasdan, "Family Sructure, Migration, and the Entrepreneur," in
Entrepreneurship and Economic Development, ed. Peter Kilby (New York: Free
Press, 1971), pp. 225–39.

9. Voss, *Periphery of Mexico*, pp. 27–29. Though agriculture developed along
the river valley in which Arizpe was located, that town's main stimulous was its
designation as administrative center for the region in 1776.

10. Francisco R. Almada, *Diccionario de historia, geografía y biografía son-
orenses* (Chihuahua, 1952), gives examples of those children sent away to school,
as well as an account of the first schools in the region.

11. For example, Lieutenant R. W. H. Hardy wrote in his journal that his
host had the appearance of an English squire (*Travels in the Interior of Mexico,
1825–1828* [London, 1829], p. 109).

12. The various schema for delineating colonial society are discussed in a series of articles in *Comparative Studies in Society and History:* John K. Chance
and William B. Taylor, "Estate and Class in a Colonial City: Oaxaca in 1792,"
19, no. 3 (1977):454–86; Robert McCaa, Arturo Grubessich, and Stuart B.
Schwartz, "Race and Class in Colonial Latin America: A Critique," 21, no. 3
(1979):421–33; Chance and Taylor, "Estate and Class: A Reply," ibid, pp. 434–
42.

13. The Aguilar brothers (Victores and Dionisio) illustrate the general pattern. Each married into separate families, and among their children, there was
only one marriage of paternal cousins, and none to their wives' families. See *Informaciones Matrimoniales, 1799–1894*, compiled from the Archivo Histórico
de la Catedral de Hermosillo by the Biblioteca y Museo de Sonora (San Miguel,
1809; Rayón, 1837); *Archivo General del Estado de Sonora, Juzgado Civil, Matrimoniales*, book 3 (Guaymas, 1873), p. 61; Fernando Galaz, *Dejaron huella en
el Hermosillo de ayer y hoy* (Mexico: A. Mijares and Brother, 1971), pp. 222–23.

14. Albert Stagg, *The First Bishop of Sonora: Antonio de los Reyes, O.F.M.*
(Tucson: University of Arizona Press, 1976), pp. 61–95, and *The Almadas and
Álamos*, pp. 22–25; Almada, *Diccionario*, pp. 239, 638–39, 710–11, 810–11. De
los Reyes had known the region as a Franciscan missionary between 1768 and
1772. Salido a few years later was appointed subdelegado for that district in the
new intendancy system. He and his nieces' father had both married daughters of
the Elías González family founder. A third daughter married into another presi-
dio family, the Urreas, while a fourth became the bride of peninsular Juan Leo-
cadio de Palomares.

15. Stagg, *Almadas and Alamos*, pp. 4–6, *First Bishop of Sonora*, pp. 74–75;
Carlota Miles, *Almada of Álamos: The Diary of Don Bartolomé* (Tucson: University of Arizona Press, 1962), pp. 3–10.

16. Voss, *Periphery of Mexico*, pp. 35–38.

17. Miguel Domínguez, *La guerra independencia en las provincias Sonora y Sinaloa* (Hermosillo, 1949), pp. 14–28; Robert C. Stevens, "Mexico's Forgotten Frontier: A History of Sonora, 1821–1846" (Ph.D. diss., University of California, 1963), pp. viii–xiii. The one real emancipation movement came from without, an insurgent expedition sent by Father Hidalgo in the winter of 1810–11 that was decisively defeated in southern Sinaloa. The emerging notable families seem to have taken their status as imperial subjects with little questioning. Under the Bourbons they had been able to prosper. The strong peninsular component among them only reinforced these ties. They felt neither the fear of groups beneath them in the social order nor the frustration of long-standing restrictions to turn them toward separation from an imperial realm. Independence came to them in 1821 as an external fact of their existence that they had no choice but to accept.

18. Voss, *Periphery of Mexico*, pp. 37–43.

19. Ibid, pp. 43–44.

20. Galaz, *Hermosillo*, pp. 40–128 passim, 265–66; Almada, *Diccionario*, pp. 21, 202, 288, 405; *Matrimoniales, AES-JC*, book 3 (Guaymas, 1874), p. 75; Hardy, *Travels*, p. 110.

21. Almada, *Diccionario*, 239–43. Simón, Ignacio, and José María Elías González attained the highest ranks in the presidial system. José María and Simón also served as commanders general, state legislators, and deputies to Congress after independence. Simón, in addition, became a governor. Another brother, Juan José, parish priest of Arizpe, also served as a state legislator. A fifth brother, Rafael, became one of the largest hacendados of northeast Sonora by the 1830s and held local, district, and state political posts.

22. Stagg, *Almada and Álamos*, pp. 19–40, 47–49, 60–62, 65–67. José María's most important mining acquisition, the La Quintera mine in 1830, he offered to exploit jointly with his brothers, two of whom accepted.

23. Felstiner, "Kinship Politics," pp. 78–80.

24. The foreign merchants too wanted autonomy to pursue their trade, though their interests extended far beyond the confines of the port's coastal district. For a detailed account of Occidente politics, see Stevens, "Forgotten Frontier," 67–98.

25. Galaz's selection of notarial archives provides abundant examples for Hermosillo during this period.

26. Wrote one exasperated notable in the mid 1830s: "I have heard persons very close to the government [in Mexico City] speak with more ignorance of Sonora than when speaking of Tunkin or Bidedulgerid" (Ignacio Zúñiga, *Rápida ojeada al Estado de Sonora* . . . [Mexico, D.F., 1948], p. 34. Zúñiga's work was originally published in Mexico City in 1835).

27. For a detailed account of this struggle to find security and beneficial extra-local connections, see Voss, *Periphery of Mexico*, chapters 3–6. Only in central

and southern Sinaloa were insecurities resulting from the tribal Indians not present.

28. The geographical surveys of José Agustín de Escudero, *Noticias estadísticas de Sonora y Sinaloa* (Mexico, D.F., 1849), of Francisco Velasco, *Noticias estadísticas del Estado de Sonora* (Mexico, D.F., 1850), and of John Russell Bartlett, *Personal Narratives of Explorations and Incidents in Texas, New Mexico, California, Sonora, and Chihuahua* (London, 1854) are the best sources for this commercial pattern.

29. Galaz, *Hermosillo*, pp. 123–347 passim. Guillermo Beato, in a paper delivered at the Sixth Conference of Mexican and United States Historians, Chicago, September 1981, "La formación (y las relaciones familiares) de la burguesia de Jalisco," has demonstrated a similar pattern in Central Mexico, and provides a survey of the changes in economic activity through the nineteenth century.

30. Galaz, *Hermosillo*, pp. 110–332 passim, 750; Almada, *Diccionario*, p. 405; Captain Guillet, "Las notas sobre Sonora del Captain Guillet, 1864–1866," trans. Ernesto de la Torre Villar, *YAN—Ciencias Antropológicas*, no. 1 (Mexico, D.F., 1953), p. 57.

31. See *La Estrella de Occidente* (Ures), 25 December 1863, in the microfilm collection of the Instituto Nacional de Antropología y Historia, Museo de Historia y Antropología, Mexico City (hereafter abbreviated as MAHm), Sonora, reel 13. One of the early partnerships was that between Hermosillo merchant entrepreneurs Agustín Muñoz, his father-in-law, Manuel Calles, and the French immigrant Juan Camou in the mid 1830s. Galaz, *Hermosillo*, p. 188.

32. Galaz, *Hermosillo*, pp. 222–23.

33. Ibid., pp. 294, 332–33. A decade later, at González's death, his wife (Carmen Serna) married the son of Manuel María Gándara (Iñigo's close political associate), and a few years thereafter González's daughter married another Gándara.

34. Hardy, *Travels*, p. 439; Escudero, *Noticias*, p. 40.

35. Almada, *Diccionario*, pp. 241, 244–46, 710–11; Alfredo Ibarra, *Sinaloa en la cultura de Mexico* (Mexico, D.F.: Editorial Hidalgo, 1944), pp. 95, 157–158.

36. Almada, *Diccionario*, pp. 806–10; Horacio Sobarzo, *Crónicas biográficas* (Hermosillo, 1949), pp. 63–68; Zúñiga, *Rapida ojeada*, pp. 51–55. For details on the military necessities arising from the circumstances of the first half century of independence, see Voss, *Periphery of Mexico*, chaps. 2–5.

37. Almada, *Diccionario*, pp. 483–84. The first efforts to establish primary schools (both public, financed by the municipios, and private) were led by the notables in the transition between the first and second generations.

38. Amado González Dávila, *Diccionario geográfico, histórico, y estadístico del Estado de Sinaloa* (Culiacán, 1959), pp. 561–62; Ibarra, *Sinaloa*, p. 81. With mining limited and commerce concentrated in Culiacán and Mazatlán, the majority studied law and letters. Among the most accomplished were Eustaquio

Buelna, Ángel Urrea, Jesús M. Gaxiola, Luis and Francisco J. del Castillo Negrete, and José C. Valadés.

39. Frank Safford, "Social Aspects of Politics in Nineteenth-Century Spanish America: New Granada, 1825–1850," *Journal of Social History* 5, no. 3 (Spring 1972):351–55; Frederick P. Bowser and Margaret Chowning, "Socio-Economic Power and Political Change in Mexico: the Case of Michoacán" (Paper delivered at the Sixth Conference of Mexican and United States Historians, Chicago, September 1981), p. 15.

40. Safford, "Social Aspects of Politics," pp. 365–67.

41. Manuel Corbalá Acuña, *Sonora y sus constituciones* (Hermosillo: Editorial Libros de Mexico, 1972), pp. 29–82; Galaz, *Hermosillo*, pp. 61–323 passim. In Hermosillo (Sonora's largest, most prosperous urban center by mid century), these three offices were dominated by the principal merchant-hacendados of the late arrivals of the first generation; thereafter, the offices were increasingly held by their sons and in-laws (many of whom were aspiring newcomers).

42. For details on these struggles over the location of the state capital, see Voss, *Periphery of Mexico*, chaps. 2–8.

43. Principal sources for these examples include: Almada, *Diccionario; Informaciones Matrimoniales, ACH; Matrimoniales, AES-JC;* and Galaz, *Hermosillo.*

44. González Dávila, *Diccionario*, pp. 64–65. A lack of adequate transportation, capital, and defined export markets restricted agricultural production around the small district towns to the local market. The once prosperous mining centers of Cosalá and Rosario were in decline, beset by the same discouraging conditions confronting that sector most everywhere else in the country.

45. Almada, *Diccionario*, p. 740; *La Voz del Estado* (Magdalena), March 1889, MAHm, Sonora, reel 9; Galaz, *Hermosillo*, pp. 353, 594. Both Dionisio González (an Opata Indian) and Pedro de la Serna (no sources consulted reveal his origins) had built up considerable fortunes from mining on the frontier in Altar district before Apache raids began devastating the area.

46. *Matrimoniales, AES-JC,* book 3 (Guaymas, 1874), p. 75, and act 47 (Hermosillo, 1867), p. 36; Max L. Moorehead, "The Birth and Death of a Legend: The Johnson 'Massacre' of 1837," *Arizona and the West* 18 (Autumn 1976): 283–85.

47. *El Sinaloense* (Culiacán), 5 November 1847, MAHm, Sinaloa, reel 4; Eustaquio Buelna, *Apuntes para la historia de Sinaloa, 1821–1882* (Mexico: Departmento Editorial de la Secretaría de Educación, 1924), pp. 16–35.

48. Galaz, *Hermosillo*, pp. 265–66; *Matrimoniales, AES-JC,* book 3 (Guaymas, 1876), p. 19.

49. The most successful of these joint enterprises was the firm of Manuel Iñigo and Company. It joined Manuel, his brother Pascual, their nephew Fernando Cubillas, Francisco A. Aguilar, and Encarnación Gándara (sister of Aguilar's brother-in-law, Manuel María Gándara).

50. The composite of this family network was drawn from a variety of sources, principal among them: Almada, *Diccionario; Informaciones Matrimoniales, ACH; Matrimoniales, AES-JC;* Galaz, *Hermosillo,* and Corbalá Acuña, *Constituciones.*

51. Almada, *Diccionario,* pp. 575–83; *La Voz de Sonora* (Ures), 23, 30 July, 13 August, 1 October 1851, MAHm, Sonora, reel 3; Rodolfo Acuña, *Sonoran Strongman: Ignacio Pesqueira and His Times* (Tucson: University of Arizona Press, 1974), pp. 14–15. After a decade of militia service, Pesqueira's leadership in a skirmish with the Apaches in 1851 launched him on a dramatic rise to state political power through a series of increasingly important military and political offices, culminating in the governorship in 1857. He held that post for the next eighteen years. The frontier he had guarded as an amateur soldier was also the locale for a growing number of enterprises including a hacienda specializing in tobacco cultivation, a marketing trade in that crop under state contract, and important mining properties.

Joaquín Corella, who along with two brothers was an important frontier militia officer, was also Pesqueira's brother-in-law. Other important amateur military officers from the second generation were Francisco Serna, Victoriano Ortiz, Cayetano Navarro, and Francisco de la Vega. See Juan Antonio Ruibal Corella, *Perfiles de un patriota* (Mexico, D.F.: Editorial Porrua, 1979), pp. 16–17; Almada, *Diccionario,* pp. 188–89, 501, 543, 740; González Dávila, *Diccionario,* p. 651.

52. The progression of these political events in Sonora is detailed in Voss, *Periphery of Mexico,* chaps. 3–5, 7–9.

53. The principal sources for this portrait of the Vega network are *El Sinaloense* (Culiacán), 5 November 1847, MAHm, Sinaloa, reel 4; González Dávila, *Diccionario,* pp. 645–51; and Buelna, *Apuntes,* pp. 16–190. The political struggle during this half century is traced in Voss, *Periphery of Mexico,* chaps. 3–5, 7–8. The Vega founder, like the founder of the Iñigo's, gravitated toward San Miguel de Horcasitas when it was capital of the province and an important presidial community (1748–76). His children married into the leading families there, and then most, along with their parents, had moved south into Sinaloa, one branch stopping in Fuerte, the rest settling in Culiacán, acquiring lands and building a prosperous commerce.

54. A kind of generational lag was experienced, especially by those in the smaller communities. Such families had to wait until the third generation for the level of notability achieved by the more successful families in the second. Moreover, they were generally precluded from meeting the new standards of notability in the third generation unless they could incorporate themselves into those successful families.

55. The best survey of political developments during the Porfiriato is that of Daniel Cosío Villegas, *Historia moderna de Mexico,* vols. 8 and 9: *El Porfiriato, La vida política interior* (Mexico, D.F.: Editorial Porrua, 1970–72). In addition, in-depth regional studies of the period are now reaching publication stage, such

as those of Mark Wasserman on Chihuahua and Allen Wells on the Yucatán. The Díaz Archives reveal the nature and process of the centralization of power that took place in Mexico during the late nineteenth century.

56. Stuart F. Voss, "Towns and Enterprise in Northwestern Mexico: A History of Urban Elites in Sonora and Sinaloa, 1830–1810," (Ph.D. diss., Harvard University, 1972), chaps. 7–9. In 1900, Sonora had the largest contingent of "public forces" among the states, and in 1910 it had nearly twice the number of federal armed forces as any other state. Dirección General de Estadística, Ministerio de Fomento, *Resumen General del Censo de la República Mexicana, 1900* (Mexico, D.F., 1905), pp. 57, 61; Dirección General de Estadística, Secretaría de Agricultura y Fomento, *Tercer Censo de Población de los Estados Unidos Mexicanos* (Mexico, D.F., 1918), 2:60–65.

57. *Tercer Censo* 1:9–13; 2:60–65; United States Department of State, *Report on the Commercial Relations of the United States with All Foreign Nations* (Washington, 1902), 2:501–3. By 1910 Sonora had a greater percentage of foreign residents than any other state and ranked second in cumulative numbers. In the first years of the twentieth century, North American investments in mining were greater in Sonora than in any other state, while Sinaloa led in North American manufactures. In total United States investment, Sonora ranked third and Sinaloa seventh. Also by 1910, internal migrants made up one-tenth of Sonora's population and four percent of Sinaloa's.

58. Secretaría de Fomento, Colonización y Industria, *Anales de Ministerio de Fomento de la República Mexicana* (México, D.F., 1881), 5:85; *Tercer Censo* 1:9–13.

59. A detailed summary of the fortunes of the various towns and districts is in Voss, "Towns and Enterprise," chaps. 8–13.

60. Galaz, *Hermosillo*, 352–69. Maximiliano López Portillo, of the notable network based in Rosario (some of whose family members had moved to Culiacán), in 1910 sold a mine in the district of Mazatlán to a North American company for 200,000 pesos. López Portillo remained head of the company store (*Diario del Pacifico* (Mazatlán), 4 June 1910).

61. See newspapers for the period and commercial directories, in particular: John R. Southworth, *El Estado de Sonora: sus industrias, comerciales, mineras y manufacturas* (Nogales, Arizona, 1897), and *El Estado de Sinaloa: sus industrias, comerciales, mineras y manufacturas* (San Francisco, 1898); Federico García y Alva, *Album directorio del Estado de Sonora* (Hermosillo, 1905–7). Arturo Aviles worked his way up to the position of manager of a French commercial house in Guaymas. Ricardo Díaz, with the accumulated capital and knowledge of the trade from clerking for various of that port's principal mercantile firms, established his own commercial business in Hermosillo (Southworth, *Sonora*, pp. 32, 43).

62. Southworth, *Sinaloa*, pp. 38, 40.

63. The best readily available sources revealing the growth of municipal revenues in the region are the *Cuentas del Erario* published by the Sonoran govern-

ment, and the *Presupuestos municipales de ingresos y egresos del Distrito de Mazatlán, 1900–1913* (Mazatlán, 1899–1912).

64. For example Captain L. S. Mix, trained in New York as a contractor,
planned and supervised the construction of many important buildings in Sonora,
including the state capitol and the municipal building in Álamos (Southworth,
Sonora, p. 60).

65. Southworth, *Sinaloa*, pp. 84–86; Luis Zúñiga Sánchez, *Apuntes para la
historia de Mazatlán* (Mazatlán, n.d.), pp. 25–28; *El Estado de Sinaloa*, 3 October 1893; Francisco Cañedo, *Memoria del Estado de Sinaloa, 1895* (Culiacán,
1896), p. 13.

66. Southworth, *Sinaloa*, pp. 43–47; *El Estado de Sinaloa*, 26 October 1878,
13 July 1888, 4 April 1898; Cañedo, *Memoria*, pp. 14, 357.

67. Southworth, *Sinaloa*, pp. 84–86.

68. Ignacio Pesqueira's son, Ramón, pursued commercial studies in Los Angeles, and upon his return was put in charge of bookkeeping for the family's principal agricultural holdings (Ruibal Corella, *Perfiles*, p. 204).

69. Hector Aguilar Camín, *La frontera nomada: Sonora y la Revolución Mexicana* (México, D.F.: Siglo Veintiuno Editores, 1977), p. 42; García y Alva, *Album;* Southworth, *Sonora*, p. 41. Almada became one of Álamos's principal
merchants, with agencies for a bank headquartered in neighboring Chihuahua
and for a large sugar refinery across the border in Sinaloa.

70. Among the wide variety of sources reflecting this increased activity of the
municipios are Corbalá Acuña, *Sonora y sus constituciones* (Hermosillo, 1972),
and the *Cuentas del Erario.*

71. Municipal election results for these years can be found in the official newspaper *El Estado de Sinaloa* and the *Archivo del Estado de Sonora* (AES), under
the section entitled "Elecciones" for each year.

72. Almada, *Diccionario*, p. 541; Southworth, *Sonora*, pp. 28–29.

73. González Dávila, *Diccionario*, 232; *El Estado de Sinaloa*, 10 October
1888, 10 March 1889; Southworth, *Sinaloa*, p. 39; Hector R. Olea, *Bréve historia de la Revolución en Sinaloa, 1910–1917* (Mexico, D.F.: Patronato del Instituto Nacional de Estudios Históricos de la Revolución, 1964), p. 13. Prominent
among these professionally trained officeholders were Heriberto Zazueta, Her-
lindo Elenes Gaxiola, Miguel and Ramón Ponce de León, Daniel Pérez Arce, and
Ignacio M. Gastelum.

74. Corbalá Acuña, *Constituciones*, pp. 261–71; García y Alva, *Album;* n.p.;
Galaz, *Hermosillo*, pp. 443, 741, 751–52; *La Evolución* (Hermosillo), 28 April
1905.

75. By comparison, in Northeast Brazil the shift from endogamous to exogamous marriages was delayed until the late nineteenth century (Lewin, "Historical Implications of Kinship Organization," pp. 286–91).

76. Emiliano Philippi, who arrived in Mazatlán in 1882, developed diverse
business interests and married the daughter of an important municipal official
and businessman in the port (Lic. Carlos F. Galán). But he returned to Germany with his family in 1910 (*Diario del Pacifico*, 22 June 1910).

77. Prominent among Greene's clients was Agustín F. Pesqueira, who operated a commercial establishment specializing in the commission trade and representation for foreign manufacturers. He was also a member of the board of directors of the Southwestern Land and Improvement Company, a real estate venture formed principally by officials of the Greene company (García y Alva, *Album*).

78. Business directories, newspaper accounts, and election results reveal this spatial flexibility and the growing interurban ties. Voss, "Towns and Enterprise," chaps. 9–13, surveys the varying fortunes of the districts.

79. Ibid, chap. 7, details the rise to power of the Torres circle. One of Corral's aunts had married a son of Don José María Almada, for whom Corral's father managed a hacienda. After his father's fatal fall from a horse, Miguel Urrea (leader of Álamos's second-generation notables) and his wife, Justina Almada, took the young Corral in and saw to his education and socialization with young third-generation notables. Torres, of humble origins from neighboring Chihuahua, was a veteran of the decade of civil war and of the porfirista opposition movements in Sinaloa in the years that followed.

Politically, Ortiz had questioned the extent of subordination to the Díaz regime and had sought to maintain alamense influence and rewards at the state level. The result was that the original quartet became a triumvirate, and the alamense network was excluded from the state level of notability.

80. Few newcomers appear in the newspapers and commercial directories. By the end of the period, the few large enterprises in Álamos—recorded in García y Alva, *Album*, and Governor Rafael Izabal, *Memoria del Estado* (Hermosillo, 1907)—overwhelmingly belonged to foreign firms. Salidos occupied state offices. Salidos were among the few alamense families who developed large agricultural holdings in the Mayo and Yaqui valleys once federal troops secured them in the 1890s.

81. This composite of the state network in Sonora is drawn from the wide variety of sources noted above for the late nineteenth century.

82. Voss, "Towns and Enterprise," pp. 470–72; García y Alva, *Album;* Southworth, *Sonora*, p. 60; Almada, *Diccionario*, p. 641; *El Trafico* (Guaymas), 9 October 1899, 6 December 1900, 22 February, 23 March 1901; Manuel Mascareñas, *Business Records of a General Merchandise Store, 1884–1891*, Special Collections Department, University of Arizona Library, Tucson. When the railroad to Guaymas was completed, all three moved to Nogales (Mascareñas and Ramírez from Hermosillo, the Sandovals from Guaymas) and quickly established their dominance. Each complemented their commission houses and wholesale trade with the pueblos, small towns, and mining camps across the frontier with mining interests, agricultural operations on large tracts of land, and real estate holdings in the town.

83. *AES*, Elecciones, 1884–1911; *El Trafico*, 25 July, 22 August 1897, 22 August, 9 October 1899, 25 July, 1 October 1900.

84. Secretaría de Gobernación, *Memoria* (Mexico, D.F., 1877), document 21; Buelna, *Apuntes*, p. 224; *El Estado de Sinaloa*, 4 February 1884.

85. *El Estado de Sinaloa*, 1880–1911 passim; interview with Candido Aviles, Culiacán, June 1974; *El Estado de Sinaloa*, 13 July, 25 August 1888. Members of the Osuna and Lafarga families occupied the office of prefect of San Ignacio district for all but eight years between 1877 and 1911.

86. Dr. Ramón Ponce de León, from Rosario, attended the colegio, taught courses there for many years, and through his position on the state junta de instrucción pública was instrumental in its growth and development. Both of his sons attended the school, one later acquiring a pharmacy in the capital. Ponce de León was a legislator for twenty-six years, and his family owned one of the principal haciendas in Rosario district (*El Estado de Sinaloa*, 28 May 1881, 19 August 1885, 20 October 1888; Southworth, *Sinaloa*, p. 39; Cañedo, *Memoria*, p. 336).

87. *El Estado de Sinaloa*, the memorias of governors Francisco Cañedo and Mariano Martínez de Castro, and González Dávila's *Diccionario* are the principal sources from which the political and marital relations of the state network are drawn.

88. Lic. Heriberto Zazueta, from San Ignacio, after attending secondary school in the state capital and then acquiring legal training in Guadalajara, returned to Culiacán, marrying a Batiz. Beginning as Cañedo's private secretary, he rose to the post of government secretary, which he occupied from 1892 to 1909 (Olea, *Revolución*, p. 13; *El Estado de Sinaloa*, 22 April 1898).

89. *El Estado de Sinaloa*, 6 June 1883, 5 May, 16 July 1887, 14 November 1888, 16 June 1891, 21 May 1896, 23 June 1899; Southworth, *Sinaloa*, pp. 30, 37, 75, 78, 84, 94; González Dávila, *Diccionario*, pp. 118–19, 520. Redo, who married a Vega and was a confidante of Díaz, became the leading businessperson in the state.

90. In 1892, having alternated with Cañedo as governor since 1880, and with the recent reform of the constitution permitting unlimited reelection, Mariano Martínez de Castro toyed with the idea of continuing in office, supported by various components of the Culiacán network. The strength of Cañedo's ties with Porfirio Díaz, however, were quickly made evident as notables in all other towns fell in behind his candidacy. Despite this political affront, the Martínez de Castro family members remained important cogs in the Cañedo regime, holding important offices and being cut in on important economic ventures. Voss, "Towns and Enterprise," pp. 387–388; González Dávila, *Diccionario*, 339; *El Estado de Sinaloa*, 25 August 1899; Secretaría de Fomento, Colonización e Industria, *Memoria, 1905–1907* (Mexico, D.F., 1909), pp. 97–170 passim.

91. *El Estado de Sinaloa*, 12 October 1887.

92. García y Alva, *Album*. A junta de mejores materiales supervised the construction of Álamos's new municipal building in 1899, two-thirds of which was financed by the state government. The ayuntamiento and businesspeople of the town staged an elaborate dedication ceremony attended by the triumvirate, many high state officials, and all of Álamos's notable families.

93. *Diario del Pacífico*, 30 December 1910; Alfonso Iberri, *El Viejo Guaymas* (1952), pp. 33–34; Alan T. Bird, *Sonora, Mexico: The Empire State of the West Mexican Coast* (Guaymas: Sonora Railroad Company, 1907), p. 14; *El Trafico*, 21 November 1898.

94. Southworth, *Sonora*, p. 33. The club was managed by Antonio B. Monteverde, assisted by a member of the Corral family. Its counterpart in Cananea, owned by the Greene interests, contained a bar with large mirrors, a library with large numbers of current periodicals and expensive paintings, a billards parlor with ivory-bordered tables and a piano, a ballroom with a grand piano, a restaurant, and baths.

95. Izabal, *Memoria*, appendixes; John R. Southworth, *Directory of Mines and Estates in Mexico* (México, D.F., 1910), Sonora; United States Bureau of Manufacturers, *Commercial Relations* (Hermosillo, 1909), p. 541, Consul Louis Hostetter (the bureau published these reports from 1903 to 1911); Pedro N. Ulloa, *El Estado de Sonora: y sus situación económica* (Hermosillo, 1910), pp. 169–77.

96. *Diario del Pacifico*, 29 July, 15, 18 August 1910.

97. Cámara Agricola Nacional del Estado de Sonora to Porfirio Díaz, Hermosillo, 21 June 1910, *Correspondencia de Porfirio Díaz*, legajo 35: 7974; Evelyn Hu-DeHart, "Resistance and Survival: A History of the Yaqui People's Struggle for Autonomy" (Manuscript revision of Ph.D. diss.), 2:392–99, 408–12, 418–24. The anti-Chinese sentiment, both economic and social, fills the pages of available newspapers from 1895 to 1911. *El Trafico* in Guaymas was the most strident. The agricultural chamber's president, Dionisio González, was an early member of the Torres circle, but in 1900 became the titular head of a municipal electoral challenge in Hermosillo.

98. See *AES*, "Elecciones" for Sonora, and lists in *El Estado de Sinaloa*.

99. Antonio G. Rivera, *Sonora en la Revolución* (Mexico, D.F.: Editorial Porrua, 1969), pp. 140, 153–60; *El Centinela* (Hermosillo), 16 February 1907. Other local officials who had questioned the governor's orders and were removed included the postmaster, the mining agent, the school inspector, the director of the town school, and two teachers.

100. Aguilar Camín, *Frontera nomada*, pp. 84–85; José C. Valadés, *Mis confesiones* (Mexico, D.F.: Editores Mexicanos Unidos, 1966), pp. 137–58; interview with Candido Aviles, June 1974; *Diario del Pacifico*, 15 June 1910; Olea, *Revolución*, pp. 16–18; Rivera, *Revolución*, pp. 163–80.

101. *Diario del Pacifico*, 26 January, 7, 8, 10, 12, 15, 16, 19, 24 April 1911; Rivera, *Revolución*, pp. 182–91; González Dávila, *Diccionario*, 119, 293–294; Olea, *Revolución*, 22ff.

102. Sources include Aguilar Camín, *Frontera nomada*, González Dávila, *Diccionario*, and Olea, *Revolución*. Maderista officeholders from network families included Maytorena, Gayou, and de la Huerta (Guaymas); Mascareñas and Iñigo (Nogales); Morales, Romo, and Araiza (Ures); Ruiz, Gaxiola, and Monte-

verde (Hermosillo); Salido, Almada, Marcor, and Mendivil (Álamos); Pesqueira and Elías (Arizpe district); Luga, Vega, Ochoa, and Zazueta (Fuerte district); and Buelna and Riveros (Mocorito).

103. Aguilar Camín summarizes the main biographical sources (*Frontera nomada*, pp. 27–29, 180–83, 221–24). Flavio Borquez, Hill's early associate and another poor relation, was related to one of the largest landholders in Álamos district (the Valderrain family, through his mother). After service as a secretary to a prefect in neighboring Chihuahua, he began a small commercial trade in Álamos, married into the Gil Samaniego family, and moved to Navajoa, where his business grew slowly (ibid., pp. 35–36).

104. Corbalá Acuña, *Constituciones*, pp. 247–50, 272–90. Although I have undertaken no organized study of postrevolutionary economic data, personal observation and discussion with natives of the region have revealed the continuing prominence of many of the nineteenth-century notable families.

Chapter Four

1. Tulio Halperín-Donghi, *Politics, Economics and Society in Argentina* (Cambridge: Cambridge University Press, 1975), p. 213.

2. For the list of the 154, see Appendix. For the original eighteen, the basic documents used were *sucesiones* (probate records); for the rest, commercial guides, directories, church records, land records, membership lists of clubs, banks, and railroads have been used. Biographical dictionaries, genealogies, and the like complemented this material. The main sources of this kind were the following: Academia Nacional de Bellas Artes, *Estancias* (Buenos Aires, 1969); Academia Nacional de Bellas Artes, *Prilidiano Pueyrredón* (Buenos Aires, 1945); *Almanak Mercantil: Guía de Comerciantes* (Madrid, 1796); *Almanak Mercantil: Guía de Comerciantes* (Madrid, 1802); *Almanaque Comercial y Guía de Forasteros para el Estado de Buenos Aires, Año de 1855* (Buenos Aires, 1855); *Almanaque Político y de Comercio de la Ciudad de Buenos Aires para el año de 1826*, ed. La Flor (Buenos Aires, 1968); Amigos del Arte, *C. H. Pellegrini* (Buenos Aires, 1946); *Argentine Standard Directory* (Buenos Aires, 1920); Roberto T. Barili, *Mar del Plata* (Mar del Plata, 1962); *Beare Plan* (1862); *Boletín Interno Instituto Argentino de Ciencias Genealógicas*, nos. 9, 10, 11, 12, 14, 17 1–26 (Buenos Aires, 1970–72); Arturo B. Carranza, *La capital de la república*, 3 vols. (Buenos Aires, 1938); Virginia Carreño, *Estancias y estancieros* (Buenos Aires, 1968); *Comisión Directiva de la Provincia de Buenos Aires, Censo General de la Provincia de Buenos Aires* (Buenos Aires: Censo de Estancias, 1881); Horacio Juan Cuccorese, *Historia del Banco de la Provincia de Buenos Aires* (Buenos Aires, 1972); Vicente Osvaldo Cutolo, *Nuevo diccionario biográfico Argentino* (Buenos Aires, 1971); Delmo F. M. Daró, *Apuntes históricos de la colonia y pueblo de Armstrong (Santa Fe) desde sus orígenes hasta 1972* (Santa Fe, 1972); Departamento Topográfico, *Planos catastrales de los partidos de la Provincia de*

Buenos Aires (Buenos Aires, 1867, 1890, 1930); *Diario de sesiones de la Cámara de Diputados de la Provincia de Buenos Aires* (Buenos Aires, 1865); *Documentos para la historia Argentina*, vol. 11: *Padrón de la Ciudad de Buenos Aires 1778*, and vol. 12: *Padrón de la Campaña de Buenos Aires 1778* (Buenos Aires, 1919); *Edelberg: Mapas de los partidos de la Provincia de Buenos Aires* (Buenos Aires, 1920s and 1930s); *Historia del Banco de la Nación Argentina en su cincuentenario* (Buenos Aires, 1941); Raúl A. Molina, *Hombres de Mayo: Genealogía*, (Buenos Aires: Revista del Instituto Argentino de Ciencias Genealógicas, 1961), vol. 16; Hugo Fernandez-Burzaco y Barrios, *La Venerable Orden Tercera de Santo Domingo en Buenos Aires* (Buenos Aires, 1963); *Guía de Criadores de Shorthorn, Herd Book Argentino* (Buenos Aires, 1888); *Guía de Sociedades Anónimas* (Buenos Aires, 1929); *Guía Senior* (Buenos Aires, 1969); Ricardo Hogg, *Guía Biográfica Argentina* (Buenos Aires, 1904); *Indice de la Sala de Representantes de Buenos Aires* (1821–52); Ricardo Levene, *Catálogo del Archivo de la Real Audiencia y Cámara de Apelación de Buenos Aires*, Archivo Histórico de la Provincia de Buenos Aires, Ministerio de Educación (La Plata, 1974); Santos Suarez Menéndez, *Historia de Mar del Plata* (Buenos Aires, 1945); *Mulhall Directory* (Buenos Aires, 1885); Jorge de Newton and Lily de Newton, *Historia del Jockey Club de Buenos Aires* (Buenos Aires: 1960); Felix Outes, *Cartas y planos inéditos de los siglos diecisiete, dieciocho y del primer decenio del siglo diecinueve conservados en el Archivo de la Dirección de Geodesia, Catastro y Mapas de la Provincia de Buenos Aires: Plano Catastral y Parcelario de las suertes de tierra y pertenencias de proprietarios situadas sobre el Río de la Plata desde el Partido de Flores hasta el pueblo y puerto de Las Conchas*, Instituto de Investigaciónes Geográficas, ser. 13, no. 3 (Buenos Aires, 1930); *Registro oficial* (Buenos Aires, 1821–22); Enrique Udaondo, *Crónica histórica de la Venerable Orden Tercera de San Francisco en la República Argentina* (Buenos Aires, 1920); Enrique Udaondo, *Diccionario biográfico Argentino* (Buenos Aires, 1938); Enrique Udaondo, *Diccionario biográfico colonial* (Buenos Aires, 1945); Jacinto R. Yabén, *Biografías Argentinas y Sudamericanas* (Buenos Aires, 1938).

3. Susan Socolow, *The Merchants of Buenos Aires 1778–1810: Family and Commerce* (Cambridge: Cambridge University Press, 1978).

4. Halperin-Donghi, *Politics, Economics, and Society*, p. 92.

5. Germán O. E. Tjarks, *El Consulado de Buenos Aires y sus proyecciones en la historia del Río de la Plata* (Buenos Aires: Universidad de Buenos Aires Facultad de Filosofía Letras, 1962), p. 896.

6. *Almanak Mercantil o Guía de Comerciantes* (Madrid, 1802), p. 401.

7. See John Fisher, "Silver Production in the Viceroyalty of Peru, 1776–1824," *HAHR* 55 (1975):25–43; and Herbert S. Klein, "Structure and Profitability of Royal Finance in the Viceroyalty of the Río de la Plata in 1790," *HAHR* 53 (1973):440–69.

8. John Lynch, *Argentine Dictator Juan Manuel de Rosas, 1829–1852* (Oxford: Oxford University Press, 1981), p. 44.

9. Bernardino Rivadavia was first principal cabinet minister (1821–24) for General Martín Rodriguez, governor of Buenos Aires, then president (1826–27).

10. Alfredo J. Montoya, *La ganadería y la industria de la Salazón de Carnes en el período 1810–1862* (Buenos Aires: Editorial El Coloquio, 1971).

11. Urban real estate was most important in the estates of first-generation merchants but at times was as important in value as the estancias in the third generation's estates.

12. See, for example, a merchant's letter in James Lockhart and Enrique Otte, eds. and trans., *Letters and People of the Spanish Indies: Sixteenth Century* (Cambridge: Cambridge University Press, 1976), p. 90; or Hoberman, "Merchants in Seventeenth-Century Mexico City," 479–503.

13. Sucesión José G. Iraola, Archivo General de la Nación Argentina Leg. 6386.

14. Sucesión Carlos Casares, AGNA Leg. 5150, 2 cuerpos.

15. Sucesión Vicente Casares, AGNA Leg. 5083.

16. Sucesión Carmen Díaz Velez, AG Tribunales Leg. 869, 2 cuerpos.

17. Facultad de Filosofía y Letras, Universidad de Buenos Aires, *Documentos para la historia Argentina*, vol. 4: *Abastos de la Ciudad de Buenos Aires*, p. 474.

18. Sucesión Santiago Lawrie, Archivo de la Provincia de Buenos Aires Leg. 83.

19. Sources for the Luro family: Instituto Argentino de Ciencias Genealógicas, *Boletín Interno*, no. 10 (Buenos Aires: Agosto, 1970); Vicente Osvaldo Cutolo, *Nuevo diccionario biográfico Argentino* (Buenos Aires, 1978); Roberto Barili, *Mar del Plata* (Mar del Plata, 1962); Santos Suarez Menendez, *Historia de Mar del Plata* (Buenos Aires, 1945); Alfredo J. Otarola, *Mar del Plata y genearquía de sus fundadores* (Buenos Aires, 1972); *Argentine Standard Directory* (Buenos Aires, 1920); *Guía de Sociedades Anónimas 1928/1929* (Buenos Aires, 1929); *Bahía Blanca: Una nueva provincia y diversos proyectos para su capitalización* (Bahía Blanca, 1972).

20. Pellegrini, a French hydraulic engineer, was brought to Argentina by Rivadavia's government to plan a water system and port for Buenos Aires. He found himself without a job when he arrived in 1828, since Rivadavia's government had fallen, and he took up portrait painting to earn a living. Since he painted the prominent of Buenos Aires, he portrays the second generation of these families as they emerge into notability. His son Carlos Pellegrini later became president of Argentina, a success story in just two generations.

Pueyrredón's family arrived early; Pellegrini came with the second wave of immigrants. Puerredón's father was the son of a French Basque merchant who immigrated to Buenos Aires, was a merchant himself, and served as director supremo after independence. Pellegrini was part of the first generation, and Pueyrredón was a member of the third. They became the two most important painters of the period under study, and they have left us some portraits of members of the 154 families. Pellegrini painted members of twelve families in the group; Pueyrredón painted fourteen.

21. In 1880, the Buenos Aires legislature and National Congress became established in separate cities: La Plata was made the provincial capital when the city of Buenos Aires was made the national capital. The domination of the Buenos Aires legislature by the Buenos Aires family network undoubtedly influenced the decision for this separation. In 1853, after the defeat of Rosas by Urquiza and the attempt to place the national capital in Entre Ríos, Buenos Aires seceded. It remained a separate state until 1861, when it once again placed itself at the head of the country. Between 1853 and 1880, or from the time it became a separate state to the time the city became the federal capital, the Buenos Aires legislature held sway. It was perhaps the only period in which the legislature was truly powerful in Argentina, at least as powerful and active as the cabildo of colonial times. So perhaps the thirty-two network families in the legislature during this period had more real power in the political system than any legislators who followed.

22. President Julio Rocas's family was represented in the clubs through a nephew, Ataliva Roca. Also his niece, daughter of his brother Ataliva, married a third-generation member of one of the 154 families, but since he is not *the* third-generation member on the list, he has not been included in the total count.

23. The voting went as follows:

Agüero	did not vote	Arana	for junta
Aguirre	for junta	Balcarce	for junta
Belgrano	for junta	Bosch	for Virrey
Castex	for junta	Castro	for junta
A. Pío de Elía	for junta	Molina	for Virrey
Quesada	for junta	Martínez de Hoz	for Virrey
Quirno	for Virrey	Ramos Mejía	not known
Saavedra	for junta	Torres	did not vote (with brother-in-law, J. S. de Agüero)

Did not vote	2
Voted for deposition of the Virrey (for Virrey's authority to be transferred to the cabildo)	9
Voted for Virrey	4
Vote note known	1

24. See Arthur S. Whitaker's *Argentina* (Englewood Cliffs, N.J.: Prentice-Hall, 1964), pp. 41–64, for a good overview of this period.

25. C. de Murrieta and Co., a bank in London that also dealt in Anglo-Argentine financing, closed in 1892. The uncles and cousins of the first generation of

the Casares had founded the firm in London. In 1903, the commercial firm Emilio Casares e Hijos opened in the same city.

26. I am indebted to Professor Vera Blinn Reber for a copy of the reports on the Casares business firm V. Casares and Sons in the Baring Brothers Archives, London (*House correspondence 16* [Buenos Aires, 1857]); the Belgian Consular Service (*Belgium Reciceil Consulaire*, vol. 9, p. 251, 1863); and a report on Carlos Casares from the Bank of London (D 35, 15 May 1878–11 March 1882, Buenos Aires to London).

27. Peter H. Smith, "Los Radicales Argentinos y la defensa de los intereses ganaderos, 1916–1930," *Desarrollo Ecónomico* 17 (April–June 1967): 805.

28. Cuccorese, *Historia del Banco de la Provincia de Buenos Aires*, pp. 103–6.

29. Acosta, Armstrong, Billinghurst, Cambaceres, Cano, Casares, Cascallares, Casey, Díaz, Velez, Drysdale, Elizalde, Guerrico, Hale, Lanús, Mendez, Luro, Madero, Molina, Peralta, Quesada, Saavedra, and Temperley.

30. Only the direct ancestors of the Jockey Club and the Sociedad Rural members are being considered; if the whole cohort was included, this group would probably show a very large number of military families.

31. Halperín-Donghi, *Politics, Economics, and Society*, p. 192.

32. The 1879 Conquista del Desierto by General Julio Roca, also a campaign against Indians to the south, did the same for the third generation.

33. Emilio Coni, *La enfiteusis de Rivadavia* (Buenos Aires, 1927).

34. Sucesión Carmen Díaz Velez, AG Tribunales Leg. 869, 2 cuerpos.

35. Sucesiónes Gaspar José de Campos, AGNA Leg. 4852; Sucesión Martín B. Campos, Archivo de Tribunales Leg. 1921.

36. The Castex and the Artayeta were both of French Basque origin and united into the Artayeta-Castex, both part of the 154 families. Francisco Castex was an oficial de milicias, Bernardo Artayeta had a tanning establishment; Francisco's brother Esteban, a merchant in France, was in the hide trade. The second-generation Castex, Alejo and Vicente, both fought in the English invasions, were diputados, and served as provisioners to the army. They had estancia land to the north of the city in Baradero. The Artayeta and the Castex eventually took sides with Lavalle against Rosas in 1839 and followed Lavalle to his exile and death. The third-generation Castex was assemblyman, congressman, and justice of the peace in Morón.

37. Sources for Belgrano family: Molina, *Hombres de Mayo: Genealogía*; Museo Mitre, *Documentos del Archivo de Belgrano* (Buenos Aires; 6 ts); Rubén G. Gonzalez, *El General Belgrano y la Orden de Santo Domingo* (Buenos Aires, 1961); Ministerio de Educación, *Archivo histórico de la Provincia de Buenos Aires* (La Plata, 1974), p. 31.

38. Ricardo Levene, *Catálogo del Archivo de la Real Audencia y Cámara de Apelación de Buenos Aires, Provincia de Buenos Aires* (La Plata, 1974), p. 31.

39. "Don Manuel Belgrano se nos presenta así en la faceta inusitada de representante de hacendados de la Banda Oriental" Tjarks, *El Consulado de Buenos Aires*, 10:46).

40. Who did the women in the 154 families marry? The few complete cohorts available show that males with estancia land seem to be the preferred marriage partners for daughters.

41. See Lewin, "Historical Implications of Kinship Organization," p. 274.

42. Lanús marriages from Instituto Argentino de Ciencias Genealógicas, *Boletín Interno*, nos. 11, 12, and 14.

43. The case probably of many of those forty-four families for whom data has not been found.

44. For sources for Luro family, see footnote 19.

45. Sources for Peralta Ramos family: Otarola, *Mar del Plata y genearquía de sus fundadores*; Cutolo, *Nuevo diccionario biográfico Argentino* (1971); Udaondo, *Diccionario biográfico Argentino*. (1938).

46. Sources for Quirno family: Molina, *Hombres de Mayo genealogía*; Udaondo, *Diccionario Biográfico Colonial* (1945); *Argentine Standard Directory* (1920).

47. Sources for Ramos Mejía family: Sucesión Ezequiel Ramos Mejía, AGNA Leg. 8057; *Morón, Planos Catastrales, del Departmento de Geodesia 1864* (Maipú, 1890); *Estancias*, Documentos de Arte Argentino, Academia Nacional de Bellas Artes, 2:69.

48. Sources for Bosch family: Sucesión Francisco B. Bosch, AG Tribunales Leg. 8945; Molina, *Hombres de Mayo: Genealogía*; Census 1778; Arturo B. Carranza, *La cuestión capital de la república* (Buenos Aires, 1938); Carlos Calvo, *Nobiliario del antiguo Virreinato* (Buenos Aires, 1936); *Argentine Standard Directory* (1920).

49. Sources for Torres family: Molina *Hombres de Mayo: Genealogía*; Udaondo, *Diccionario biográfico Argentino* (1938); *Mullhall Directory* (Buenos Aires, 1885).

50. Sources for Lawrie family: Sucesión Santiago Lawrie, Archivo General de la Provincia de Buenos Aires, Leg. 83; Lawrie Family Papers in possession of Nelly Pearson Lawrie, La Plata, Buenos Aires; Cecilia Grierson, *Primera y única colonia formada por escoceses en la Argentina* (Buenos Aires, 1925).

51. Sources for Malcolm family: Sucesión Juan Malcolm (1865), AGNA Leg. 6841; Juan Malcolm (1898), AGNA Leg. 7143; Juan Malcolm (1923), AG Tribunales Leg. 9647, 9648.

52. Data on Ortiz Basualdo quinta from Sucesión Manuel Ortiz Basualdo, AGNA Leg. 7281, and María de la Cruz Segurola, AGNA Leg. 7280.

53. Data on Carlos Casares estancia house from Sucesión Carlos Casares, AGNA Leg. 5150, 2 cuerpos.

54. These construction booms, with their abrupt turn in type and style and size, parallelled those of a powerful group of families in New York City in the 1870s and 1880s.

55. George E. Marcus, "Law in the Development of Dynastic Families among American Business Elites: The Domestication of Capital and the Capitalization of Family," *Law and Society Review* 14:4 (Summer 1980):859–60.

Chapter Five

1. See, for example, Brading, *Miners and Merchants*, in particular chapter 9, "The Elite"; and Socolow, *The Merchants of Buenos Aires*, in particular chapter 1, "The Merchant Population," and chapter 2, "Women, Marriage, and Kinship."

2. Eric Van Young, *Hacienda and Market in Eighteenth-Century Mexico: The Rural Economy of the Guadalajara Region, 1675–1820* (Berkeley: University of California Press, 1981).

3. Lesley Byrd Simpson *Many Mexicos*, 3d ed. (Berkeley: University of California Press, 1957), p. 232.

4. Lockhart and Otte, *Letters*, pp. 18, 24, 89, 90, 111.

5. See Hoberman "Merchants in Seventeenth-Century Mexico City."

6. Campbell, "A Colonial Establishment," p. 21.

7. Kuznesof, "Clans, the Militia, and Territorial Government." See also Stuart B. Schwartz, "Magistracy and Society in Colonial Brazil," *HAHR* (1970) 4:116.

8. German Colmenares, *Historia económica y social de Colombia* (Cali: Universidad del Valle, 1973), pp. 93, 274.

9. Ibid., pp. 93–132, 277, 304, 307–9.

10. François Chevalier, *Land and Society in Colonial Mexico: The Great Hacienda*, trans by Alvin Eustis, edited with a Foreword by Lesley Byrd Simpson (Berkeley, University of California Press, 1963), p. 12.

11. Brading, *Miners and Merchants*, pp. 212–19.

12. Barbier, "Elites and Cadres," pp. 419–21.

13. Ibid., p. 435.

14. German Colmenares, *Cali: Terratenientes, mineros y comerciantes siglo xviii* (Cali: Universidad del Valle 1975), pp. 179, 180.

15. Doris M. Ladd, *The Mexican Nobility at Independence, 1780–1826*, Latin American Monographs no. 40 (Austin: University of Texas Press, 1976), p. 27.

16. Van Young, *Hacienda and Market*.

17. Ibid., pp. 173–75.

18. Bowser and Chowning, "Socio-Economic Power," p. 3.

19. Brading, *Miners and Merchants*, p. 319.

20. Elizabeth Anne Kuznesof, "The Role of the Merchants in the Economic Development of São Paulo 1765–1850 *HAHR* 60 (1980): 579–90; John Norman Kennedy, "Bahian Elites, 1750–1822" *HAHR* 53, No. 3 (August 1973), 431–439.

21. Bowser and Chowning, "Socio-Economic Power," p. 4.

22. Manuel Romero de Terreros, *El Conde de Regla* (Mexico: Ediciones Xochitl, 1943), pp. 10–11; See also Couturier, "Hacienda of Hueyapán."

23. Ibid., p. 110; Edith B. Couturier, "Women in a Noble Family: The Mexican Counts of Regla, 1750–1830," in *Latin American Women: Historical Perspectives*, ed. Asunción Lavrín. (Westport, Conn.: Greenwood Press, 1978), pp. 129–49.

24. Ladd, *The Mexican Nobility*; D. A. Brading, "Government and Elite in Late Colonial Mexico," *HAHR* 53, (1973):396.

25. Franklin W. Knight, "Origins of Wealth and the Sugar Revolution in Cuba, 1750–1850" *HAHR* 57 (1977):231–53; Allan J. Kuethe, "The Development of the Cuban Military as a Sociopolitical Elite, 1763–83" *HAHR* 61 (4), 1981, 695–704.

26. Socolow, *The Merchants of Buenos Aires*, pp. 16–17.

27. Wells, "Family Elites," p. 227.

28. Edwards, *La fronda aristocrática*; Barbier, "Elites and Cadres," pp. 416–35; Felstiner, "Kinship Politics," pp. 58–80; Robert Oppenheimer, "From Family to Corporation: Merchant Family Organization in Nintheenth-Century Santiago, Chile." (Paper given at meeting of the American Historical Association 30 December 1980).

29. Rae Flory and David Grant Smith, "Bahían Merchants and Planters in the Seventeenth and Early Eighteenth Centuries," *HAHR* 58 (1978):572.

30. Ibid., 576.

31. Ibid.

32. María Teresa Huerta, "La familia Yermo, 1750–1850" (Paper delivered at the Conference of Mexican and United States Historians, Chicago, Illinois, 10 September 1981).

33. Brading, "Government and Elite," p. 396.

34. Ibid., 409.

35. Twinam, "Enterprise and Elites," p. 475.

36. Charles H. Harris, *A Mexican Family Empire: The Latifudio of the Sanchez Navarros, 1765–1867* (Austin: University of Texas Press, 1975), p. 94.

37. Wells, "Family Elites," p. 225.

38. Ibid., 227.

39. Ibid., 226.

40. Ciro F. S. Cardoso, ed., *Formación y desarrollo de la burguesía en Mexico siglo xix* (Mexico: Siglo Veintiuno, 1978).

41. Ibid., 57, 108, 140.

42. Ibid., 267.

43. See Ibid., 231, for Milmo. Henry Swayne story in Juan Rolf Englesen, "Social Aspects of Agricultural Expansion in Coastal Peru, 1825–1878" (Ph.D. diss., University of California at Los Angeles, 1977), p. 577.

44. Lewin, "Historical Implications of Kinship Organization," p. 288.

45. Kuznesof, "The Role of Merchants in São Paulo," p. 571.

46. See Linda Greenow, "Spatial Dimensions of the Household and Family Structure in Eighteenth-Century Spanish America," *Discussion Series Paper 35*, (Department of Geography, Syracuse University, 1977), p. 18.

47. Cardoso, *Formación y desarollo*.

48. Linda Greenow, "Spatial Dimensions of the Credit Market in Eighteenth-Century Nueva Galicia," in *Social Fabric and Spatial Structure in Colonial Latin America*, ed. David Robinson (Syracuse: University Microfilms International,

1979); Richard P. Hyland, "A Fragile Prosperity: Credit and Agrarian Structure in the Cauca Valley, Colombia, 1851–87," *HAHR* 62 (1982):369–406.

49. Huerta, "La familia Yermo."

50. Hyland, "A Fragile Prosperity," pp. 394–95.

51. Ibid., 30.

52. Richard Parry Lindley, "Kinship and Credit in the Structure of Guadalajara's Oligarchy, 1800–1830" (Ph.D. diss., University of Texas at Austin, 1978), p. 262.

53. Ibid., 288.

54. Ibid.

55. Kuznesof, "The Role of Merchants in São Paulo, p. 583.

56. Blank, "Patrons, Clients, and Kin," p. 3, and "Political Participation and Kinship Patterns in Seventeenth-Century Caracas" (Paper presented at American Historical Association meeting, December 1981).

57. Blank, "Political Participation," p. 2.

58. Edith Couturier and Asunción Lavrín, "Dowries and Wills: A View of Women's Socioeconomic Role in Colonial Guadalajara and Puebla, 1640–1790," *HAHR* 59 (1979):281.

59. Lewin, "Historical Implications of Kinship Organization," p. 277.

60. Lewin, ibid., pp. 270, 275.

61. Cardoso, *Formación y desarollo*, p. 231.

62. Felstiner, "Kinship Politics," p. 60.

63. Cardoso, *Formación y desarollo*, p. 267.

64. Marzahl, "Creoles and Government," pp. 655–56.

65. Hoberman, "Merchants in Seventeenth-Century Mexico City," pp. 482, 494.

66. Kuznesof, "Clans, the Militia, and Territorial Government," p. 185.

67. Felstiner, "Kinship Politics," p. 80.

68. Wells, "Family Elites," p. 19.

69. Felstiner, "Kinship Politics," pp. 74–75.

70. Ladd, *The Mexican Nobility*, pp. 168, 170.

71. Lewin, "Historical Implications of Kinship Organization," p. 265.

72. Ibid., pp. 266, 272, 284. a letter by the state governor lamented that "all the mayors divide among the members of their families the revenues of their municipalities."

73. Peter Dobkin Hall, "Family Structure and Economic Organization; Massachusetts Merchants, 1700–1850," in *Family and Kin in Urban Communities, 1700–1930*, ed. Tamara Hareven (New York: New Viewpoints, 1977), pp. 38–61; "The Model of Boston Charity: A Theory of Charitable Benevolence and Class Development," *Science and Society* 38 (Winter 1974–75):464–77; and "Three Generations: Family Strategy and Modernization in Massachusetts Merchant Families, 1740–1799" (Paper presented at American Historical Association meeting, December 1980).

74. Thomas L. Purvis, "High-Born, Long-Recorded Families: Social Origins of New Jersey Assemblymen, 1703–1776," *William and Mary Quarterly,* 3d ser., 37 (October 1980):608.

75. Ibid., p. 613.

76. Englesen, "Social Aspects of Agricultural Expansion," p. 433.

77. Ibid., pp. 436–40.

78. Ibid., p. 441.

79. Ibid., pp. 423, 438.

80. Hyland, "A Fragile Prosperity," p. 20.

81. Michael T. Hamerly, "A Social and Economic History of the City and District of Guayaquil during the Late Colonial and Independence Periods" (Ph.D. diss., University of Florida, 1970). This work sheds no light on families in the area but does show the breaking up of regions and their attempt at alliances with other areas. For the colonial background, see Altman and Lockhart's excellent work, *Provinces of Early Mexico: Variants of Spanish American Evolution,* UCLA Latin American Center Publications (Los Angeles: University of California, 1976).

82. David Cubitt, "La Composición social de una elite Hispanoamericana a la independencia: Guayaquil en 1820," *Historia de América* 94 (1982):7–31.

83. John Frederick Wibel, "The Evolution of a Regional Community within Spanish Empire and Peruvian Nation: Arequipa, 1780–1845," (Ph.D. diss., Stanford University, 1975).

84. Ibid., p. 94 (emphasis added).

85. Ibid., p. 128–30.

86. Ibid., 464.

87. Ibid., 463.

88. Englesen, "Social Aspects of Agricultural Expansion," p. 475.

89. Roger M. Haigh, "The Creation and Control of a Caudillo," *HAHR* 44 (1964): 483, 490. See also Haigh's *Martin Güemes.*

90. Frederick Alexander Hollander, "Oligarchy and the Politics of Petroleum in Argentina: The Case of the Salta Oligarchy and Standard Oil, 1918–1933" (Ph.D. diss., University of California, Los Angeles, 1976). Though Hollander's thesis has a good overview of competition among regional family networks in the nineteenth century, the specific study of the Standard Oil negotiations leaves this view out and becomes a conventional account of political maneuvers.

91. See for example, Torcuato S. Di Tella, *Reflection on the Argentine Crisis,* Occasional Paper no. 3 (Center for Hemispheric Studies, January 1982): "In a capitalist country, above all, in our stage of development, there must of necessity be oligarchies. What is important is there exist several, not one, and that between them and the other structures of power . . . there be some element of competition" (p. 18). "This system [of single member constituencies in the lower house of Congress] deprives provincial electoral machines of much of their power, passing it on to local *notables* or leaders. The ascendancy of the latter, capable of aggregating the interests of the community, is not necessarily

bad. . . . The term 'local notables' may smack of conservative associations, but in order for the dominant classes to become a party to the democratic process, it is necessary to offer some advantages to compensate for the natural results of their minoritarian role in the central balloting process" (p. 23; italics added).

92. Nils P. Jacobsen, "The Wool Export Economy of Peru's Altiplano Region's Livestock Haciendas, 1850–1920" (Paper delivered at the Annual Meeting of the American Historical Association, New York, 29 December 1979); Frederick A. Hollander, "Oligarchy and the Politics of Petroleum in Argentina: The Case of the Salta Oligarchy and Standard Oil, 1918–1933" (Ph.D. diss., University of California, Los Angeles, 1976); Hyland, "A Fragile Prosperity," pp. 369–406; Wells, "Family Elites," pp. 224–53; Wasserman, "Capitalists and Caciques."

93. Larissa Adler Lomnitz and Marisol Pérez Lizaur, "The History of a Mexican Urban Family," *Journal of Family History* 3, (1978):392–409; Julia Alfaro Vallejos and Susana Chueca Posadas, "El processo de hacer la America: una familia italiana en el Peru" (M.A. thesis, Pontificia Universidad Catolica del Peru, Lima, 1975); Billy Jaynes Chandler, *The Feitosas and the Sertão dos Inhamuns: The History of a Family and a Community in Northeast Brazil, 1700–1930* (Gainesville: University of Florida Press, 1972); Levi, "The Prados of São Paulo."

94. Lewin, "Historical Implications of Kinship Organization," pp. 262–92; Robert Oppenheimer, "From Family to Corporation: Merchant Family Organization in Nineteenth-Century Santiago, Chile" (Paper delivered at the Annual Meeting of the American Historical Association, Washington, 30 December 1980). Oppenheimer has coauthored with Diana Balmori, "Family Clusters."

95. Hyland, "A Fragile Prosperity"; Jacobsen, "Wool Export Economy"; Chandler, *The Feitosas and the Sertão;* Hollander, "Oligarchy and the Politics of Petroleum"; Lawrence James Nielsen, "Of Gentry, Peasants, and Slaves: Rural Society in Sabará and Its Hinterland, 1780–1930" (Ph.D. diss., University of California, Davis, 1975).

96. Unlike most networks at the state level, which became subordinated to the growing power and presence of the national government, that headed by the powerful Terrazas family in Chihuahua retained a considerable measure of perogative. It was able to weather periods of economic stagnation and political challenges (the opposition allied with the Díaz regime nationally) from the mid 1870s to 1902 and then achieve hegemony within the state and hold its own vis-à-vis Mexico City and foreign entrepreneurs as more than a dependent satellite (Wasserman, "Capitalists and Caciques," pp. 73–75, 127–31, 159, 221, 227).

For the Prados and other notable families in central and southern Brazil (and to a lesser extent for Chihuahua notables), foreign presence was pervasive, including large numbers of immigrants. In the Mexican state of Jalisco and the Argentine province of Salta, foreign presence was more restricted, in the form of individual entrepreneurs. In southern Peru, the Cauca Valley (Colombia) and the Yucatán, foreign contact was mainly in the form of markets controlled by foreign companies.

In southern Peru and the Inhamuns district in Northeast Brazil, technological transformation was restricted largely to the construction of single railroad lines. By contrast, for notable families in such bustling metropolitan centers as São Paulo, Guadalajara, and Santiago, there were abundant opportunities and adjustments to be made.

Levi and Lomnitz and Pérez-Lizaur trace the stratification within families (both using class designations). Wasserman shows the flexibility of the Terrazas network in adjusting to significant alterations in labor relations, while retaining customary strategies where circumstances did not warrant change (Levi, "The Prados of São Paulo," pp. 67–68, 328–29, 332–35; Lomnitz and Pérez-Lizaur, "The History of a Mexican Urban Family," pp. 396–403; Wasserman, "Capitalists and Caciques," pp. 246–86).

97. Jacobsen, "Wool Export Economy," pp. 30–34; Hollander, "Oligarchy and the Politics of Petroleum," pp. 146–70, 616–19; Wasserman, "Capitalists and Caciques," pp. 9–58, 89–131; Alfaro Vallejos and Chueca Posadas, "Una familia italiana en el Peru," pp. 73–142.

98. Oppenheimer, "From Family to Corporation," pp. 8–9. See also, Hyland, "A Fragile Prosperity," pp. 399–404, and Beato, "La formación de la burguesía," pp. 12–13.

99. Levi, "The Prados of São Paulo," pp. 188–89, 256–63; Joseph Sweigart, "The Planter as Entrepreneur: Rio de Janeiro, 1870–1889" (Paper delivered at the Annual Meeting of the American Historical Association, New York, 29 December 1979), pp. 4–8; Wells, "Family Elites," pp. 235, 241–51.

100. Levi, "The Prados of São Paulo," pp. 266–69; Wasserman, "Capitalists and Caciques," pp. 110–17; Vallejos and Chueca Posadas, "Una familia italiana en el Peru," pp. 87–88, 111–42, 159–86.

101. In general, public service ventures can be found scattered through many of the studies. Only Wasserman and Edith Couturier, however, analyze in depth their complementary role in the family enterprise (Wasserman, "Capitalists and Caciques," pp. 117–19; Couturier, "Hacienda of Hueyapán," pp. 117–25, 188–92.

102. Alfaro Vallejos and Chueca Posadas, "Una familia italiana en el Peru," pp. 88–96, 100–102.

103. Wasserman, "Capitalists and Caciques," pp. 79–89, 221, 227, 299; Wells, "Family Elites," pp. 227–52; Hyland, "A Fragile Prosperity," pp. 395, 398–99; Jacobsen, "Wool Export Economy," pp. 8–17. Arnold Bauer Jacobs details how Chilean notables acquired rural estates (or used existing holdings) to serve as collateral in securing capital for investments in other economic sectors, particularly in urban real estate and stock in new corporations. See "Chilean Rural Society in the Nineteenth Century" (Ph.D. diss., University of California, Berkeley, 1969), pp. 86–87, 97.

104. Oppenheimer, "From Family to Corporation," pp. 7–9. See also Beato, "La formación de la burguesía, pp. 23–25; Alfaro Vallejos and Chueca Posadas,

"Una familia italiana en el Peru," pp. 107, 142–72; and Englesen, "Social Aspects of Agricultural Expansion," pp. 315–22, 418–23.

105. Wasserman, "Capitalists and Caciques," pp. vi–vii, 119–24, 159–80; Wells, "Family Elites," pp. 235–40; Hollander, "Oligarchy and the Politics of Petroleum," chaps. 4–5.

106. Marc J. Hoffnagel, "From Monarchy to Republic in Northeast Brazil: The Case of Pernambuco, 1868–1895" (Ph.D. diss., Indiana University, 1975), pp. 2–4; Chandler, Feitosas and the Sertão, pp. 56–57, 106–11, 143–44; Lewin, "Historical Implications of Kinship Organization," pp. 286–90; Roberto C. Hernández Elizondo, "Comercio e industria textil en Nuevo León, 1852–1890: Un empresario—Valentín Rivero," in Formación y desarrollo, ed. Cardoso, p. 272; Levi, "The Prados of São Paulo," pp. 76, 157, 332–34. These and other case studies reveal the declining role of the military as a professional career (or even part-time endeavor) in the third generation.

107. Sweigart, "Planter as Entrepreneur," p. 9; Hoffnagel, "From Monarchy to Republic," pp. 16–17; Wasserman, "Capitalists and Caciques," 176–79; Chandler, Feitosas and the Sertão, pp. 111–15, 168–69; Oppenheimer, "From Family to Corporation," pp. 11–12; Levi, "The Prados of São Paulo," pp. 96, 101–11, 311–12; Lomnitz and Pérez-Lizaur, "The History of a Mexican Urban Family," pp. 394–95.

108. Barão de Vila Bela to Luis Felipe de Sousa Leão, Rio de Janeiro, 14 September 1878, Arquivo Sousa Leão, Instituto Histórico e Geográfico Brasileiro, Rio de Janeiro, in Hoffnagel, "From Monarchy to Republic," p. 36.

109. Levi, "The Prados of São Paulo," pp. 101–5, 169–84, 195, 217–20, 291–92, 323–27.

110. Oppenheimer, "From Family to Corporation," pp. 10–11; Wasserman, "Capitalists and Caciques," pp. 56–59, 127–31.

111. Wasserman, "Capitalists and Caciques," 130.

112. Lewin, "Historical Implications of Kinship Organization," p. 290.

113. Ibid., pp. 281–91; Levi, "The Prados of São Paulo," pp. 62–69, 96–101, 328–29, 339–42. Lewin notes the following factors in the shift to exogamous marriages among notables in Northeast Brazil: (1) new channels of mobility opened by the foundation of professional faculties; (2) the introduction of competitive politics, which meant "a sophisticated political system that more broadly projected family networks at each tier of office-holding and bureaucracy"; and (3) economic growth and the spoils of patronage, which reinforced the politicization of the family as a unit.

114. Lewin, "Historical Implications of Kinship Organization," p. 290.

115. Hoffnagel, "From Monarchy to Republic," pp. 16–17; Hollander, "Oligarchy and the Politics of Petroleum," p. 97; Alfaro Vallejos and Chueca Posadas, "Una familia italiana en el Peru," pp. 111–42; Wasserman, "Capitalists and Caciques," pp. 9–27, 36–41, 58, 64–65. Englesen provides another case of a large third-generation family, the Elias, whose twelve sons and additional daughters, working as a cohesive unit, expanded and diversified the family's interests ("Social Aspects of Agricultural Expansion," pp. 467–75).

116. Oppenheimer, "From Family to Corporation," pp. 5–6.

117. Lewin, "Historical Implications of Kinship Organization," pp. 265–266; Hollander, "Oligarchy and the Politics of Petroleum," pp. 74–96; Wasserman, "Capitalists and Caciques," pp. vi, 32–36, 41–53, 73–75. Wasserman's research reveals the levels and interconnections from those families in between state and national levels, through the state network, down to the localities.

118. Lewin, "Historical Implications of Kinship Organization," pp. 265–66; Chandler, *Feitosas and the Sertão*, pp. 60–63, 77–78, 81–83, 111–24; Hoffnagel, "From Monarchy to Republic," pp. 31–53, 221–63; Angus Lindsay Wright, "Market, Land, and Class: Southern Bahía, Brazil, 1890–1942" (Ph.D. diss., University of Michigan, 1976), pp. 38–56, 170–74; Wasserman, "Capitalists and Caciques," 181–82, 186–93; Hollander, "Oligarchy and the Politics of Petroleum," pp. 183–93. Neilsen offers a similar example of state intervention in the localities for the Sabará area of Minas Gerais ("Of Gentry, Peasants, and Slaves," pp. 88–89, 124–26, 131–38).

119. Levi, "The Prados of São Paulo," pp. 332–36.

120. Wright analyses the change from a personal to an impersonal context in Brazilian politics in the wake of the Depression ("Market, Land, and Class," pp. 140–41, 149–51). Fourth-generation notables in southern Bahía tried to organize various pressure groups and cooperatives to link up with small and medium-sized farmers in order to bring about a return to regional autonomy. In addition, their political activities became centered around the use of law and government programs, most prominently the creation of the Cacao Institute of Bahía in 1931. Howard L. Karno touches on a similar theme in analyzing the political rise of Agusto Leguía in Peru in the 1920s. Leguia broke with fellow notables and formed his own popular party, which advocated social reforms along with economic growth. See Karno, "Agusto B. Leguía: The Oligarchy and the Modernization of Peru, 1870–1930" (Ph.D. diss., University of California, Los Angeles, 1970), pp. 169–246.

121. Lewin, "Historical Implications of Kinship Organization," p. 291; Levi, "The Prados of São Paulo," pp. 108, 112–14, 131–32, 249, 284–86; Lomnitz and Pérez-Lizaur, "The History of a Mexican Urban Family," pp. 396–403; Alfaro Vallejos and Chueca Posadas, "Una familia italiana en el Peru," pp. 164–72.

122. Alfaro Vallejos and Chueca Posadas, "Una familia italiana en el Peru," p. 107; Lomnitz and Pérez-Lizaur, "The History of a Mexican Urban Family," pp. 400–403.

123. Wasserman, "Capitalists and Caciques," pp. 198–200, 291–99; Levi, "The Prados of São Paulo," chaps. 5, 9–11.

124. Mark Wasserman, "Persistant Oligarchs: Vestiges of the Porfirian Elite in Revolutionary Chihuahua, Mexico, 1920–1935" (Paper delivered at the Sixth Conference of Mexican and United States Historians, Chicago, 10 September 1981), pp. 2–9, 14–15; Levi, "The Prados of São Paulo," p. 280; Hollander, "Oligarchy and the Politics of Petroleum," pp. 170–83, chaps. 4–8.

BIBLIOGRAPHY

Recent Publications with Relevant Materials on Families

Altman, Ida, and Lockhart, James, eds. *Provinces of Early Mexico*. Los Angeles: Latin American Center, University of California, 1976. In particular see: "Introduction" by James Lockhart; chapter 1: "Yucatán" by M. Espejo-Ponce Hunt; chapter 4: "Texcoco" by L. Lewis; chapter 5: "Tlaxcala" by D. M. Szewczyk; chapter 7: "Valleys of Mexico and Toluca" by J. M. Tutiño; chapter 8: "Zacatecas" by P. J. Bakewell; chapter 9: "Querétaro" by J. C. Super; chapter 10: "A Family and a Region in the Northern Fringe Lands" by I. Altman.

Arrom, Silvia M. "Marriage Patterns in Mexico City, 1811." *Journal of Family History* 3 (Special Issue: The Family in Latin America) (1978):376.

_____. "Cambios en la condición juridica de la mujer mexicana durante el siglo XIX." In *Memoria del II Congreso de Historia del Derecho*. Mexico City: Universidad Nacional Autonomista Mexicana, 1981.

_____. *Women in Mexico City, 1790–1857*. Palo Alto: Stanford University Press, 1984.

Balmori, Diana, and Oppenheimer, Robert. "Family Clusters: The Generational Nucleation of Families in Nineteenth-Century Argentina and Chile." *Comparative Studies in Society and History* 21 (1979):231–61.

Barbier, Jacques A. "Elite and Cadres in Bourbon Chile." *Hispanic American Historical Review* 52 (1972):416–35.

Barman, Roderick, and Barman, Jean. "The Prosopography of the Brazilian Empire." *Latin American Research Review* 13 (1978):78–97.

Berquist, Charles. *Coffee and Conflict in Colombia*. Durham, N.C.: Duke University Press, 1978.

Blank, Stephanie. "Patrons, Client and Kin in Seventeenth Century Caracas: A Methodological Essay in Colonial Spanish American Social History." *Hispanic American Historical Review* 54 (1974):260–83.

Borah, Woodrow, and Cook, Sherburne F. "Marriage and Legitimacy in Mexican Culture, Mexico and California." *California Law Review* 54 (1966):946–1008.

Brading, D. A. *Miners and Merchants in Bourbon Mexico, 1763–1810.* Cambridge: Cambridge University Press, 1971. In particular see chapter 9, "The Elite."

_____. "Government and Elite in Late Colonial Mexico." *Hispanic American Historical Review* 53 (1973):390.

_____. *Haciendas and Ranchos in the Mexican Bajío: Leon, 1700–1860.* Cambridge: 1978. In particular see chapter 6: "Landlords" and chapter 7: "Rancheros."

Brading, D. A., and Wu, Celia. "Population Growth and Crisis: Leon, 1720–1860." *Journal of Latin American Studies* 5 (1973):1–36.

Bromley, Rosemary. "The Functions and Development of 'Colonial' Towns: Urban Change in the Central Highlands of Ecuador, 1698–1940." *Transactions of the Institute of British Geographers* 4 (1979):30–43.

Brown, Jonathan C. *A Socio-economic History of Argentina, 1776–1860.* Cambridge: Cambridge University Press, 1979. In particular see chapter 8: "Formation of the Anchorena Cattle Business."

Burkett, E. C. "Indian Woman and White Society: The Case of Sixteenth Century Peru." In *Latin American Women: Historical Perspectives*, edited by Asunción Lavrin. Westport, Conn.: Greenwood Press, 1978.

Burkholder, Mark. "Titled Nobles, Elites and Independence." *Latin American Research Review* 13 (1978):290–95.

Cancian, Francesca M.; Goodman, Louis Wolf; and Smith, Peter H. "Capitalism, Industrialization, and Kinship in Latin America: Major Issues." *Journal of Family History* 3 (Special Issue: The Family in Latin America) (1978):319.

Cardoso, Ciro F. S., ed. *Formación y desarrollo de la burguesía en Mexico, Siglo XIX.* Mexico City, 1978.

Carlos, Manuel L., and Sellers, Lois. "Family, Kinship Structure and Modernization in Latin America." *Latin American Research Review* 7 (1972):95–124.

Cavariozzi, Marcelo. "El Orden Oligárquico en Chile, 1880–1910." *Developing Economies* 18, 70 (July–September 1978):231–62.

Chance, John K., and Taylor, William B. "Estate and Class in a Colonial City: Oaxaca in 1792." *Comparative Studies in Society and History* 19 (1977):454–86.

_____. "Estate and Class: A Reply." *Comparative Studies in Society and History* 21 (1979):434–42.

Chandler, Billy Jaynes. *The Feitosas and the Sertão Dos Inhamuns—The History of a Family and a Community in Northeast Brazil, 1700–1930.* Gainesville: University of Florida, 1972.

Chaney, Elsa M. "Old and New Feminists in Latin America: The Case of Peru and Chile." *Journal of Marriage and the Family* 35 (1973):331–42.

Chipman, Donald. "The Oñate-Moctezuma-Zaldívar Families of Northern New Spain." *New Mexico Historical Review* 52, 4 (October 1977):297–310.

Christie, Keith H. "Antiqueño Colonization in Western Colombia—A Reappraisal." *Hispanic American Historical Review* 58 (1978):260–83.

Costa de la Torre, Arturo. *Ensayo Genealógico de la Familia de la Torre: Sucesión y descendencia en Bolivia*. La Paz, 1971.

Couturier, Edith B. "The Philanthropic Activities of Pedro Romero de Terreros: First Count of Regla (1753–1781)." *Americas* 32 (1976):13–30.

_____. *La Hacienda de Hueyapán 1550–1936*. Mexico City: Sepsetentas, 1976.

_____. "Women in a Noble Family: The Mexican Counts de Regla, 1750–1830." In *Latin American Women: Historical Perspectives*, edited by Asunción Lavrin. Westport, Conn.: Greenwood Press, 1978.

Couturier, Edith, and Lavrin, Asunción. "Doweries and Wills: A View of Women's Socio-economic Role in Colonial Guadalajara and Puebla, 1640–1790." *Hispanic American Historical Review* 59 (1979):280–304.

Cubitt, David J. "La Composición Social de una elite hispanoamericana a la independencia Guayaquil en 1820." *Revista de Historia de América* 94 (1982):7–31.

Dean, Warren. *The Industrialization of Sao Paulo 1880–1945*. Austin: University of Texas Press, 1969. In particular, see chapter 3: "Social Origins, The Plantation Bourgeoisie"; chapter 4: "Social Origins, The Immigrant Bourgeoisie"; and chapter 5: "The Merger of Emerging Elites."

Deere, Carmen Diana. "The Differentiation of the Peasantry and Family Structure: A Peruvian Case Study." *Journal of Family History 3* (Special Issue: The Family in Latin America) (1978):422.

Duke, Cathy. "The Family in Eighteenth Century Plantation Society in Mexico." In *Comparative Perspectives on Slavery in New World Plantation Societies*, edited by Vera Rubin and Arthur Tuden. New York: New York Academy of Sciences, 1977.

Felstiner, Mary Lowenthal. "Kinship Politics in the Chilean Independence Movement." *Hispanic American Historical Review* (1976):58–80.

Fifer, J. Valerie. "The Empire Builders: A History of the Bolivian Rubber Boom and the Rise of the House of Suárez." *Journal of Latin American Studies 2* (1970):113–46.

Flory, Rae, and Smith, David Grant. "Bahían Merchants and Planters in the Seventeenth and Early Eighteenth Centuries." *Hispanic American Historical Review* 58 (1978):571–94.

Gallagher, Ann Miriam, R.S.M. "The Indian Nuns of Mexico City's Monasterio of Corpus Christi." In *Latin American Women: Historical Perspectives*, edited by Asunción Lavrin. Westport, Conn.: Greenwood Press, 1978.

Goldston, Angela. "The Children in the Family and Society, Late Eighteenth and Early Nineteenth Century Mexico." University of Texas. In progress.

Gonzalez, Elda R., and Mellafe, Rolando. *La función de la familia en la historia social hispanoamericana colonial, América colonial: Población y Economía.* Rosario, Argentina, 1965.

Gorman, Stephen M. "The State, Elite, and Export in Nineteenth Century Peru: Towards an Alternative Reinterpretation of Political Change." *Journal of Inter-American Studies* 21, 3 (August 1979):395–417.

Greenow, L. L. "Spatial Dimensions of the Credit Market in Eighteenth Century Nueva Galicia." In *Social Fabric and Spatial Structure in Colonial Latin America*, edited by David Robinson. Ann Arbor: University Microfilms International, 1979.

Greenow, Linda. "Family, Household and Home: A Micro-Geographic Analysis of Cartagena (New Granada) in 1777." *Discussion Paper Series, Department of Geography, Syracuse University* 18 (1976):1–51.

_____. "Spatial Dimensions of Household and Family Structure in Eighteenth Century Spanish America." *Discussion Paper Series, Department of Geography, Syracuse University* 35 (1977):1–31.

_____. "Women, Convents and Family Networks in the Credit Market of Late Colonial Guadalajara." Forthcoming.

Haigh, Roger M. *Martin Güemes: Tyrant or Tool.* Fort Worth: Texas Christian University Press, 1968.

_____. "The Creation and Control of Caudillo." *Hispanic American Historical Review* 44 (November 1964):481–90.

Halperín-Donghi, Tulio. *The Aftermath of Revolution in Latin America.* New York: Harper and Row, 1973.

_____. *Politics, Economics and Society in Argentina in the Revolutionary Period.* Cambridge: Cambridge University Press, 1975.

Hareven, Tamara K. "Postscript: The Latin American Essays in the Context of Family History." *Journal of Family History* 3 (Special Issue: The Family in Latin America) (1978):454.

_____. "The History of the Family as an Interdisciplinary Field." *Journal of Interdisciplinary History* 2 (1971):399–414.

Harris, Charles H. *A Mexican Family Empire: The Latifundio of the Sanchez Navarros, 1765–1867.* Austin: University of Texas Press, 1975.

Hoberman, Louisa Schell. "Merchants in Seventeenth-Century Mexico City: A Preliminary Portrait." *Hispanic American Historical Review* 57 (1977):479–503.

Horton, F. W. O. "The Military and Society in Bahía—1800–1821." *Journal of Latin American Studies* 7 (1975):249–69.

Hyland, Richard P. "A Fragile Prosperity: Credit and Agrarian Structure in the Cauca Valley, Colombia, 1851–87." *Hispanic American Historical Review* 62 (1982):369–406.

Johnson, Ann Hagerman. "The Impact of Market Agriculture on Family and Household Structure in Nineteenth-Century Chile." *Hispanic American Historical Review* 58 (1978):625–48.

Johnson, L. L., and Socolow, S. M. "Population and Space in Eighteenth Century Buenos Aires." In *Social Fabric and Spatial Structure in Colonial Latin America*, edited by David Robinson. Ann Arbor: University Microfilms International, 1979.

Joseph, Gilbert M., and Allen Wells. "Corporate Control of a Monocrop Economy: International Harvester and Yucatan's Henequen Industry during the Porfiriato." *Latin American Research Review* 17 (1982):69–99.

Kennedy, John Norman. "Bahian Elites, 1750–1822." *Hispanic American Historical Review* 53 (1973):415–39.

Kicza, John E. "The Great Families of Mexico: Elite Maintenance and Business Practices in Late Colonial Mexico City." *Hispanic American Historical Review* 62 (1982):429–57.

_____. *Colonial Entrepreneurs: Families and Business in Bourbon Mexico City.* Albuquerque: University of New Mexico Press, 1984.

Kinsbruner, Jay. "The Political Status of the Chilean Merchants at the End of the Colonial Period: The Concepción Example, 1790–1810." *Americas* 29 (1972):30–36.

Klein, Herbert S. "The Structure of the Hacendado Class in Late Eighteenth Century Alto Peru: The Intendencia de la Paz." *Hispanic American Historical Review* 60 (1980):191–212.

Kuznesof, Elizabeth Anne. "The Role of the Merchants in the Economic Development of São Paulo, 1765–1850." *Hispanic American Historical Review* 60 (1980):571–92.

_____. "Household Composition and Headship as Related to Changes in Mode of Production: São Paulo, 1765 to 1836." *Comparative Studies in Society and History* 22 (1980):79–109.

_____. "The Role of the Female-Headed Household in Brazilian Modernization: São Paulo, 1765 to 1836." *Journal of Social History* 13 (1980):589–613.

_____. "Clans: The Militia and Territorial Government: The Articulation of Kinship with Policy." In *Social Fabric and Spatial Structure in Colonial Latin America*, edited by David Robinson. Ann Arbor: University Microfilms International, 1979.

Ladd, Doris. *The Mexican Nobility at Independence, 1780–1826.* Austin: University of Texas Press, 1976. See in particular the following chapters: "The Origins of the Mexican Nobility," "Nobles as Plutocrats," "The Noble Life Style: Social Determinants of Investment Preferences," and "Reconciling Social and Economic Investments."

Lavrin, Asunción. "In Search of the Colonial Woman in Mexico." In *Latin American Women: Historical Perspectives*, edited by Asunción Lavrin. Westport, Conn.: Greenwood Press, 1978.

Levi, Darrell. *A Família Prado.* São Paulo: Cultura 70—Editora Brasiliense, 1977.

Lewin, Linda. "Some Historical Implications of Kinship Organization for Family-Based Politics in the Brazilian Northeast." *Comparative Studies in Society and History* 21 (1979):262–92.

Lockhart, James, and Otte, Enrique, eds. and trans. *Letters and People of the Spanish Indies: Sixteenth Century.* Cambridge: Cambridge University Press, 1976. In particular see the following letters: 3: "The Woman as Conqueror"; 11: "An Encomendero's Establishment"; 17: "The Tanner and His Wife"; 18: "The Troubadour"; 19: "The Nephew"; 20: "The Garden and the Gate"; 21: "The Woman as Settler"; 22: "The Farmer"; 23: "The Petty Dealer"; 29: "How a Governor Operates"; and 37: "The Petty Administrator."

Lomnitz, Larissa Adler, and Lizaur, Marisol Pérez. "The History of a Mexican Urban Family." *Journal of Family History* 3 (Special Issue: The Family in Latin America) (1978):392.

McAlister, L. N. "Social Structure and Social Change in New Spain." *Hispanic American Historical Review* 43 (1963):349–70.

McCaa, Robert; Grubessich, Arturo; and Schwartz, Stuart B. "Race and Class in Colonial Latin America: A Critique." *Comparative Studies in Society and History* 21 (1979):421–33.

_____. "Modeling Social Interaction: Marital Miscegenation in Colonial Spanish America." *Historical Methods* 15 (1982):45–66.

_____. *The Demographic Transition in Chile: The Population History of the Petorca Valley.* Boulder: Westview Press, 1983.

_____. "Tamaño de la familia en la historia de Latinoamerica, 1562–1950." *Histórica* 4 (1980):3–19.

Martínez-Alier, Verena. *Marriage, Class and Colour in Nineteenth Century Cuba: A Study of Racial Attitudes and Sexual Values in a Slave Society.* Cambridge: Cambridge University Press, 1974.

Marzahl, Peter. "Creoles and Government: The Cabildo of Popayán." *Hispanic American Historical Review* 54 (1974):636–856.

_____. *Town in the Empire: Government, Politics and Society in Seventeenth Century Popayán.* Latin American Monographs 45. Austin: University of Texas Press, 1978.

Metcalf, Alida. "Family and Society in a Brazilian Community: An Analysis of Social Structures and Their Meanings, 1700–1850." University of Texas. In progress.

Moraes, Maria Augusta Sant'Anna. *Historia de uma oligarquía: Os Bulhoes.* Goiania, Brazil, 1976.

O'Brien, Tomas. "Chilean Elites and Foreign Investors: Chilean Nitrate Policy, 1880–1882." *Journal of Latin American Studies* 11 (1979):101–21.

Oppenheimer, Robert B. "The Urbanization Process in Nineteenth Century Chile: The Railroad and Rural-Urban Migration. In *Population Growth and Urbanization in Latin America: The Rural-Urban Interface,* ed. John Hunter et al. 55–75. New York: Schenkman Press, 1983.

Pinto, Rodriquez, J. *Dos estudios de la población chilena en el siglo XVIII: Distribución y crecimiento regional y tamaño de la familia.* Santiago, 1981.

Ramos, Donald. "City and Country: The Family in Minas Gerais, 1804–1838." *Journal of Family History* 3: (Special Issue: The Family in Latin America) (1978):361–75.

_____. "Marriage and the Family in Colonial Vila Rica." *Hispanic American Historical Review* 55 (1975):200–225.

Rial, J. *La población uruguaya y el crecimiento económico-social entre 1850 y 1930: Cambio demográfico y urbanización en un pequeño pais.* Montevideo, 1981.

Ridings, Eugene W. "Elite Conflict and Cooperation in the Brazilian Empire: The Case of Bahia's Businessmen and Planters." *Luso-Brazilian Review* 12 (1975):80–99.

Robinson, David, ed. "Introduction to Themes and Scales." *Social Fabric and Spatial Structure in Colonial Latin America.* Ann Arbor: University Microfilms International, 1979. In particular see chapter 3: "The Spatial Dimensions of a Social Process Marriage and Nobility in Late Colonial Northern Mexico" by M. Swann; chapter 4: "Clans, the Militia and Territorial Government: The Articulation of Kinship with Polity in Eighteenth Century São Paulo" by Elizabeth Kuznesof; chapter 5, "Spatial Dimensions of the Credit Market in Eighteenth Century Nueva Galicia" by Linda Greenow; chapter 8: "Population and Space in Eighteenth Century Buenos Aires" by Lyman L. Johnson and Susan Migden Socolow.

Robinson, David J. "Latin American Family Life in the Nineteenth Century." Paper delivered at World Conference on Records: Preserving Our Heritage, August 1980; reprinted in *Proceedings of World Conference on Records: Preserving Our Heritage*, vol. 9. Salt Lake City: Church of Jesus Christ of Latter Day Saints, 1981.

Russell-Wood, A. J. R. "Female and Family in the Economy and Society of Colonial Brazil." In *Latin American Women: Historical Perspectives*, edited by Asunción Lavrin. Westport, Conn.: Greenwood Press, 1978.

_____. "Class, Creed and Colour in Administration." In *Fidalgos and Philanthropists: The Santa Casa de Misericordia of Bahia, 1550–1755.* Berkeley: University of California Press, 1968.

_____. "Dowries." In *Fidalgos and Philanthropists: The Santa Casa de Misericordia of Bahia, 1550–1755.* Berkeley: University of California Press, 1968.

Safford, Frank. "Bases of Political Alignments in Early Republican Spanish America." In *New Approaches to Latin American History*, ed. Richard Graham and Peter Smith. Austin: University of Texas Press, 1974.

_____. "Social Aspects of Politics in Nineteenth Century Spanish America: New Granada, 1825–1850." *Journal of Social History* 5 (1972):344–70.

Salinas Meza, Rene. "Reconstitución de familias en San Felipe y La Ligua durante los siglos VIIII y XIX." *Cuadernos de Historia* 2 (1981):63–71.

Smith, Peter H. "The Mexican Revolution and the Transformation of Political Elites." *Boletín de Estudios Latin Americanos* 25 (December 1978):3–20.

Smith, Raymond T. "The Family and the Modern World System: Some Observations from the Caribbean." *Journal of Family History* 3 (Special Issue: The Family in Latin America) (1978):337.

Socolow, Susan. "The Merchant Population." In *The Merchants of Buenos Aires, 1778–1810.* Cambridge: Cambridge University Press, 1978.

———. "Women, Marriage and Kinship." In *The Merchants of Buenos Aires, 1778–1810.* Cambridge: Cambridge University Press, 1978.

———. "Marriage, Birth, and Inheritance: The Merchants of Eighteenth-Century Buenos Aires." *Hispanic American Historical Review* 60 (1980):387–406.

Soeiro, Susan. "The Feminine Orders in Colonial Bahia, Brazil: Economic, Social, and Demographic Implications." In *Latin American Women: Historical Perspectives,* edited by Asunción Lavrin. Westport, Conn.: Greenwood Press, 1978.

Stagg, Albert. *The Almadas and Alamos, 1783–1867.* Tucson: University of Arizona Press, 1978.

Swann, Michael. "The Spatial Dimensions of a Social Process: Marriage and Mobility in Late Colonial Northern Mexico." In *Social Fabric and Spatial Structure in Colonial Latin America,* edited by David Robinson. Ann Arbor: University Microfilms International, 1979.

Szuchman, Mark. "The Limits of the Melting Pot in Urban Argentina: Marriage and Integration in Cordoba, 1869–1909." *Hispanic American Historical Review* 51 (1977):24–50.

Tutiño, John. "Hacienda Social Relations in Mexico—The Chalco Region in the Era of Independence." *Hispanic American Historical Review* 55 (1975):496–528.

———. "Power, Class, and Family: Men and Women in the Mexican Elite, 1750–1810." *Americas* 39 (January 1983):359–82.

Twinam, Ann. "Enterprise and Elites in Eighteenth Century Medellín." *Hispanic American Historical Review* 59 (1979):444–75.

Van Young, Eric. *Hacienda and Market in Eighteenth Century Mexico: The Rural Economy of the Guadalajara Region, 1675–1820.* Berkeley: University of California Press, 1981.

Vaughan, Mary K. "Women, Class and Education in Mexico, 1880–1928." *Latin American Perspectives* 4 (1977):135–52.

Voss, Stuart F. *On the Periphery of Nineteenth Century Mexico: Sonora and Sinaloa, 1810–1877.* Tucson: University of Arizona Press, 1982.

Wainerman, Catalina H. "Family Relations in Argentina: Diachrony and Synchrony." *Journal of Family History* 3 (Special Issue: The Family in Latin America) (1978):410.

Wasserman, Mark. "Capitalists and Caciques: Elite and Foreign Enterprise in Chihuahua, Mexico, 1821–1911." Manuscript.

———. *Capitalists, Caciques and Revolution: The Native Elite and Foreign Enterprise in Chihuahua, Mexico, 1854–1911.* Chapel Hill: University of North Carolina Press, 1984.

———. "Foreign Investment in Mexico, 1876–1910: A Case Study of the Role of Regional Elites." *Americas* 1 (1979):3–21.

———. "Oligarquía e Intereses Extranjeros en Chihuahua Durante el Porfiriato (Terrazas-Creel Family)." CM/HM *Historia Mexicana* 22 (1973):279–319.

Wells, Alan. "Family Elites in a Boom-and-Bust Economy: The Molinas and Peóns of Porfirian Yucatán." *Hispanic American Historical Review* 62 (1982): 224.

_____. *Yucatan's Golden Age: Haciendas, Henequen and International Harvester, 1860–1915.* Albuquerque: University of New Mexico Press. Forthcoming.

Wolf, Eric, and Edward Hansen. "Caudillo Politics: A Structural Analysis." *Comparative Studies in Society and History* 9 (1967):168–79.

Wortman, Miles L. *Government and Society in Central America, 1680–1840* (New York: Columbia University Press, 1982).

Zorilla, Ruben. *Extracción Social de los Caudillos 1810–1870.* Buenos Aires: 1972.

Papers Presented at the Workshop Panel No. 114, "Family in Nineteenth-Century Latin America," Latin American Studies Association Meeting, Mexico City, September 1983

Chandler, B. J. "Impact of Political and Legal Changes on Family Structure and Marriage Options."

Escoria, Jose. "Familia, politica y economía en el siglo XIX colombiano."

Greenow, Linda. "Micro-Geographic Analysis as an Index to Family Structure."

Guy, Donna. "Sources for the Study of Lower Class Family."

Johnson, Ann H. "Impact of the Changing Modes of Production on the Family."

Kicza, John. "Family as the Agent of Economic Development."

Kuznesof, E. A., and Oppenheimer, R. B. "The Family in the Nineteenth Century."

Seed, Patricia. "The Role of Race and Marriage in Family Strategies."

Tutiño, Joseph. "Family as a Mode of Analyzing Agrarian History: Mexico."

Commentators: Silvia Arrom (Yale), Diana Balmori (Visiting Fellow, Yale), Peter Smith (MIT).

Doctoral Dissertations

Anthropology

Brownrigg, Leslie Ann. "The Nobles of Cuenca: The Agrarian Elite of Southern Ecuador." Ph.D. dissertation, Columbia University, 1972. 589 pp.

Carman, Julia Elizabeth Rogers. "An Urban Family in Brazil: A Case Study of Upward Mobility." Ph.D. dissertation, Rice University, 1973. 297 pp.

Crespi, Muriel Kaminsky. "The Patrons and Peons of Pesillo: A Traditional Hacienda System in Highland Ecuador." Ph.D. dissertation, University of Illinois at Urbana-Champaign, 1968. 467 pp.

Goode, Judith Granich. "Changes in the Nature of an Elite Status: The Development of the Legal Professions in Antioquía, Colombia." Ph.D. dissertation, Cornell University, 1968. 277 pp.

Greaves, Thomas Custer. "The Dying Chalán: Case Studies on Four Haciendas of the Peruvian Coast." Ph.D. dissertation, Cornell University, 1968. 485 pp.

Hutchinson, Harry William. "Vila Reconcavo: A Brazilian Sugar-Cane Plantation Community." Ph.D. dissertation, Columbia University, 1954. 415 pp.

Johnson, Allen Willard. "Economics and Dependence on a Plantation in Ceara, Brazil." Ph.D. dissertation, Stanford University, 1968. 175 pp.

Kirk, Rodney Carlos. "San Antonio, Yucatán: From Henequén Hacienda to Plantation Ejido." Ph.D. dissertation, Michigan State University, 1975. 406 pp.

Lobo, Susan Bloom. "Kin Relationships and the Process of Urbanization in the Squatter Settlements of Lima, Peru." Ph.D. dissertation, University of Arizona, 1977. 546 pp.

Maeyama, Takashi. "Familialization of the Unfamilar World: The Family, Networks, and Groups in a Brazilian City." Ph.D. dissertation, Cornell University, 1975. 315 pp.

Miller, Charlotte Ingrid. "Middle Class Kinship Networks in Belo Horizonte, Minas Gerais, Brazil: The Functions of the Urban Parentela." Ph.D. dissertation, University of Florida, 1976. 247 pp.

Miller, Solomon. "The Hacienda and the Plantation in Northern Peru." Ph.D. dissertation, Columbia University, 1964. 165 pp.

History

Balmori, Diana (Hernando). "Casa y Familia: Spatial Biographies in Nineteenth Century Buenos Aires." Ph.D. dissertation, University of California, 1973. 761 pp.

Barbier, Jaques Armand. "Imperial Reform and Colonial Politics: A Secret History of Late Bourbon Chile." Ph.D. dissertation, University of Connecticut, 1973. 306 pp.

Bauer, Arnold Jacob. "Chilean Rural Society in the Nineteenth Century." Ph.D. dissertation, University of California at Berkeley, 1969. 331 pp.

Brennan, Eileen McAuliffe. "Demographic and Social Patterns in Urban Mexico: Guadalajara, 1876–1910." Ph.D. dissertation, Columbia University, 1978.

Brown, Jonathan Charles. "The Commercialization of Buenos Aires: Argentina's Economic Expansion in the Era of Traditional Technology, 1776–1860." Ph.D. dissertation, University of Texas at Austin, 1976. 319 pp.

Burbach, Roger Joseph. "The Chilean Industrial Bourgeoisie and Foreign Capital, 1920–1970." Ph.D. dissertation, Indiana University, 1975. 284 pp.

Chapman, John G. "Steam, Enterprise and Politics: The Building of the Veracruz-Mexico City Railway, 1837–1880." Ph.D. dissertation, University of Texas, 1971.

Chueca Posadas, Susana; Vallejos, Alfaro; and Julia, Florinda. "El Proceso de hacer la América: Una familia italiana en el Peru." M.A. thesis, Pontificia Universidad Católica del (Lima) Peru, 1975.

Colson, Roger Frank. "The Destruction of a Revolutionary Polity, Economy and Society in Brazil, 1750–1895." Ph.D. dissertation, Princeton University, 1979.

Crider, Ernest. "Modernization and Human Welfare: The Asistencia Pública and Buenos Aires, 1883–1910." Ph.D. dissertation, Ohio State University, 1976.

Couturier, Edith Boorstein. "Hacienda of Hueyapán: The History of a Mexican Social and Economic Institution, 1550–1940." Ph.D. dissertation, Columbia University, 1965. 321 pp.

Englesen, Juan Rolf. "Social Aspects of Agricultural Expansion in Coastal Peru, 1825–1878." Ph.D. dissertation, University of California at Los Angeles, 1977.

Felstiner, Mary Alexandra Lowenthal. "The Larraín Family in the Independence of Chile, 1780–1830." Ph.D. dissertation, Stanford University, 1970. 284 pp.

Ferry, Robert J. "Cacao and Kindred: Transformations of Economy and Society in Colonial Caracas." Ph.D. dissertation, University of Minnesota, 1980.

Flory, Rae Jean. "Bahian Society in the Mid-Colonial Period: Sugar Planters, Tobacco Growers, Merchants and Artisans of Salvador and the Reconçavo: 1680–1725." Ph.D. dissertation, University of Texas, 1978.

Gallagher, Ann Miriam, R.S.M. "The Family Background of the Nuns of Two Monasterios in Colonial Mexico: Santa Clara Querétaro and Corpus Christi, 1724–1822." Ph.D. dissertation, Catholic University, 1972.

Gallagher, Mary. "Social Class and Social Change in the Colombian Family." Ph.D. dissertation, Saint Louis University, 1964.

Gifun, Frederick Vincent. "Ribeirão Preto, 1880–1914: The Rise of a Coffee County, or the Transition to Coffee in São Paulo as Seen through the Development of Its Leading Producer." Ph.D. dissertation, University of Florida, 1972. 239 pp.

Guy, Donna. "Politics and the Sugar Industry in Tucumán, Argentina: 1870–1900." Ph.D. dissertation, University of Indiana, 1973.

Haigh, Roger Malone. "Martin Güemes: A Study of the Power Structure of the Province of Salta, 1810–1821." Ph.D. dissertation, University of Florida, 1963. 183 pp.

Hamerly, Michael T. "A Social and Economic History of the City and District of Guayaquíl during the Late Colonial and Independence Periods." Ph.D. dissertation, University of Florida, 1970.

Hansen, Elizabeth Riggs. "Santana: Middle Class Families in São Paulo, Brazil." Ph.D. dissertation, City University of New York, 1977. 381 pp.

Hoffnagal, Marc J. "From Monarchy to Republic in Northeast Brazil—The Case of Pernambuco, 1868–1895." Ph.D. dissertation, Indiana University, 1975.

Hollander, Frederick Alexander. "Oligarchy and the Politics of Petroleum in Argentina: The Case of the Salta Oligarchy and Standard Oil, 1918–1933." Ph.D. dissertation, University of California at Los Angeles, 1976. 709 pp.

Hollander, Nancy C. "Women in the Political Economy of Argentina." Ph.D. dissertation, University of California at Los Angeles, 1976.

Hunt, Marta Espejo Ponce. "Colonial Yucatan: Town and Region in the Seventeenth Century." Ph.D. dissertation, University of California at Los Angeles, 1974. 677 pp.

Johnson, David Church. "Social and Economic Change in Nineteenth Century Santander, Colombia." Ph.D. dissertation, University of California at Berkeley, 1975. 421 pp.

Karno, Howard Laurence. "Augusto B. Leguia: The Oligarchy and the Modernization of Peru, 1870–1930." Ph.D. dissertation, University of California, 1970. 322 pp.

Kaye, Harvey J. "The Political Economy of Seigneurialism: An Interpretation of the Historical Development of Rural Spanish America." Ph.D. dissertation, Louisiana State University, 1976.

Kirsch, Henry W. "The Industrialization of Chile, 1880–1930." Ph.D. dissertation, University of Florida, 1973. 347 pp.

Ladd, Doris Maxine. "The Mexican Nobility at Independence, 1780–1826." Ph.D. dissertation, Stanford University, 1972. 415 pp.

Langston, William Stanley. "Coahuila in the Porfiriato, 1893–1911: A Study of Political Elites." Ph.D. dissertation, Tulane University, 1980. 267 pp.

Levi, Darrell Erville. "The Prados of São Paulo: An Elite Brazilian Family in a Changing Society, 1840–1920." Ph.D. dissertation, Yale University, 1974. 400 pp.

Lindley, Richard Barry. "Kinship and Credit in the Structure of Guadalajara's Oligarchy, 1800–1830." Ph.D. dissertation, University of Texas at Austin, 1978. 345 pp.

Lutz, Christopher. "Santiago de Guatemala, 1541–1773: The Sociodemographic History of a Spanish American Colonial City." Ph.D. dissertation, University of Wisconsin, 1976.

Marcella, Gabriel. "The Structure of Politics in Nineteenth Century Spanish America: The Chilean Oligarchy, 1833–1891." Ph.D. dissertation, University of Notre Dame, 1973. 159 pp.

Marzahl, Peter Gottfried. "The Cabildo of Popayán in the Seventeenth Century: The Emergence of a Creole Elite." Ph.D. dissertation, University of Wisconsin at Madison, 1970. 226 pp.

Meyers, William K. "Interest Group Conflict and Revolutionary Politics: A Social History of La Comarca Lagunera, Mexico, 1880–1911." Ph.D. dissertation, University of Chicago, 1980.

Nielsen, Lawrence, J. "Of Gentry, Peasants, and Slaves: Rural Society in Sabará and Its Hinterland, 1780–1930." Ph.D. dissertation, University of California, 1975. 320 pp.

Nwasike, Dominic A. "Mexico City Town Government, 1590–1650: A Study in Aldermanic Background and Performance." Ph.D. dissertation, University of Wisconsin, 1972.

Oppenheimer, Robert Ballen. "Chilean Transportation Development: The Railroad and Socio-economic Change in the Central Valley, 1840–1885." Ph.D. dissertation, University of California at Los Angeles, 1976. 532 pp.

Palmer, Ronald B. "Politics and Modernization: A Case Study of Santa Cruz, Bolivia." Ph.D. dissertation, University of California at Los Angeles, 1979.

Pinsdorf, Marion Katheryn. "German-Speaking Immigrants: Builders of Business in Brazil's South." Ph.D. dissertation, New York University, 1976. 397 pp.

Pregger-Roman, Charles G. "Dependent Development in Nineteenth Century Chile." Ph.D. dissertation, Rutgers University, 1975. 332 pp.

Ramos, Donald. "A Social History of Ouro Preto: Stresses of Dynamic Urbanization in Colonial Brazil, 1695–1726." Ph.D. dissertation, University of Florida, 1972. 464 pp.

Rector, John Lawrence. "Merchants, Trade, and Commercial Policy in Chile: 1810–1840." Ph.D. dissertation, Indiana University, 1976. 296 pp.

Rice, Jacqueline. "The Porfirian Political Elite: Life Patterns of the Delegates to the 1892 Union Liberal Convention." Ph.D. dissertation, University of California at Los Angeles, 1979.

Saragoza, Alexander M. "The Formation of a Mexican Elite: The Industrialization of Monterrey, Nueva León, 1880–1920." Ph.D. dissertation, University of California at San Diego, 1978.

Smith, David Grant. "The Mercantile Class of Portugal and Brazil in the Seventeenth Century: A Socio-economic Study of the Merchants of Lisbon and Bahia, 1620–1690." Ph.D. dissertation, University of Texas at Austin, 1975. 452 pp.

Stann, Eugene J. "Caracas, Venezuela, 1891–1936: A Study of Urban Growth," Ph.D. dissertation, Vanderbilt University, 1975.

Sweigart, Joseph F. "Financing and Marketing: Brazilian Export Agriculture and the Coffee Factors of Rio de Janeiro, 1850–1888." Ph.D. dissertation, University of Texas, 1980.

Tutiño, John Mark. "Creole Mexico: Spanish Elites, Haciendas, and Indian Towns, 1750–1810." Ph.D. dissertation, University of Texas at Austin, 1976. 462 pp.

Twinam, Ann. "Miners, Merchants and Farmers: The Roots of Entrepreneurship in Antioquía, 1763–1810." Ph.D. dissertation, Yale University, 1976. 368 pp.

Villamarin, A. "Encomenderos and Indians in the Formation of Colonial Society in the Sabana de Bogotá, 1537–1740." Ph.D. dissertation, Brandeis University, 1972.

Waldron, Kathleen. "A Social History of a Primate City—The Case of Caracas, 1750–1810." Ph.D. dissertation, Indiana University, 1977. 319 pp.

Walker, David Wayne. "Kinship, Business and Politics: The Martínez de Rio Family in Mexico, 1824–1864." Ph.D. dissertation, University of Chicago, 1981.

Wibel, John Frederick. "The Evolution of a Regional Community within Spanish Empire and Peruvian Nation—Arequipa, 1780–1845." Ph.D. dissertation, Stanford University, 1975.

Wright, Angus Lindsay. "Market Land and Class: Southern Bahía, Brazil, 1890–1942." Ph.D. dissertation, University of Michigan, 1976. 279 pp.

INDEX

Agriculture. *See* Land ownership
Agüero family, 143, 166, 171 ,173
Aguilar family, 91, 103, 104, 118, 123,
  242n.13
Aguirre family, 170
Álamos, 86–88, 89, 103–4, 117, 118
Alcalde (local judge and executive), 99
Alcalde mayor (district office), 8
Alfaro, Julia. *See* Alfaro Vallejos,
  Julia
Alfaro Vallejos, Julia, 220, 221, 222,
  229
Almaceneros (wholesalers), 198–99
Almada family, 18, 86–88, 91–92,
  104, 113–14, 118, 123
Almanaques (Commercial Guides of
  Buenos Aires), 136–37
Alvear family, 153, 168
Anchorena family, 151, 168, 170, 171
Arequipa, Peru, 215–16
Argentine Industrial Union, 139
Arrivillaga family, 71–73
Arvizu family, 97
Astiazarán family, 102, 103
Audiencia, 33, 237n.9
Aviles family, 120, 126

Aycinena family, 61–69, 72–78
  passim, 237n.2, 239n.17
Ayuntamientos, 93, 99

Bahía (Brazil), 197–98, 265n.120
Balmori, Diana, 174, 176, 177, 180
Banks, banking, 19, 138, 152, 153–54,
  201–5, 220–21
Barbier, Jacques, 191, 196
Barona family, 202–3, 214
Barracas (warehouses), 137
Barracas de cuero (hide warehouses),
  137, 142
Barrundia family, 76, 78
Barrutias family, 74, 75
Batres family, 73, 74
Belgrano family, 161–63
Blank, Stephanie, 206
Bolivia, 216
Bosch family, 170–71
Boston Brahmins, 212
Bourbons, reforms of, 8–9, 10, 30–34;
  in Central America, 57, 58, 63, 64;
  in Northwest Mexico, 83, 84
Bourgiere, André, 23
Bowser, Frederick P., 192–93

281